*Training Plans for*

# Multisport
# ATHLETES

By *Gale Bernhardt*

*Foreword by Michelle Blessing*

**VELO**
*press*

BOULDER, COLORADO USA

International Standard Book Number: 1-884737-82-X

Library of Congress Cataloging-in Publication Data:

Bernhardt, Gale, 1958-
    Training plans for multisport athletes/by Gale Bernhardt ; foreword by Michelle Blessing.
        p. cm. -- (The ultimate training series from VeloPress)
    Includes bibliographical references and index.
    ISBN 1-884737-82-X
     1. Physical education and training. 2. Triathlon -- Training. I. Title. II. Series
GV1060.7 .B47 2000
613.7'11--dc21

00--32075

Distribute in the United States and Canada by Publishers Group West.

**PRINTED IN THE USA**
10 9 8 7 6

*Cover Design: Erin Johnson*
*Interior layout/production: Paulette Livers-Lambert*

**VELO**
*press*

1830 N. 55th Street • Boulder, Colorado • 80301-2700 • USA
303/440-0601 • FAX 303/444-6788 • E-MAIL velopress@7dogs.com

To purchase additional copies of this book or other Velo products,
call 800/234-8356 or visit us on the Web at www.velogear.com

# DISCLAIMER

The information and ideas in this book are for educational and instructional purposes and are not intended as prescriptive advice.

*To Delbert:*
*I cannot find enough words to express*
*my gratitude for your support.*
*Thank you.*

# TABLE OF CONTENTS

# FOREWORD

Congratulations! By buying this book, you have taken a significant step up in your commitment to training smarter and racing faster. Gale Bernhardt has written a significant training manual that is not only an abundant source of good and accurate information, but is also a practical guide to setting up training plans. The concise training plans are really what set this book apart from the other books that are out on the market. In fact, there are already a number of excellent books on training for multisport events. But *Training Plans for Multisport Athletes* takes the information and makes it useful to the reader. It is an excellent tool for both athletes who are looking to train and for coaches who are looking for some new ideas. As an athlete, I picked up many new training and racing tidbits. And as a coach, I found many sections of this book to be quite useful in my work with Olympic-format triathletes.

I am a voracious reader of everything involving multisport training, and, therefore, have been following Gale's career for some time. I read anything and everything she writes. Her columns that are in the various cycling and triathlon magazines are always well-written and brimming with great ideas and information. When I was told that she was publishing a book, I was excited. When I was asked to write this foreword, I was honored. And, finally, when I read the manuscript, I was pleasantly surprised. The chapter on nutrition is valuable in and of itself and warrants the purchase of this book. Gale's no-nonsense approach to nutrition is a refreshing change from the "secret pill" approach to diet that we see in so many other books. Like the rest of the book, the nutrition chapter stresses consistency and sound training principles.

Another innovative section of the book is on treadmill workouts. Many athletes find running on a treadmill to be monotonous and uninspiring. The treadmill workouts outlined in this book are not only unique and make the workouts more fun, but they make sense from a training standpoint. I have tried them myself and have tried them with some of the elite athletes I work with, and the response has been overwhelmingly positive.

I could go on with specific praise for *Training Plans for Multisport Athletes,* but do yourself a favor: if you have not yet purchased the book, do so. Then, read it from cover-to-cover. While the training plans are excellent, you will sell yourself short if you do not take full advantage of Gale's vast knowledge of training and racing. However, if you are looking for miracle shortcuts or training secrets, this is not your book. But if you are looking for sound advice on training and racing from one of the premier multisport coaches in the U.S., then this book is for you. Enjoy!

  *—Michelle Blessing,* 2000 Olympic coach for
    both the men's and women's U.S. triathlon teams

# PREFACE

Jerry was my first multisport training partner. In our preteen years we could be found at the pool nearly every day of summer vacation. Before we knew what goggles were, we swam with our eyes open playing games until our bloodshot, tearing eyes demanded a timeout. The play continued as we rode our bicycles everywhere, on- and off-road. Jerry was the champ at off-road maneuvers. On the bike or running, my younger sibling could really sprint. More often than not, the sprint concerned an argument, so sprint training usually turned into strength training—a wrestling match until one or the other of us was pinned, but both refusing to beg for mercy. Our family fitness carried over into neighborhood activities like baseball, football, ice-skating and other assorted sports. We both understood that being strong and fast had advantages.

As a preteen I noticed fitness in other people, particularly adults. One adult role model was Susie Poeschal. Susie taught swim lessons and held the glorious job of lifeguard. At 12 years old I thought, "I want to grow up to be a lifeguard." Between the ages of 12 and 18, I continued to marvel at Susie's fitness. I noticed she could do fun things other adults had long since given up, like hiking mountain trails and riding her bicycle long distances. I recall listening as she told us she rode her bike 15 miles and it was pretty easy. Wow, what a feat considering she was almost 30 years old! I wanted to be that fit when I got older—say, 30 years old.

Susie influenced my desire to remain fit and teach sporting activities, and Dick Hewson influenced my desire to coach. Dick coached the Loveland Swim Club and made certain that all of the kids had a chance to participate and reach their personal best performances. As I continued into high school, Dick remained my swim coach. He coached in a manner that made people want to swim fast, as opposed to driving their performance with fear and intimidation. I recognized that difference in coaching techniques early on and wanted to find out how to help people reach beyond what they thought possible, through their desire.

Throughout the remainder of high school and college and into my early twenties, I was able to maintain some sort of fitness and I kept my hand in teaching or coaching various sports. In 1987 after entering the "real job" world, I met Joyce Friel. She knew I taught aerobics, cycled to work and ran enough to complete a running race now and then. She also knew of my previous swimming background. She insisted I "must" do a triathlon. A what? I wondered.

Swim, bike and run all combined into one event for time, she explained, changing clothes was timed as well. It sounded like fun, but I recall that my biggest concerns were about mascara and contacts. At that time in my life, I was not seen in public without mascara—which I am happy to say is no longer the case. Additionally, I did not want to lose my contacts in the swimming pool—then how would I see anything on the bike ride?

I managed to overcome these two initial concerns and with six weeks of swim training, I did the Fort Collins Triathlon, a sprint event. The event was great fun and triggered a new concern—"How do I go faster and get better?"

I read everything about triathlon training I could get my hands on. Joyce let me know that her husband Joe coached triathletes and that he could help me get faster. A triathlon coach? I was just an age-group athlete, with no illusions of getting paid to do this fun sport. Did I really need a coach?

As it turns out, hiring Joe as my coach was an excellent decision. Our athlete-coach relationship eventually evolved into a business partnership. I found he shared my interest in helping endurance athletes reach beyond what they thought possible.

Due to my experience in coaching individual athletes, *Triathlete* magazine asked if I would be interested in writing a column for their June 1995 issue. This was a chance to extend my knowledge and experience to more athletes. The column, "Going from One to Du," instructed runners and cyclists on how to become duathletes. It generated a big response from readers, who were excited to have a daily guide to help them train.

Athletes using *Triathlete* magazine as a training resource continued to request specific training plans to guide their multisport journeys. Each column seemed to generate requests for more plans. Some athletes did not want to take the time required to design their own plan and some wanted someone with experience to guide them. The magazine columns were excellent for plans six to twelve weeks long; however, a magazine column cannot explain detailed, advanced training plans. Hence, this book was conceived.

# ACKNOWLEDGMENTS

I must thank *Triathlete* magazine, editors and staff, for their column request in 1995. That June column was the seed for this book. John Duke, Christina Gandolfo, T. J. Murphy and Lisa Park have been instrumental in publishing my training materials to guide the masses.

I would like to thank VeloPress and all its editors who contributed expertise to this book. Thank you, as well, to all the athletes who took the time to provide their insightful comments. And thanks to all the photographers and to Saturn Cycling, GT Bicycles and Trek Bicycles for their great photographs.

I am quite indebted to my immediate and extended family and friends for their support and encouragement. I cannot begin to inscribe this extensive list.

Joe Friel, Cathy Sloan and Tom Manzi gave generously of their time and suggestions to improve the book's content. Joe also influenced the text as a mentor and business partner. In addition to offering editing suggestions, Cathy helped keep me sane by assisting in my business. Her value as a training partner, buddy and Buffy No.1 make her irreplaceable. Tom, also a business partner, offered fresh perspective on my writing and provided plenty of entertainment at coaching clinics.

Chris Book, a registered dietitian, was of tremendous help in the transformation of my own diet and furnished a good deal of information for the nutrition chapter of this book. Athletes and nonathletes alike value her expertise. Dr. Deborah Shulman, registered dietitian, exercise physiologist and elite-distance runner, reviewed the majority of data in the nutrition chapter. She supplied useful information based on firsthand experience and her work with endurance athletes.

In 1996 I had a major shift in my training philosophy concerning periodization concepts as applied to endurance athletes. Fran Bell, Brian Quale and Greg Jensen, with the Colorado Acceleration Program, were instrumental in that change. They taught me the value of overspeed training on the treadmill, plyometrics and power training. Together we figured out how to apply those training tools to endurance athletes, some of which work is reflected in this book.

Nick Hansen not only improved my personal swim times, but also made significant contributions to Chapter 18. A small taste of his extensive knowledge and experience is in the sample workouts in Appendix F. Plan to see more from this excellent coach in the future.

Certainly, this project would not have been possible without Amy Sorrells. She supported the concept for the book and managed the publication process. Clancy Drake edited what I meant to say into readable text, Lori Hobkirk kept the project moving forward, and Paulette Livers Lambert provided book design expertise.

I am grateful to all the athletes who have allowed me into their lives and allowed me to influence their athletic endeavors. Without them this book would not have been possible.

Words of thanks must also go to all the athletes who contributed quotations to the beginning of each chapter.

Finally, I must mention Shelby, who relieved all episodes of writer's block with her timely urgings to go for a run. Her constant companionship provides security from all things scary, allowing my mind to wander in peace.

For more information on educational coaching seminars and certification, contact USA Triathlon at www.usa-triathlon.org.

*Shelby*

# INTRODUCTION

*"Getting faster is a matter of wisely investing time, not simply spending more time."*

—Gale Bernhardt

When I began to train for my first triathlon, I searched all the bookstores for a text that contained a plan. I had roughly six weeks to get ready for my first race and I wanted a guide for the preparation. What I found were books explaining what the sport was, what equipment was necessary and how to find it, the physiology of endurance training and lots of sample weeks or sample training workouts. But I wanted a plan—the whole enchilada. What should I be doing every day between the start of training and race day? And for how long? How fast? I was busy, so what was the minimum training necessary? What I wanted, a detailed, progressive plan—not just sample training days—was not available.

If you are searching for a book with training plans, you are in the right place. This tome contains 14 plans to guide the training of multisport athletes, from novices to experts. Each plan details specific workouts, with each workout's time and intensity placed within an organizational structure for the plan as a whole. Some athletes will use the plans as they are, verbatim. For others, the plans may require small changes to fit personal needs. The ability to see each plan in its entirety, along with your knowledge of your personal schedule and level of fitness, allows you to make calculated modifications to any of the plans. The name of each plan and its length in weeks are in the table of contents.

To begin use of this manual, read Part I, which contains information that is vital to all of the training plans. It covers the concepts of training and racing periodization and intensity, the limits of the notion that "one plan fits all" and a nutrition primer. Once training intensities are grasped, the workout codes in Part V have more meaning. There are codes for swimming, cycling, running and strength training workouts, and the codes for each sport are covered in separate chapters within Part V. These codes are referenced in nearly every plan, though not all codes are used in every plan. It is, however, attempting to define every workout of value with a handful of codes, this limits variety and progression. Hence, every plan also includes special instructions for some of the workouts within the text of its accompanying chapter.

If you thumb through the book to find the training plans, you may find the code-filled columns and rows a little overwhelming. Take a deep breath and look at only one week at a time. Each plan has an underlying logic and a pattern that repeats. The pattern may vary a bit from phase to phase on the longer plans, but it remains a pattern as well as a progression. On the longer plans, it may be helpful to use a highlighter to define three- to four-week training blocks. This visual separation helps to break the whole plan into smaller segments of accomplishment.

Each of the plan chapters begins with an athlete profile, which describe the person for whom the plan was designed and the goal to be accomplished at the end of the plan. The goals for plans in Part II are accomplished in six to 13 weeks. These plans are written for athletes with limited training time, limited experience, limited fitness or some combination of those circumstances. These early plans contain stashes of information useful to athletes of all experience levels. In fact, I recommend skimming the text for all plans, as each chapter contains useful tips not repeated elsewhere in the book.

The plans in Part III are for athletes with more preparation time between the beginning of structured training and race day. These plans outline between 11 and 24 weeks of training. There is only one plan in Part IV. This plan is a full 52 weeks long and, if completed in total, would be challenging to many seasoned triathletes. Whether the plan you choose spans a few months or an entire year, there will more than likely need to be modifications.

After all, real life doesn't always stick to a schedule. Tips for modification are included with each plan and in Appendix D, which contains general questions and answers. If you decide to attempt the design of your own plan, *The Triathlete's Training Bible* by Joe Friel, available from VeloPress, is a good resource.

The plans within this book are intentionally different in design. I have yet to discover a single training plan that fits everyone's needs. The only "standard" used in all the plans is the principle of periodization—adding increments of training volume or intensity followed by rest, in a structured format, to achieve athletic improvement. For some this means having the fitness to comfortably survive an event while for others it entails pushing the limits of speed. For still others, it means maintaining a fitness level that allows participation in a variety of sports, including triathlon. No matter which description fits you, I hope the book is a valuable training tool, one that you'll refer to time and time again.

# PART I

Before your dig right into a training plan, it is advantageous to read the first three chapters. Chapter 1 covers the concepts of training periodization and intensity. It reviews the body's means of energy production and discusses how to establish training zones through use of a heart rate monitor and/or the Borg scale, or rating of perceived exertion (RPE).

Chapter 2 discusses the factors that influence performance—some of which we can control, others of which we can't. Those factors mean there are benefits and limitations to any generic training plan. As we all know, one size does not fit all—but several sizes can fit many quite well, with a few alterations. Chapter 3 deals with nutrition, since a faulty nutrition plan can derail even the best athlete. Good athletes need to be as intentional about fueling and hydration as they are about training.

# CHAPTER ONE

# Levels
# *of Exercise*

*"Individualization in training is one of the main requirements of contemporary training and it refers to the idea of each athlete, regardless of level of performance, being treated individually according to his or her abilities, potential, learning characteristics and specificity of the sport.... Quite often coaches apply a completely unscientific approach in training by literally following training programs of successful athletes, completely disregarding his or her athlete's personality, experience and abilities.*
—Tudor Bompa,
Theory and Methodology of Training, *1994*

You may want to complete your first triathlon or perhaps travel faster or farther than you have done in past races. It doesn't matter which goal you are trying to achieve; the road to each has similarities. However, too often athletes take that wrong left turn and end up disappointed with their performance. For endurance athletes, some of the most common mistakes are:

• *Training at the same speed all the time*
• *Having no specific goals and no plan to achieve success*
• *Following careless nutrition and hydration practices*

This book will address all three common errors and give athletes tools to help them succeed. Most of the book is composed of goals and plans to guide your journey, which will help you avoid error No. 2. Chapter 3 will help you avoid error No. 3 by addressing some basics about nutrition. The first error, which happens most frequently, is the tendency to train at a fast pace all the time.

It seems to make sense that if you want to be fast in a race you have to train fast. That is true to some extent; however, you cannot train fast *all* the time and make progress. Athletes who are trying to train fast all the time end up going one mediocre speed—not too fast, not too slow. They are too tired for their arms and legs to turn over a fast pace, yet they feel enough spunk to go a decent pace. This chapter will help you avoid that rut by discussing training and racing intensities, as well as giving you some self-tests to estimate training zones. Chapters 18 through 20 will give you tools to find out if you are making progress.

Perhaps you have been on a group ride or run, or in a particular lane at a group practice, where the speeds were sizzling from the start. For a few moments you were right there, hanging with the pack. Then, you were dropped like a rock. Your heart was pounding, your legs were burning, and you gave it all you had. The group intensity, or speed, was obviously too fast for you to sustain. But other people were going that fast, so it is humanly possible to keep such a pace. What were they doing that you were not?

Building and improving fitness is analogous to building a

house. The first part, the foundation, must be constructed properly or the rest of the house will not hold up—at least not for very long. After the foundation is laid, a strong frame and roof can be built. The best results come from an orderly process in the initial stages of the construction. When it comes to the finishing details, the order of some tasks can be changed somewhat to accommodate the construction schedule's needs. Then, once the house is constructed, it must be maintained. If the house is properly maintained, improvements can be made to suit the needs and wants of the owner. These improvements are typically done a few at a time.

So it goes with fitness. A solid base is needed before long duration or long bouts of speed are added. If long duration is attempted prior to a gentle increase in training volume, there is high risk of injury. If long bouts of speed are added before a good base of fitness is achieved, one can expect short-lived success and also high injury risk. Once a certain level of fitness is achieved, it needs to be maintained. Each season, further improvements can be made to well-kept fitness. It can take years to build a world-class multisport athlete.

## PERIODIZATION

You may or may not be striving to be world class. Either way, a periodization plan will help guide your journey to faster or longer races. Briefly, a periodization plan manipulates exercise volumes and intensities over the course of weeks, months and years. A periodization plan for an Olympic athlete will span the course of several years. This type of plan is designed to have the athlete at peak fitness and speed for the Olympic Games. No athlete, even an Olympic-caliber athlete, can maintain peak fitness year-round. Peak performances are planned and can occur about two or three times per year.

The training plans in Chapters 4 through 17 are periodization plans. For some plans, the depth of fitness will be enough for "survival." For other plans, the depth of fitness will be geared toward increasing speed on an already established base.

All plans intentionally stress the body with increasing volume or intensity, then allow it to rest, so the fitness level after the rest is greater than before the stressful workout. This concept is called "overcompensation" or "supercompensation."

Supercompensation, however, is a fine line. Too much stress and the body will break down, resulting in illness or injury. Too little stress and no progress is made. Getting yourself into peak condition will require science and art. Science comes from laboratory studies. Art is knowing when to follow a plan exactly and when to make deviations. Each training plan in this book will guide you in blending science and art.

## INTENSITY

So how do you know how fast to swim, bike or run? Table 1.1 lists seven heart rate training zones. The percent of lactate threshold heart rate those zones represent are: the Borg scale of perceived exertion, the correlation of breathing to the various levels of exertion and descriptions of the purpose of

TABLE 1.1. TRAINING AND RACING INTENSITIES BASED ON LACTATE THRESHOLD HEART RATE

| Zone (Intensity) | Percent of Lactate Threshold (Bike) | Percent of Lactate Threshold (Run) | Rating of Perceived Exertion (Borg Scale) | Breathing Rate | Terms Commonly Used to Describe Purpose of Each Zone |
|---|---|---|---|---|---|
| 1 | 65–81 | 65–84 | 6–9 | Hardly noticeable | Aerobic, Recovery |
| 2 | 82–88 | 85–91 | 10–12 | Slightly noticeable | Aerobic, Extensive Endurance |
| 3 | 89–93 | 92–95 | 13–14 | Aware of breathing a little harder | Tempo, Intensive Endurance |
| 4 | 94–100 | 96–100 | 15–16 | Starting to breathe hard | Subthreshold, Muscular Endurance, Threshold Endurance |
| 5a | 100–102 | 100–102 | 17 | Breathing hard | Superthreshold, Muscular Endurance, Threshold Endurance |
| 5b | 103–105 | 103–105 | 18–19 | Heavy, labored breathing | Aerobic Capacity, Speed Endurance, Anaerobic-Endurance |
| 5c | 106+ | 106+ | 20 | Maximal exertion in breathing | Anaerobic Capacity, Power |

From The Cyclist's Training Bible by Joe Friel, VeloPress, 1996. Adapted by permission.

each training zone. Because we will use the pace clock for swimming, lactate threshold heart rates are not given for the pool, but the Borg scale is applicable in the pool and should be correlated with the pool workouts in Chapter 18.

## ENERGY PRODUCTION

Before we discuss each training zone, it is important to understand a bit about energy production within the body. Our bodies need to have a continuous supply of energy— even to sleep. Energy is supplied by complex chemical reactions. The end result of these chemical reactions is a rich compound called adenosine triphosphate or ATP. The potential energy within the ATP molecule is utilized for all energy-requiring processes of the cells of your body.

There are two basic methods your body uses to produce ATP. One method is aerobic, or with oxygen, and the second method is anaerobic or without the presence of oxygen. The method of energy production your body uses depends on the rate of demand for energy, or intensity, and the length of demand for energy, or duration. Short bursts of high speed utilize the anaerobic system of energy production to fuel the muscles. For longer efforts, fat and glycogen are burned in the presence of oxygen to create ATP.

A small amount of energy is readily available to be utilized "on demand." For example, when you sprint to make it through an intersection before the light changes, a small amount of energy is needed instantly. The majority of the energy necessary for this sprint is created anaerobically. After you have made it through the intersection and a slower speed is resumed, energy is created mostly by aerobic means.

For short sprints, energy is created anaerobically and uses ATP stored in the muscle cells to complete the work. ATP is stored in the cells in limited quantities. It is readily available but is used quickly. Aerobically produced ATP, on the other hand, takes more time for the body to produce, but it is available in huge quantities. These large quantities of energy allow an athlete to exercise for several hours at easy to moderate speeds.

The energy production system within the body is quite complex. It is important to note that although an athlete may be swimming, riding or running along at a moderate pace, some of the energy it takes to do so is produced anaerobically. In other words, both systems are working at the same time. As the intensity or speed increases, energy production and utilization need to happen more rapidly. Remember, the aerobic system needs time to produce energy; it is not as quick as the anaerobic system. So the body relies more on anaerobic energy production as the pace increases.

A by-product of the anaerobic energy production system is lactic acid. Lactic acid is often viewed as an evil demon, but in fact it is an energy source for the body. When given enough time, the body can process and use lactic acid to produce ATP. Lactate (a salt of lactic acid) is present in the blood at rest. Even while you are sitting and reading this book, there are low levels of lactate circulating in your blood stream.

At low levels, lactic acid is not a problem. As you continue to increase your workout intensity, your body increases energy production, relying more heavily on anaerobic metabolism. More reliance on anaerobic metabolism means the lactate level in your blood begins to increase. When your body can no longer process lactic acid fast enough, lactate begins to accumulate at an increasing rate in the blood, the condition is called "onset of blood lactate accumulation" (OBLA) or "lactate threshold." This accumulation is closely correlated with heart rate and ventilatory rate. Athletes can often tell when they have reached lactate threshold because their breathing becomes labored and they begin to feel "burning" in their muscles.

If athletes exceed lactate threshold pace, they can only sustain the increased pace for a few minutes before the discomfort forces them to slow down. The margin by which lactate threshold is exceeded is inversely proportional to the time the athlete is able to sustain that pace. In other words, if an athlete's lactate threshold heart rate is 162 and heart rate is pushed to 172, he or she will be able to hold that pace for a shorter period of time than if working at a heart rate of 164. Lactate threshold can be understood as the pace, and correlating average heart rate, that an athlete can sustain for approximately one hour while participating in a single sport. For example, the lactate threshold for a highly fit cyclist is approximately the pace and average heart rate that that athlete can hold for a 40km-time trial on the bicycle. Research has found that lactate threshold heart rate varies depending on the particular sport. Generally speaking, running lactate threshold heart rates tend to five five to 10 beats higher than cycling lactate threshold heart rates.

Lactate threshold typically occurs at 55 to 65 percent of $VO_2$ max in healthy, untrained people. In highly trained endurance athletes, lactate threshold is often greater than 80 percent of $VO_2$ max. Lactate threshold is trainable, and that's good news. In other words, you can train your body to process lactate at higher percentages of $VO_2$ max, which means increased levels of speed before the onset of discomfort forces an end to the effort.

Studies have shown lactate threshold to be a reliable predictor for endurance race performance. $VO_2$ max is not nearly as reliable. So, if you have been tested for $VO_2$ max and your numbers weren't stellar, do not panic.

## TESTING

There are various ways to estimate your lactate threshold and the corresponding heart rate. One way is to go to a laboratory for a graded exercise test. In this test, the exercise workload is incrementally increased and blood samples are taken at specific intervals to measure the level of lactate in the blood. During a graded exercise test at a laboratory, the ratio of oxygen to carbon dioxide being expelled from your respiratory system can also be measured and used to estimate lactate threshold.

There are also ways to estimate lactate threshold heart rate in the field. For all of the tests, you need a wireless heart rate monitor. In order to get the best estimates, you need to be rested and highly motivated. If you do the test when tired, the results may be inaccurate. These tests, however, are not intended to find maximum heart rate. If you have any concerns about doing such tests, seek the advice of a physician first. It is not wise to conduct the tests during the first workouts after you've been inactive for a long period of time.

Before beginning the tests to estimate lactate threshold heart rate, look at Table 1.1 on page 7. It has a column titled "Rating of Perceived Exertion (Borg Scale)" and one titled "Breathing Rate." The Borg scale was originally designed to correlate with heart rate for young athletes and was derived by dividing the heart rate by 10. For example, easy exercise at a perceived exertion value of 6 was intended to correlate to a heart rate of 60. Although the numbers do not always correlate exactly to heart rate, the perceived exertion scale can be very valuable and is still widely used. For athletes training for their first triathlon and using Chapter 4 as a guide, the rating of perceived exertion (RPE) can be used to estimate training zones until high interest in triathlon warrants the purchase of a heart rate monitor.

The heart rate monitor is one tool available to estimate exercise intensity. Monitors come in a variety of models and price ranges. The least expensive model simply reads heart rate. The more expensive models have the capability to store several hours' worth of data, then download that data into a computer for analysis.

The heart rate monitor consists of a transmitter belt worn strapped around the chest just below the breasts and a receiver worn on the wrist or mounted on the handlebar of the bike. The transmitter belt picks up electrical impulses from the heart and relays the information to the receiver via an electromagnetic field. The receiver then displays the heart rate. It's like having a tachometer for the body, similar to the one on a sports car.

When trying to determine your own lactate threshold record your rating of perceived exertion, breathing rate and heart rate. When doing the test, keep a copy of Table 1.1 handy, so you can refer to the Borg numbers and their correlated breathing rate. Specific field tests for estimating cycling lactate threshold heart rate are in Appendix A. Field tests for running are in Appendix B.

The methods outlined in Appendices A and B are ways to

estimate lactate threshold (LT). There are other methods, but these work well. It is possible to use either the cycling or the running test to estimate LT heart rate for one sport and then use that value to estimate the LT heart rate for the other sport. As mentioned previously, for multisport athletes, running LT is often 5 to 10 beats higher than cycling LT. Hence, if you did the cycling test and found your LT heart rate to be around 168, your running LT heart rate would probably be around 173 to 178.

Can an individual's lactate threshold heart rates change? Yes. Does everyone's body follow the 5- to 10-beat rule for the difference between cycling and running? Most of the time, yes; however, there are exceptions. So, if the numbers seem "off" in your training, you can hone in on a more precise number by doing a separate LT test in each sport and by noticing your heart rates during training and racing.

In this book, heart rate is one tool used, in conjunction with rating of perceived exertion, to quantify training and racing intensities for cycling and running. Other tools for determining workloads on the bike include power readings produced by CompuTrainer and Power-Tap. Instructions on how to use those tools are in Appendix C.

For swimming, use a time trial test to establish baseline fitness. Then use the results of this time trial, in conjunction with a pace clock, as a tool for swimming intensity. Instructions on how to conduct the time trial, along with a few swimming workouts, are in Chapter 18.

## TRAINING ZONES

Once you've done the tests outlined in Appendices A and B and Chapter 18, you will be armed with an estimated LT and seven training zones for each sport. Here's a bit about each zone:

### Zone 1

Zone 1 is used for early fitness building and recovery purposes. It is also used in conjunction with Zone 2 to build volume of training hours and base fitness in experienced athletes.

### Zone 2

Zone 2 training is used for building base fitness and maintaining current levels of fitness.

### Zone 3

Zone 3 training is used for early season tempo work to begin lactate threshold improvement. Zones 1 through 3 are used extensively for events lasting longer than about three hours.

### Zone 4

This zone is used in conjunction with intervals, hill work and tempo work to improve lactate threshold speed and muscular-endurance. It is common for the intervals in this zone to have a work-to-rest ratio of 3:1 or 4:1 in cycling and running.

### Zone 5a

This zone is used in conjunction with intervals, hill work and tempo work to improve lactate threshold speed and muscular endurance. It is typically used after some Zone 4 work has already been done.

### Zone 5b

The major use for this zone is to improve anaerobic endurance. The cycling and running intervals in this zone often have a work-to-rest ratio of 1:1. This zone is also used in hill work.

### Zone 5c

Zone 5c is fast—really fast—or powerful swimming, cycling or running. For example, sprinting to grab a competitor's wheel in a draft-legal race or climbing hills out of the saddle both elicit heart rates in Zone 5c. Exercise in Zone 5c cannot be maintained for long periods of time. It is common for the intervals in this zone to have a work-to-rest ratio of 1:2 or more.

The preceding comments for each zone are not all-inclusive, but they do give an idea of the uses for each particular training zone. We will use the seven training zones to measure speed and help you avoid mediocre workouts. Remember that anyone can train and race "hard," but not everyone is fast.

### REFERENCES

Bernhardt, G. *The Female Cyclist: Gearing up a Level.* Boulder, CO: VeloPress, 1999.

Burke, E. R., Ph.D. *Serious Cycling.* Champaign, IL: Human Kinetics, 1995.

Edwards, S. *The Heart Rate Monitor Book.* Polar Electro Oy, 1992.

Friel, J. *The Cyclist's Training Bible.* Boulder, CO: VeloPress, 1996.

Friel, J. *The Triathlete's Training Bible.* Boulder, CO: Velo-Press, 1998.

Janssen, P. G. J. M. *Training Lactate Pulse-Rate.* Polar Electro Oy, 1987.

Martin, D. E., Ph.D. and Coe, P. N. *Better Training for Distance Runners,* Second Edition. Champaign, IL: Human Kinetics, 1997.

McArdle, W. D., et al. *Exercise Physiology, Energy, Nutrition, and Human Performance.* 3d ed. Lea & Febiger, 1991.

# CHAPTER TWO

# Can
# *One Plan*
# *Fit All?*

*Gale has painstakingly gone through the literature and applied scientific theory to sound coaching practice. This is what the multisport world has needed for years.*
*–James M. Green, Asheville, North Carolina*

In all the years I've been coaching individual athletes, I've never written two training plans exactly the same—even if two athletes had the same race schedule. This is because there are sundry elements that enter into creating a training plan, including the athlete's work schedule, family obligations, ability to recover from training and racing, individual fitness areas that limit performance, experience level, desire, nutrition or genetics, as examples. But just how much of our performance can we control and how much is fate?

## "I PICKED THE WRONG PARENTS!"

Sometimes parents are blamed for an athlete's endurance performance. The parents *are* responsible—for a portion of the performance. Several scientific studies have been conducted to determine if genetics are responsible for great athletic performances. Claude Bouchard, Ph.D. and a team of researchers at Laval University in Québec, looked at monozygotic (identical) twins and put a group of 20, or 10 pairs, on a 20-week training program. The twins trained four to five times per week, for 45 minutes per session, at an average intensity of roughly 80 percent of maximal heart rate. The result? Identical twins did in fact respond nearly identically to the training program. One pair gained 10 and 11 percent, respectively, on their $VO_2$ max, or aerobic capacity, while a second pair gained 22 and 25 percent. Most of the variation in performance gains was between, not within, sets of twins.

Although this study on twins revealed that 82 percent of the variation in $VO_2$ max was due to genetics, it also revealed that only 33 percent of the differences found in ventilatory threshold (another benchmark of improvement) was attributable to genetics. This is important, since ventilatory threshold and the closely related lactate threshold are frequently found to be the best predictors of actual performance. This is good news for all of us, because lactate threshold tends to be more "trainable" than $VO_2$ max.

The researchers at Laval conducted other studies in addition to the one just mentioned. Overall, they concluded that genetic factors account for only around 20 percent of the variation in the performances of endurance athletes. Nongenetic factors, however, were found to influence 40 percent of the variation. Nongenetic factors include nutrition, lifestyle, past exercise patterns, age, socioeconomic status and mental skills to name a few. Gender differences accounted for 10 percent. The final 30 percent of variation was due to how a particular set of genes reacts to a particular training program. That is, some people will respond to one training program, but not to another.

Bottom line? Two things: You can control around 70 percent of your performance; and what works for you won't necessarily work as well for the multisport athlete next to you.

## Training Response Rates

Speaking of that person next to you, what about the differences between athletes on the same program? The researchers at Laval conducted another study to determine how much variation there would be in fitness gains if people followed the same training program. In this study, 24 similar subjects (initially sedentary) followed the same training program for 20 weeks. After 20 weeks, there were some big changes. The average gain in $VO_2$ max was 33 percent, and one person in the group gained a whopping 88 percent! Unfortunately, another individual sweating on the same plan increased $VO_2$ max by a mere 5 percent.

The same study, scientists measured power output on a bicycle ergometer, on which subjects pedaled away for 90 minutes. Their mean power output was measured before the training program began and again at the completion of the 20 weeks. The average power improvement was a nice 51 percent. One happy person gained a gigantic 97 percent, while another gained only 16 percent.

Why do some people seem to make big gains while others make minimal gains? And do their gains happen at even rates?

The studies at Laval led researchers to believe people can be divided into "responders" and "nonresponders." Those who are considered to be responders make big improvements in aerobic capacity and power as a result of their training, while non-responders barely show a gain, even after 20 weeks of hard work. The scientists estimate around 5 percent of us are high responders who can make improvements over 60 percent, while about the same number are low responders and may only expect a 5 percent improvement.

In addition to identifying responders and nonresponders, the studies revealed a gradation in response rates—a scale of responsiveness. Some people made nice gains after just four to six weeks of training, but seemed to plateau and made minimal gains in weeks 7 to 20. Others were late bloomers who were at a standstill for 6 to 10 weeks but then improved their aerobic capacities by 20 to 25 percent after 10 weeks of additional training.

### The Limitations and Benefits of Generic Training Plans

An important point is that given any single training program, not all individuals will react exactly the same. Some people will make big gains, while others may make marginal gains. Some will make their gains quickly, while others do so after more time has passed. Learning how your body responds to training and how to make adjustments will help you optimize your performance.

While there are limitations to using a generic training program, I've found that a good number of athletes can be quite successful using my plans as a guide. Some of the plans have been tried and tested by the masses because some of them are versions of plans I've written for *Triathlete* magazine over the years. Other plans are a combination of several athletes' individual training plans—which is exactly what the *Triathlete* magazine plans were prior to publication.

At the beginning of each plan in this book is an athlete profile—a description of the person the plan is written for—and a goal—what the athlete should expect to do if he or she follows the plan. Each chapter gives tips on how to modify the particular training plan featured in that chapter. For additional help in modifying the plans, there is a list of common questions and answers included in Appendix D. Armed with the tools and information provided in this book, you should be well on the way to new or improved performances.

## REFERENCES

American Council on Exercise. *Research Matters.* No. 1 (May 1995).

Anderson, O. "Are women better than men in the long run?" *Running Research News* 10, No. 6 (November-December 1994).

Anderson, O. "Question and Answer Section." *Running Research News* 11, No. 4 (May 1995).

Anderson, O. "Dad, Mom, and You: Do Your Genes Determine Your Performances?" *Running Research News* 11, No. 8 (October 1995).

Bernhardt, G. *The Female Cyclist: Gearing up a Level.* Boulder, CO: VeloPress, 1999.

McArdle, W. D. et al. *Exercise Physiology, Energy, Nutrition, and Human Performance.* Ed ed. Lea & Febiger, 1991.

Seiler, S. "Gender Differences in Endurance Performance Training" (Web site). MAPP, March 1998.

# CHAPTER THREE

# Basic Nutrition *to* *Survive* Endurance Training

> *When I finally decided to start eating, at the age of 40, I went from a 98-pound weakling to a healthy female athlete. I felt strong for the first time ever. If you don't eat, you won't be able to endure. Don't wait until you are a master's athlete to learn the value of consuming enough food.*
> —Cathy Sloan,
> Loveland, Colorado, age 45

The story about Windy on the next page is one I share with many of the athletes I coach. It's a good story because it illustrates many of the "Nutrition Rules" in the sidebar on page 26—rules that the rest of this chapter will cover in depth. Furthermore, Windy's story shows how:

- *Extreme calorie restriction and chronic dieting slows metabolism.*
- *Very low fat and/or very low protein diets are correlated with amenorrhea in women. (Many studies correlate amenorrhea in female athletes to loss in bone density.)*

# A Story of Change

Windy Ann was a competitive racer, trying to get better. She wanted to lose some weight to help her edge toward faster race speeds and more podium spots. It seemed the women who were faster were thinner than she was. Maybe if she were lighter, she could race even faster? She was well read on diet and nutrition. Literature throughout the 1980s told her she could lose weight by following a low-fat diet of no fewer than 1200 calories per day, and exercising. So that is what she did.

Windy carefully monitored her calories and opted for high-value foods—those that were chock-full of vitamins and minerals, but also low in fat. Foods fitting this description were fruits and vegetables. She knew she needed protein, but she was well aware that statistics said the average American consumes entirely too much protein. She got most of her protein from nonfat dairy products and an occasional piece of fish or poultry.

After several years of competition and training, she was unable to change her body weight. How could that be, she wondered? She exercised between 6 and 10 hours each week, worked between 48 and 55 hours each week and watched what she ate: why did her body not look like the body of a fit athlete? Why did she not feel right? She had no energy and it seemed she had one small, nagging injury each year that kept her from developing her full speed potential.

Frustrated with her situation, she sought the help of a registered dietitian in the early 1990s. The dietitian, Chris, asked her to keep food logs for a week and did an analysis. Keeping a food log was easy for Windy; she had meticulously counted calories for years. She could estimate portions without weighing them, though she occasionally checked her portions with a measuring cup or a scale. Chris found Windy's diet to be very high in vitamins and minerals, low in fat (only 10 percent of total caloric intake), low in protein (only 10 percent of total calories) and high in carbohydrate (80 percent of total calories). Her daily intake averaged around 1300 calories per day, which she felt was perfect for losing weight (or perhaps 100 calories per day too high). It was also perfect, she believed, for an endurance athlete and for someone trying to keep her cholesterol, which ranged between 195 and 198, from getting any higher. Yet, if this diet was so perfect, why did her body not have that svelte, strong, athletic look promoted in magazines?

Chris told Windy she thought her caloric intake was too low. Based on Windy's work and exercise routine, Chris recommended Windy increase her daily caloric intake to around 2300 calories. Not surprisingly, Windy wondered how she would ever lose weight this way.

Chris also thought Windy's fat and protein intake was too low. Windy suspected this as well. She had read about the work that Barry Sears did with the Stanford swim team. He helped them change their diet to 30 percent fat, 30 percent protein and 40 percent carbohydrates Windy wanted Chris's opinion about such a "30-30-40" diet. Chris had also read about this new (at the time) diet and agreed Windy should give it a try. Windy would eat more food with higher proportions of fat and protein and lower levels of carbohydrate.

After one week, Windy returned to Chris's office to find she had lost three pounds. She felt better physically, although it felt like she was eating a ton of food. Now convinced she should make changes to her diet, Windy continued eating more calories and maintaining a macronutrient split that included more fat and more protein.

When Windy began her diet change, it was November. In the weeks and months following her diet change, she began to take notice of some big changes in parts of her life she had not known were affected by her diet. She had more energy and was sleeping through the night, not getting up three to five times, as she had before—sometimes for a snack. Her hair was growing faster and needed to be cut more often. She simply felt good.

Three years before starting the new diet, Windy had quit taking birth control pills. After this, her menstrual cycle was never regular. She just thought it was due to her being on the pill for so long. Within five months of changing her diet, Windy had regularly occurring menstrual cycles.

By the time the next racing season arrived, in May, Windy was feeling better than ever and had made it through a winter of training with no nagging injuries. The initial three pounds were all Windy lost, but the numbers on the scale now meant less to her. They meant less because she felt better and she was racing faster. Throughout the entire race season following her diet change, her racing times improved.

During the race season, she found she could consume a daily diet of approximately 30-30-40 proportions, but that she needed to change that regimen during races. She found she needed to consume a sports drink during longer races or she felt terrible. She also found she needed more carbohydrate in the hours following a hard workout or race, to speed her recovery.

She was happy about her faster race times, regular menstrual cycle, lack of injuries, and how she felt better in general, but she was worried about her cholesterol level. She decided that if this new diet was good for her athletics but was putting her at risk for heart disease, she would head back to the old, low-fat diet. Fourteen months after her diet change, she had blood work done and was surprised to find her total cholesterol to be improved at 160.

Two years after changing her eating habits, Windy had lost an additional seven pounds. She was still getting faster race times, her menstrual cycle remained regular, she remained injury free and she felt great.

Although she no longer keeps food logs, Windy tries to balance her snacks and meals by eating some protein, fat and carbohydrate. Her diet changes were based on her health and training needs. She no longer lives on nonfat yogurt, bagels, fruits and vegetables. Fruits and vegetables are still a good part of her diet, but now she consumes lean meats and nuts as well. Fat is no longer an enemy. She minimizes her intake of highly processed foods and says she will never go back to her low-fat, low calorie style of eating.

- *A body that receives inadequate nutrition will break down. This can mean more frequent colds and flu, or it can mean more serious physical injuries. The ill and injured cannot train or burn as many calories as they'd like, nor can they be competitive athletes reaching their full potential.*

On a positive note, Windy knew something was wrong and took action. She had too many things she wanted to do and had no time for injury or illness.

The beginning of Windy's story is a common one. Athletes, both female and male, want to lose weight to increase speed. The first thing they do is cut calories from their diets. No one wants to diet for any extended time, so they cut a lot of calories for a short period of time to get this diet thing over with. When athletes cut significant calories from their diets in order to lose weight, the results are often counterproductive.

In a specific study on triathletes, the dietary habits of four male and two female elite triathletes were examined. An analysis of a seven-day diet record showed their daily intake of calories and carbohydrates to be insufficient to support their estimated requirements. Their diets were also found to be low in zinc and chromium. The researchers recommended diet changes to increase food intake. Follow-up seven-day diet records found the athletes had increased average daily calories, increased carbohydrate consumption and met their daily requirements for zinc, chromium and all other nutrients. Their race results also displayed an improvement in performance.

## Nutrition Rules

*Rule No. 1: Eat adequate calories.*

*Rule No. 2: Do not try to lose weight with extreme calorie restrictions.*

*Rule No. 3: Eat a balance of macronutrients.*

*Rule No. 4: Drink plenty of water.*

*Rule No. 5: There are no "bad" foods, however, some foods should be consumed with discretion.*

*Rule No. 6: Fat in the diet is essential to optimal health.*

*Rule No. 7: A healthy diet should contain a wide variety of minimally processed foods.*

In a separate study on trained cyclists, a high-fat diet was found to increase endurance. Five trained cyclists followed either a high-fat diet (70 percent fat, 7 percent carbohydrate, 23 percent protein) or a high-carbohydrate diet (74 percent carbohydrate, 12 percent fat, 14 percent protein) for two weeks. Endurance at 60 percent of $VO_2$ max was measured before and after the dietary changes and the high-fat diet was associated with "significant" increases in endurance.

If performance is not your only concern—perhaps you want to live to be 100 years old—consider the people who live in Lerik, Azerbaijan, a small mountain town near the Iranian border. This village is famous for people living 100 years and more. There are scores of old people living in the town; how do they do it?

The town is poorly served by medicine, most of the people are uneducated, and they eat very little and work like beasts of burden. Vegetables, fruit and sour cheeses make up the majority of their diet. When Azerbaijan was part of the Soviet Union, doctors visited the town and took numerous blood samples, looking for some secret to longevity. The tests were inconclusive. Researchers theorized the villagers' longevity was related to genetics and clean, stress-free living.

Confused yet? How is it that these athletes, whether their discipline is triathlon, cycling, or merely surviving, can all follow completely different diets and all have improved or sustained high performance? Some of the athletes studied ate a 30-30-40 diet, others simply increased calories, and still others ate a high-fat diet, and they all had performance increases. Then there are the Lerik "athletes," toiling each day and outliving most people, displaying sustained high performance. What are athletes supposed to do? What is the perfect diet?

If there were one golden diet that worked for everyone on earth, the person who discovered that diet would be rich and famous. If we talk about diet in very general terms, perhaps there is one perfect diet—eat and drink enough to build and maintain a healthy body. It's simple, but not easy. The difficult part comes when people want to know exactly what to eat. How many carbohydrates, how much fat and protein? How many calories? Precisely which foods should we eat each day to guarantee optimal health? An appropriate diet for an individual depends on:

- *Genetics*
- *Activity level—past, present and future*
- *Lifestyle, including stress level*
- *Quality of food consumed*

Most of us do not have the lifestyle of the people living in Lerik, so perhaps they are not a fair comparison. People living in modern cities deal with pollution, job-related toxins, job- and family-related stress and water and foods that have been processed. Given the variables, how do we know what our own optimal diet is? The remainder of this chapter will attempt to give information you can use to evaluate and improve your diet. A single chapter cannot cover all the information necessary to understand the topic of nutrition (and as technology develops, we will have new and more accurate information). But this chapter gives a good overview of macro- and micronutrients, some nutritional concerns common to athletes and some tools to evaluate diet. Let us begin with macronutrients.

## MACRONUTRIENTS

Depending on which book you read, there are either three or four macronutrients. The commonly agreed-upon macronutrients are carbohydrates, fat and protein. Some sources consider water to be a fourth macronutrient, and we'll discuss it in this section.

### Water

Between 40 and 60 percent of an individual's body weight is water. Water is typically 65 to 75 percent of the weight of muscle and less than 25 percent of the weight of fat. This water is essential to a functioning body. A body can survive many days without food; however, it can survive only a few days without water.

Many people do not stay well hydrated. Most literature recommends drinking between eight and 10 glasses of water each day. If you are drinking 8 to 10 glasses each day and your urine is dark yellow in color and foul smelling, you are not drinking enough. A general guideline is to drink enough water so that your urine is light in color and has minimal odor. Other signals of dehydration are constipation, fatigue and headaches.

Caffeinated coffees, teas and soft drinks have a diuretic effect, which means they increase the normal urinary output, leaving less fluid in the body for normal functioning. Limiting daily intake of caffeine helps keep the body hydrated. Caffeine has also been shown to increase calcium losses, so limiting its intake will help preserve precious bone.

A well-hydrated athlete also performs better. Dehydration levels as low as 2 percent of body weight are thought to impair athletic performance—perhaps by as much as 20 percent. Hence Nutritional Rule No. 4: Drink plenty of water.

### Carbohydrates

Carbohydrates are almost exclusively found in plants and their processed by-products. Fruits, vegetables, beans, peas and grains are sources of carbohydrates. The only animal sources that have significant carbohydrates are milk and yogurt.

Carbohydrates are made of sugar molecules and are divided into two major groups—complex carbohydrates and simple carbohydrates. Complex carbohydrates consist of many sugar molecules linked together. Foods in the complex group include vegetables, whole grains, beans and peas. These foods contain fiber and starches and are made of long complex chains of sugar molecules. They are more difficult than are simple carbohydrates for the body to break down into fuel

Simple carbohydrates, sometimes referred to as simple sugars, include fructose (fruit sugar), lactose (milk sugar), sucrose and glucose. Notice all of them end in the suffix "ose," which means a "carbohydrate." A food product that has several "ose" ingredients listed separately on its label actually contains that many simple sugars or combinations of sugars of different origin.

The body absorbs sugars and eventually converts them into glucose, the body's useable form of sugar. Sugar is absorbed into the blood, heart, skeletal muscle and liver—in that order. When blood sugars reach homeostasis, or a state of balance in the blood, the heart and skeletal muscles accept glucose. The always-working heart uses glucose for energy and the skeletal muscles can also use it for energy. Skeletal muscles also have the capability to store glucose as glycogen, to use for work at a later time. The liver can also absorb glucose from the blood and convert it to glycogen. The glucose not immediately needed or stored by functioning body parts is converted to fat.

Insulin is a pancreatic hormone that regulates blood sugar, and its effects are most beneficial when it does so at a moderate pace. When insulin continuously spikes and dips or is produced in inadequate quantities, health problems arise, including hypoglycemia (low blood sugar), diabetes (high blood sugar) and some of the health issues related to coronary heart disease. It is preferable to maintain blood sugars and insulin response so that there are not large peaks and valleys.

The rate at which carbohydrates in a food are digested and their effect on the rise of blood glucose is described by the food's glycemic index. Foods that are easily digested and cause a pronounced rise in blood sugar have high glycemic-index values. This pronounced rise of blood sugar initiates an insulin surge and stimulates body cells to store glucose as fat.

Foods that are more slowly digested have lower glycemic-index value and do not cause the paired glucose and insulin spikes. The glycemic-index value of some common carbohydrate foods is shown in Table 3.1. It is important to note that foods containing fats and proteins have lower glycemic-index values because fat and protein take more time to digest.

High glycemic-index foods are most valuable during exercise and post-exercise recovery. Otherwise, they should be used in moderation or in combination with fat and protein. When high glycemic-index foods are combined with fat and protein, their absorption rate is slowed. As Nutritional Rule No. 4 states, there are no "bad" foods; however, some foods should be consumed with discretion.

### Fat

Fat is essential for normal body functions. It also makes foods taste good, is enjoyable to eat and makes us feel satisfied after its consumption. Fats are constructed of building blocks called fatty acids. The three major categories of fatty acids are saturated, polyunsaturated and monounsaturated.

| TABLE 3.1: GLYCEMIC INDEX | | | |
|---|---|---|---|
| HIGH GLYCEMIC INDEX (80% or higher) | MODERATE GLYCEMIC INDEX (50-80% or higher) | LOW GLYCEMIC INDEX (30-50% or higher) | VERY LOW GLYCEMIC INDEX (Less than 30%) |
| Apricots | All-bran cereal | Apple | Cherries |
| Corn Flakes | Navy beans | Black-eyed peas | Grapefruit |
| Honey | Pasta | Yogurt | Peanuts |
| Oat bran | Spaghetti | Peaches, pears | Plums |
| Rice | Baked beans | Sweet potatoes | Soybeans |
| White bread | Oatmeal | Apple juice | |
| Banana | Pinto beans | Figs | |
| Crackers | Yams | Lentils | |
| Mango | Beets | Milk | |
| Pastries | Oranges | Barley | |
| Rye crisps | Potato chips | Grapes | |
| Whole wheat bread | Garbanzo beans | Lima beans | |
| Carrots | Orange juice | Rye bread | |
| Corn | PowerBar | | |
| French bread | | | |
| Molasses | | | |
| Potatoes | | | |
| Shredded wheat | | | |
| Corn chips | | | |
| Grapenuts | | | |
| Muesli | | | |
| Raisins | | | |
| Soda pop | | | |

The body can use all three kinds, but, as with carbohydrates, there are some fats that should be consumed in moderation.

Some of the fatty acids necessary for good health are called essential fatty acids (EFAs). EFAs contribute to a healthy body by improving hair and skin texture, reducing cholesterol and triglyceride levels, preventing arthritis and contributing to healthy hormone levels. EFAs are found in large quantities in the brain, where they aid in the transmission of nerve impulses and overall brain function. EFAs are also essential for rebuilding and producing new cells.

The body cannot manufacture EFAs—they must be obtained through the diet. Omega-3 and omega-6 fats are the two basic categories of EFAs. Omega-3 fats are found in cold-water fishes like salmon, mackerel, menhaden, herring and sardines. They are also found in canola oil, flaxseed oil and walnut oil. Omega-6 fats are found primarily in raw nuts, seeds, grapeseed oil, sesame oil and soybean oil. To supply essential fatty acids, omega-6 fats must be consumed in raw or supplement form, or as pure liquid; they can't be subjected to heat in processing or cooking. Wild game, not subjected to chemical-laden, fatten-them-up feedlot-style diets, is rich in both omega-3 and omega-6 fats.

The fats that should be consumed in moderation are the saturated variety. Excess consumption of saturated fats can raise cholesterol levels, particularly LDL (low-density lipoprotein) or "bad" cholesterol. Saturated fats are found in animal products and some tropical oils, like coconut and palm. Also, when some unsaturated oils are partially hydrogenated (a process that turns a liquid fat into a solid one), the new fat is more saturated. Hydrogenated fats contain trans-fatty acids, which are not well digested by the body and are thought to contribute to coronary artery disease. Hydrogenated and partially hydrogenated fats are prevalent in many processed foods like crackers, cookies and some canned products. Read the label on your food products and look for the word "hydrogenated."

Polyunsaturated fats are found in corn, safflower, soybean, canola and sunflower oils. Consumption of the polyunsaturated family may actually lower total cholesterol; however, it appears that large amounts of polyunsaturated fats also lower HDL (high-density lipoprotein) or "good" cholesterol. Some of the polyunsaturated oils do contain essential fatty acids or EFAs.

Monounsaturated fats are also thought to positively influence health. They are found in nuts and some vegetables, and also in the oils of those foods, such as almond, avocado, olive, canola and walnut oils.

### Protein

Protein in the diet is absolutely necessary for growth and development of the body. Next to water, protein makes up the greatest portion of our body weight. All our cells contain protein. Some food protein sources are considered "complete proteins" because they include all of the amino acids the body cannot manufacture on its own (the "essential" amino acids). Complete protein foods include meat, milk, eggs, poultry, fish, cheese, yogurt and soybean products.

People who chose to be vegetarians need to be well educated on combining foods to achieve complete proteins. This is because most plant products—with the exception of soybeans—are incomplete proteins, meaning they are missing one or more of the essential amino acids. If a diet consistently omits one or more of the essential amino acids, a deficiency will develop, resulting in illness or injury.

## MICRONUTRIENTS

Vitamins and minerals are considered to be "micronutrients" because they are needed in smaller quantities than the macronutrients—water, carbohydrates, fat and protein. Some vitamins and minerals are coenzymes, enabling the body to produce energy, grow and heal.

Vitamins regulate metabolism and assist in the biochemical processes that release energy from digested food. Some vitamins are known for their antioxidant, cancer prevention and cardiovascular disease protection properties. Vitamin E and vitamin C are two of the vitamins scientists believe we should supplement in our diet, because we probably do not get enough of these vitamins from our food. Some sources of vitamin E include nuts, seeds, whole grains, cold-pressed vegetable oils and dark green leafy vegetables. Vitamin C is found in green vegetables, citrus fruits and berries, to name a few sources.

Minerals are necessary for the correct composition of body fluids, the formation of blood and bone, the regulation of muscle tone and the maintenance of healthy nerve function. Calcium and iron are two of the minerals of most concern. Adequate calcium is necessary to ward off osteoporosis. Calcium can be found in dairy products, tofu, fortified orange juice, soymilk and canned fish with bones (such as sardines and salmon.) Iron is incorporated in hemoglobin and myoglobin and aids in the oxygenation of red blood cells and muscle. It is found in the largest quantities in the blood. Menstruating women lose blood and iron each month with their periods. Care must be taken to consume adequate iron so as not to become anemic. The best dietary sources of iron are red meat, eggs and beans.

## ANTIOXIDANTS AND PHYTOCHEMICALS

Scientists have recognized for years that diets rich in fruits, vegetables, grains and legumes appear to reduce the risk of a number of diseases, including cancer, heart disease, diabetes and high blood pressure. Researchers have found these foods to contain antioxidants, which protect cells against oxidation. Oxidation is damage to cells similar to rust on metal.

Phytochemicals are another group of health-promoting nutrients thought to prevent a number of diseases and aid in the repair of cells when disease strikes. Phytochemicals give plants their rich color, flavor and disease protection properties. There are literally thousands of phytochemicals—tomatoes alone are thought to contain over 10,000 different varieties.

The recent discovery of phytochemicals illustrates how science continues to discover more and more about whole foods and their valuable properties. Dietary supplements cannot replace the value of whole foods, because supplements represent some of our current knowledge—and humankind's quantity of knowledge is still quite small. Therefore, as Nutritional Rule No. 4 states, a healthy diet should contain a wide variety of minimally processed foods.

## HOW MUCH OF WHAT?

Now things get sticky. We need carbohydrates, fat and protein to sustain good health, but how much of each? How many calories are enough? How can one go about losing weight without compromising health? Should we take vitamin and mineral supplements? Long bouts of exercise need calorie supplementation, but how much and from what kind of foods? Long or exhausting exercise requires quick recovery—how is that best accomplished? The answer to all of these questions is an easy "Well, it depends."

If we first establish our dietary and fitness goals, prioritize those goals and determine how to measure them, then the answers become clearer. Consider the following goals, prioritized here in order of importance to long-term wellness. Consume a diet that:

1. *Builds and maintains a healthy body in the short term and minimizes the risk of disease in the future*
2. *Allows you to feel good physically and mentally*
3. *Considers your genetic makeup*
4. *Takes into account your lifestyle, fitness and activity level*
5. *Enhances your athletic capabilities*

If we eat with the main goal of building a healthy body, chances are good we will live a full and active life.

Before changing your diet, evaluate your current diet. If you consult a registered dietitian, he or she will ask you to keep a food diary. If you decide to evaluate your diet on your own, you will need to do the same thing. Use a reference book (such as *The NutriBase Nutrition Facts Desk Reference*) to measure the calories and macronutrients in your current diet. Log what foods you eat, how much and when. Begin with tabulating just calories or log the grams of carbohydrate, fat and protein as well. Record your information honestly and try not to change your eating behaviors just because you're keeping a food log. It may turn out you have been maintaining a healthy weight and eating 3000 calories per day, and there's no reason for you to change anything. Or you may constantly feel weak and tired while eating 3000 calories per day; in this case something needs to change. For now, you're just recording, so suspend your judgment.

Next, answer the questions in the Health Questionnaire in Appendix E. After filling out the questionnaire, you will have information that will help you and your doctor determine how healthy you are. If you are not as healthy as you'd like to be, consider changing your diet or lifestyle or both, in consultation with a registered dietitian who specializes in sports medicine.

## BENCHMARK FORMULAS

So far, we have established a set of nutrition rules, prioritized the goals of a healthy diet, determined what you are currently eating and recorded your current health status on the Health Questionnaire. You know where you are and, in general, where you want to go. Now how do you get there?

If you are satisfied with your current diet, if it meets both your needs and the goals of a healthy diet, celebrate! If you think your diet needs fine-tuning, or if you just want more information about measuring your intake of micro- and macronutrients, read on.

Some people prefer general dietary guidelines, while others want numbers. What follows is a bit of each.

### How Many Calories Do I Need to Consume?

One of the common formulas used to determine daily caloric intake needed to maintain body weight is 30 calories per kilogram of body weight. To find your weight in kilograms, take your weight in pounds and divide by 2.2. For example, if your weight is 140 pounds, your weight in kilograms is 140/2.2 = 63.6 or 64 kg. Your daily caloric needs are 64 x 30, or 1920 calories.

Modify this formula as appropriate:

- *Add more calories (about 100 to 300) if you lead a highly active lifestyle.*
- *Add about 0.13 to 0.16 calories per minute, per kilogram of body weight, for swimming. (For example, 0.16 calories per minute-kilogram x 60 minutes x 64 kilograms equals 614 calories needed for an hour of fast swimming.)*
- *Add about 0.15 to 0.17 calories per minute, per kilogram of body weight, for cycling. (For example, 0.17 calories per minute-kilogram x 60 minutes x 64 kilograms equals 653 calories needed for an hour of fast cycling.)*
- *Add about 0.14 to 0.29 calories per minute (roughly the range from an 11 minute pace per mile to a 5 minute, 30 second pace per mile), per kilogram of body weight, for running. (For example, 0.2 calories per minute-kilo-*

*gram x 60 minutes x 64 kilograms equals 768 calories needed for an hour of fast running.)*
- *Add about 0.1 calories per minute, per kilogram of body weight, for strength training. (For example, 0.1 calories per minute-kilogram x 60 minutes x 64 kilograms equals 384 calories needed for an hour of strength training.)*
- *Subtract calories (about 100 to 300) if your lifestyle or job is sedentary.*

So, the 140-pound person in our example would need to consume somewhere between 1620 and 2820 calories each day to maintain her weight, perhaps even more if she is training for an Ironman. She needs to consume more calories on active training days, then consume fewer calories when her body does not need them.

### What if You Want to Lose Weight?

You can calculate how many calories it takes to maintain your current weight from your food log, assuming your weight has been constant. To lose weight, decrease your daily caloric intake by 200 to 300 calories, not dropping total caloric intake below 1500. This slow approach to weight loss, through reduced food intake, reduces the risk of compromising health.

### What Source for Calories?

There currently appears to be a range for macronutrient consumption that will maintain or improve health and athletic training:

Carbohydrates:   40 to 65 percent of total calories
Fat:               15 to 30 percent of total calories
Protein:         15 to 30 percent of total calories

Exactly how much of each macronutrient each person should eat depends on the individual's health risks, dietary goals and current mode of training. Health and athletic training needs are constantly changing, so diet must also change. Nutrition needs on a heavy training day are not the same as when an athlete is resting and exercising very little. Consider the following suggested diet modifications:

- *Carbohydrate consumption should be on the higher end of the range when training fast miles (Zones 4 and 5) or long miles (90 minutes or more).*
- *Carbohydrate consumption should be in the middle range when training in Zones 1 to 3.*
- *Carbohydrate consumption should be on the lower end of the range when trying to lose weight. (Do not try to lose weight and race at the same time. This can result in emotional instability or decreased performance.)*
- *Protein consumption should be between 1.5 and 2.0 grams per kilogram of body weight. Use values on the higher end when training hard, trying to build muscle mass, doing very long exercise (over 3 hours) or trying to maintain muscle mass when dieting.*

There are different ways to estimate calorie and nutrient needs. Some sources refer to macronutrient consumption as a percentage of calorie intake, while others talk about consuming a certain number of grams of each macronutrient. It can get confusing when the measuring systems are talked about interchangeably. It helps to know that not all food grams have equal energy value:

- *1 gram of carbohydrate contains about 4 calories*
- *1 gram of protein contains about 4 calories*
- *1 gram of fat contains about 9 calories*
- *1 gram of alcohol contains about 7 calories*

## Formulas for Energy Needs During Exercise

For exercise longer than about an hour, consume, at minimum, 30 to 60 grams of carbohydrate per hour of intense or long exercise. Some athletes need to consume more than 500 calories per hour, such as the athlete profiled on page 44. How much you need to consume depends on body size, pace, pre-event muscle glycogen storage and individual metabolism. This energy can be taken in through fluid or solid sources. Be certain to consume adequate fluids as well: approximately 4 to 8 ounces of fluid every 15 to 20 minutes.

For exercise over about 3 hours, anecdotal evidence says athletes prefer to include fat and protein. The exact macronutrient proportions necessary for optimum performance are not clear. However, many ultraendurance athletes prefer more balanced foods that are not as heavily loaded with carbohydrates. Hydration needs to be maintained at 4 to 8 ounces every 15 to 20 minutes.

To speed recovery after long or exhausting workouts, consume liquid or solid fuel within 20 to 30 minutes after exercise. This fuel should contain 1.5 to 1.6 grams of carbohydrate

# Nutrition Case Study

JAY MARSCHALL, SIX-TIME IRONMAN FINISHER, 5-FEET 11-INCHES, 38 YEARS OLD, 165 POUNDS IN RACING SHAPE
BEST TIME: 9:11:58 (1993)
BEST FINISH: 46TH OVERALL, 9:27:06, THIRD MALE IN THE 35–39 AGE GROUP

"One of the most frequently asked questions I address is 'What and how do you eat in the Ironman?' Well, over the years I have come up with my nutritional strategy through trial and error as well as research and pestering questions to other athletes.

"I start by calculating the total number of calories I will burn in the race. I estimate this number to be 800 calories per hour on average (the swim is the least and the run is the most per hour). I then multiply this number by my projected finish time, in my case around nine hours, and come up with a total calorie expenditure of 7200. I then subtract the amount of carbohydrate calories I estimate are stored in my body (approximately 2000) and come up with around 5200 calories that I will need to ingest to remain in energy balance. Now the question is, how do I get that many of calories down, and through what type of food or drink?

"In the early days I would stack a pile of PowerBars on my bike handlebar and watch them melt throughout the 112-mile ride. I never had the stomach to claw off even a mouthful. Then I decided to ask Mark Allen what he ate and he said 'Exceed Meal Replacement,' which is the same thing as Ensure, a drink used primarily for the elderly. I thought this was a great idea. I only had to drink two large chocolate milk shakes during the bike to get 2000 calories (one large bottle holds about 1000 calories of Ensure). I decided to consume Ensure throughout the bike in small swallows and also sip water or a sports drink.

"Some of my calories come from a sports drink mixed to a 6-percent solution, which I again consume in frequent small swallows on the bike and on the run. In addition to the fluid calories, I have found that a bit of solid food seems to help digestion and calm a queasy stomach. In the last couple of races I used peanut butter on a whole-wheat roll as a good filler on the bike.

"The remainder of my calories come from more sports drink and/or carbohydrate gels, which I ingest every 20 to 30 minutes on the run. Oh yes: When I finish, I love to sit by the pool and have a grilled cheese sandwich, French fries and a cold beer. Of course this is consumed within the 30-minute to 1-hour optimal window for recovery!"

per kilogram of body weight and 0.4 to 0.5 grams of protein per kilogram of body weight.

To further enhance recovery after long or exhausting workouts, consume liquid or solid fuel over the 24 hours after exercise that contains 6 to 8 grams of carbohydrate per kilogram of body weight

Recovery-type foods include milkshakes, chocolate milk, bagels and cottage cheese or lean meat, fruit and protein powder smoothies, yogurt smoothies with fruit or beef jerky combined with a sports drink. Some studies indicate that regular snacks of approximately 50 grams of carbohydrate, eaten every two hours, may optimize recovery. (Of course an evening meal containing adequate carbohydrates would be necessary to get you through a night's sleep. In other words, do not try to set an alarm to wake up every two hours to eat.)

## Putting It Together

Let's say our 64-kilogram athlete is doing a long ride of three hours. We would assume her total calories today should be about 3743. (1920 + (0.16 calories per minute-kilogram x 64 kilograms x 60 minutes per hour x 3 hours)). This moderately tough group ride requires 1843 calories of energy. If today's caloric needs are about 3743 and we break down the macronutrients by percentages:

- *Due to the long ride, she'll place 60 percent of the calories as carbohydrates, or 3763 x 0.60 to equal 2257 carbohydrate calories.*
- *At 20 percent of the calories for fat, 3763 x 0.20 equals 753 fat calories.*

- *At 20 percent of the calories for protein, 3763 x 0.20 equals 753 protein calories.*

On her long ride today, she will consume 350 carbohydrate calories per hour, or 1050 calories total and she will consume a post-ride recovery food containing 1.5 to 1.6 grams of carbohydrate per kilogram of body weight, totaling about 90 grams of carbohydrate (1.6 x 64). This will give her 360 more carbohydrate calories, or 90 x 4. The total ride calories and post-ride recovery calories consumed equal 1410. This falls short of meeting her cycling emery requirements of 1843. She will need to make up the calories in other snacks or meals if she expects to maintain her weight.

Since her ride was a moderately fast group ride, she will need to consume between 6 and 8 grams of carbohydrate per kilogram of body weight, over the next 24 hours, to restore her glycogen levels. At 6 grams, she would need 384 grams of carbohydrate (including the post ride recovery drink), and at 8 grams per kilogram of body weight, she would need 512 grams of carbohydrate. Choosing 512 grams, she needs to consume about 2000 carbohydrate calories over 24 hours to restore her glycogen. She can consume some of those calories today and the remaining calories tomorrow.

Recall she was aiming to consume 2257 carbohydrate calories today. So, subtracting the 1410 carbohydrate calories associated with riding and post-ride recovery, she would need to be sure to consume and additional 847 carbohydrate calories today.

Notice the two sets of formulas provided for estimating macronutrient needs don't always mesh. If our sample athlete consumed 20-percent of her 3763 calories as protein, that 753 calories (0.20 x 3763) translates to 2.9 grams of protein per kilogram of body weight. [(750 calories x 1 gram of protein per 4 protein calories) divided by 64-kilogram athlete]

The perfect diet and nutrient breakdown depends on many factors. The best place to start is to simply log what you are doing now and use your Health Questionnaire in Appendix E to determine if your current diet is serving your needs or not. If your diet is not meeting your needs, then consider a change.

## NUMBERS, NUMBERS, NUMBERS

Now that you have formulas to estimate caloric needs, macronutrient breakdowns, fueling during a long ride and post-ride fueling strategies, here are some words of caution:

- *The word "estimate" is critical. Do not worry about getting the exact numbers when consuming calories. There is a margin of error on food product labels and there is a margin of error when estimating personal nutrition needs. Again, use the Health Questionnaire to determine if your nutrition program works for you.*
- *If you have determined you need 100 grams of carbohydrate and 33 grams of protein for post-ride recovery and a food source has 115 grams of carbohydrate and 25 grams of protein, it will work fine, don't worry.*
- *I do not advise becoming a food log addict. Use food logs to establish good eating behaviors or as spot-checks to see what is going on with your diet. It is possible to drive yourself nuts weighing and counting everything. Let food logs serve their purpose, then give them a rest.*

• *Body weight is a number and simply that. Do not weigh yourself every day and look for changes. In fact, if you lose several pounds from one day to the next, it is probably due to dehydration. Try to remedy the situation by drinking like a camel and putting some numbers back on the scale. At most, weigh yourself weekly. Review the Questionnaire to gauge how you feel. Your overall health is a better measure of nutritional success than numbers on a scale.*

## SUPPLEMENTS

*The American Heritage Dictionary* defines the word supplement as "something added to complete a thing or to make up for a deficiency." Notice it does not say, "a substitute for…." No amount of vitamin and mineral supplementation will make up for a crummy diet, something people do not seem to understand. As a case in point, I was talking with a young person sacking my groceries recently. He was inquiring about the volume and variety of vegetables I was purchasing. "Are you a vegetarian or something?" he asked.

"No, at our house we eat lots of different vegetables because they taste good and their vibrant colors make an exciting plate," I replied.

"Oh, I don't like vegetables, so I just eat meat and potatoes and take vitamins. Anyway, one vitamin pill has all the stuff I really need, so I don't have to worry about it. I'm training to be a boxer, so I need all the vitamins."

His thought process is all too common. While he continued sacking the groceries I explained about fiber, phytochemicals and the unknown, healthy substances probably also contained in real food. I explained how recent the discovery of phytochemicals was and that although we humans are pretty smart, we are a long way from knowing everything. The study of nutrition is still a young science. I further explained that supplements are meant to complement a diet high in whole foods but that no supplementation plan will make up for a diet high in processed foods, saturated fat, sugar and salt and low in fiber and variety. The young man asked if I would let him take my groceries to the car, so he could ask more questions. I answered, "You bet!" I am unsure if he will change his habits, but at least he was thinking.

Researchers are continually finding out more information about vitamin and mineral supplementation. A survey among top researchers asked what they, themselves, take for vitamin and mineral supplementation and the answers were not uniform. Some of the supplements that continue to receive attention among scientists include:

- *A multivitamin and mineral tablet*
- *Vitamin C*
- *Vitamin E*
- *Calcium*
- *Iron*

## Multivitamins

Most experts agree a multivitamin and mineral supplement is recommended. Some experts still hold a strong belief we should be able to meet all of our vitamin and mineral needs from food, but more research is telling us it does not happen for most folks. U.S. Department of Agriculture data indicates that at least 40 percent of the people in the U.S. routinely consume a diet containing only 60 percent of the recommended daily allowances (RDA) of 10 selected nutrients. We would likely fare worse if more nutrients were evaluated.

There continues to be controversy as to whether or not athletes' requirements for vitamins and minerals exceed those of the average population. If athletes are consuming a balanced and varied diet, and taking some supplements, perhaps that is enough.

### Vitamins C and E

The current recommendation is to supplement a multivitamin with 1000 milligrams of vitamin C and 400 IU of vitamin E. Both of these are antioxidants, substances that block oxidative damage to the cells of our body. To maintain constant concentrations of vitamin C in the blood, it is best to take two doses, eight to 12 hours apart.

### Calcium

The current recommendation is to consume somewhere between 1000 and 1500 milligrams of calcium daily. In order for calcium to be well-absorbed, protein and vitamins C, D, E and K all play a role. Several of the minerals also play important roles in calcium absorption. For example, too much magnesium, sodium and/or phosphorus (found in many soft drinks and processed foods) can inhibit the absorption of calcium.

Just supplementing the diet with calcium is not the cure-all. Weight-bearing exercise plays an important role, though more is not necessarily better. Even men, who seem to be less prone to bone loss, can suffer when exercise levels are excessive. One study of University of Memphis male basketball players found they were losing about 3.8 percent of their bone mass from preseason to midseason of a single year. Bob Klesges, the head scientist, determined the ballplayers were losing substantial amounts of calcium in their sweat. He concluded this by collecting the sweaty T-shirts of the players and carefully wringing out their contents to be analyzed. (Yuck!)

He found the players gained back 1.1 percent of their bone mass during summer, but they lost an additional 3.3 percent when practices resumed, making their total losses now about 5.8 percent. With supplemental calcium, they were able to regain the losses.

In summary, try to get 1000 to 1500 milligrams of calcium from your diet. (As an example, an 8-ounce glass of milk contains 290 milligrams of calcium.) If you are not getting enough through your diet, consider a supplement on the days when your food consumption does not give you the recommended requirements. The superior supplement is calcium citrate malate, found in many calcium-enriched juices. On average, people absorb 35 percent of the calcium in calcium citrate malate, compared to 30 percent of the calcium in other supplements.

## Iron

Iron is an essential component of hemoglobin and myoglobin and functions in the oxygenation of red blood cells and muscle. Women, especially, can have problems with low levels of iron, developing anemia. One of the common causes of anemia is excessive menstrual flow. Aggravating the deficiency due to blood loss, some women consume inadequate dietary iron. Good food sources of iron are fish, meat, beans, whole grains, enriched breads and enriched cereals. Iron supplements should not be self-prescribed but should be taken on the advice of a physician.

Constant fatigue is one the common symptoms of anemia. Anemia can be easily identified with a simple blood test. In fact, blood tests can detect many problems associated with diet, health and wellness. For athletes serious about wellness and competition, an annual blood test—in the off or restorative season—is an excellent source of information. This baseline test can then be used to diagnose changes to blood chemistry when a competitive season seems to have gone awry.

## ERGOGENIC AIDS

The items I receive the most questions about are sports drinks, energy bars and caffeine.

### Sport Drinks

The simple rule of thumb here is to drink the one that tastes best to you and does not cause extra potty stops. If you select a drink that tastes good and use it for workouts over an hour long, generally, it is beneficial. Be aware that some athletes have gastrointestinal problems with fructose-based sports drinks. If you are having difficulties, check to see if fructose is one of the main ingredients of the sport drink.

## Energy Bars

Energy bars are useful for long rides, pre- and post-workout snacks and pre-race snacks. They are not, however, one of the major food groups. Some athletes use them as a major source of calories, choosing them over fruits and vegetables because they are an easy food to acquire and prepare. Use them as supplements for sporting activities; they are not appropriate as meals. Eat minimally processed foods and, whenever possible, chose whole foods over highly refined foods—including energy bars.

## Caffeine

Caffeine may be the most widely used drug in the world. It stimulates the central nervous system, the adrenal system and the muscular system. It has also been shown to influence the metabolic system by stimulating fat metabolism during aerobic exercise. The results include lowered levels of perceived pain at a given pace and the sparing of glycogen as a fuel. Additionally, when used in conjunction with exercise, caffeine appears not to have the diuretic effect that it has when consumed in a nonexercise situation.

A dose of 5 to 7 milligrams of caffeine per kilogram of body weight, given one hour prior to exercise, has been the typical protocol for most studies. Additional studies, where the focus is on the measurement of free fatty acid metabolism, show the response to fat-burning may not be optimal until 3 to 4 hours after ingestion.

There can be negative side effects to caffeine consumption. Some people do not tolerate caffeine well and become shaky, jittery and unable to focus. It also is bothersome to some people's stomachs. Caffeine is banned by the U.S. Olympic Committee, at levels measuring 12 mcg/ml of urine. To reach this level would require the ingestion of nearly 1200 mg of pure caffeine.

If you decide to use caffeine, experiment with it during a training ride. It is best not to wait until a race or big event to test your tolerance and advantage levels. For racing, consume the caffeine approximately one hour before race start. Major sources for caffeine are:

| Product | Caffeine (mg) |
| --- | --- |
| Coffee (8 oz) | 100–250 |
| Espresso (1 oz) | 35–60 |
| Cappuccino (8 oz) | 35–60 |
| Caffe latte (8 oz) | 35–60 |
| Colas (8 oz) | 38–46 |
| Mountain Dew (12 oz) | 55 |
| Pocket Rocket | 50 |
| Chocolate (one packet) | |
| No-Doz, regular (1 tablet) | 100 |
| Excedrin (2 tablets) | 130 |

## REFERENCES

Balch, J. F, and P. A. Balch. *Prescription for Nutritional Healing.* Garden City Park, NY: Avery Publishing Group, 1997.

Barr, S. "Women, Nutrition and Exercise: A Review of Athletes' Intakes and a Discussion of Energy Balance in Active Women." *Progress in Food and Nutrition Science 11,* Nos. 3–4 (1987): 307–361.

Book, C. McKee Medical Center, Loveland, Colorado. Interview by Gale Bernhardt, July 7, 1998.

Burke, L. *The Complete Guide to Food for Sports Performance.* Allen & Unwin, 1995.

Coleman, E. *Eating for Endurance.* Palo Alto, CA: Bull Publishing Company, 1997.

Colgan, M. *Optimum Sports Nutrition.* Ronkonkoma, NY: Advanced Research Press, 1993.

Correll, D. "Young Girls Attempt To Mimic Model Bodies." *Sunday Loveland Reporter-Herald,* June 21, 1998.

Coyle, E. F. "Substrate Utilization During Exercise In Active People." *American Journal of Clinical Nutrition* 1995: b1(Suppl)968S–979S.

Eades, M. R. and M. Eades. *Protein Power.* New York, NY: Bantam Books, 1996.

Frentosos, J. A., and J. T. Baer. "Increased Energy and Nutrient Intake During Training and Competition Improves Elite Triathlete's Endurance Performance." *International Journal of Sports Nutrition* 1 (March 1997): 61–71.

Friel, J. *The Cyclist's Training Bible.* Boulder, CO: VeloPress, 1996.

Klesges, R. C. "Changes In Bone Mineral Content In Male Athletes. Mechanisms Of Action And Intervention Effects." *Journal of the American Medical Association* 276, No. 3 (July 1996): 226–230.

Lampert, E. V., et al. "Enhanced Endurance In Trained Cyclists During Moderate Intensity Exercise Following 2 Weeks *Of Adaptation To A High Fat Diet,"* European Journal of Applied Physiology 69, No. 4 (1994): 287–293.

Liebman, B. "Avoiding the Fracture Zone. Calcium: Why Get More?" *Nutrition Action,* Center for Science in the Public Interest, April, 1998.

Liebman, B. "3 Vitamins and a Mineral: What to Take." *Nutrition Action,* Center for Science in the Public Interest, May, 1998.

Lutter, J. M. and L. Jaffee. *The Bodywise Woman.* 2d ed. Human Kinetics, 1996.

McArdle, W. D., et al. *Exercise Physiology, Energy, Nutrition, and Human Performance.* 3d ed. Malverne, PA: Lea & Febiger, 1991.

_____. "The Big Jolt: Mountain Biking's Love Affair With Coffee," *Mountain Biker.* February 1998.

Ryan, M. "Less Is More, Taking The Sensible Approach To Shedding Weight." *Inside Triathlon,* July 1998.

Sabo, D., et al. "Modification of Bone Quality By Extreme Physical Stress. Bone Density Measurements In High-Performance Athletes Using Dual-Energy X-Ray Absorptiometry." *Z Orthop Ihre Grenzgeb* 143, No. 1 (January–February 1996): 1–6.

Sears, B. *The Zone.* New York: HarperCollins Publishers, 1995.

Sharkey, B. J. *Fitness and Health.* Champaign, IL: Human Kinetics, 1997.

Shulman, D., exercise physiologist. Interviews by Gale Bernhardt, July 1998.

Ulene, A. *The NutriBase Nutrition Facts Desk Reference.* Garden City Park, NY: Avery Publishing Group, 1995.

*USA Cycling Elite Coaching Clinic Manual.* Colorado Springs, CO: USA Cycling, February 17–19, 1997.

# PART II

The plans in Part II generally take three to four months of training to get to race day. The plans in this section are for "Level I" athletes, which means they are designed for people who have not raced multisport at all, or athletes who have minimal race experience at a given distance. All plans are for people who have minimal time to devote to training.

The layouts of the plans differ somewhat, but all of them have the week number listed in the left-hand column and each day of the week has its own column. The format for Table 4.1 on page 62 has the sport, the workout code and workout time all listed together. For example, on Wednesday of week 3, the athlete will run for 13 minutes following the instructions for an E1 workout. Many of the workout codes are listed in a separate chapter for each sport. Some chapters explain a handful of the codes within the text, and these codes are also indicated in bold type on the corresponding plans. Because swimming workouts entail so much detail, only a few sample swimming workouts and codes are in Chapter 23. *Workouts in a Binder*™ contains many more options for swimming workouts. Cycling workouts and codes are in Chapter 19; running workouts and codes are in Chapter 20; the codes for strength training and descriptions for stretching routines are in Chapter 21.

It is highly recommended that you read through all of Part V and familiarize yourself with the codes before beginning any of the plans. The code chapters are placed near the end of the book for easy reference. All workouts should start out with a rating of perceived exertion of 1 and end with a perceived exertion of 1. That means do not bolt out of the starting gate and start swimming, cycling or running as fast as you can. Allow your body a chance to warm up. Yes, that warm up and cool down time is included in the total workout time. I recommend athletes stretch after their cool down period at the end of every workout.

A second example of plan layout is Table 9.1 on page 104-105. The left column again has the week number, however each day of the week has two columns. One column lists the time of the workout in a specific sport and the second column has the workout code. Each sport or activity is listed in a separate row and repeats for each week. For example, Wednesday of week 3 will be a form workout on the bike lasting an hour and a half.

Tips for hydration and refueling are covered in Chapter 3 and apply to all the plans.

# CHAPTER FOUR

# Sprint Distance *Triathlon for Those with Limited Time and Fitness*

*I'm a Venezuelan girl who likes triathlon, but believe me when I say it's very hard for me to just get a magazine in my country.... I never thought it would be possible for me to become a triathlete, but after I read Bernhardt's article, I felt like someone was saying to me, "You can do it if you want to!"*
—Helena Mendoza, Venezuela,
quoted in Triathlete *magazine, April 1999*

Hey, there is a sprint triathlon in about three months, why don't you come along and do the race?""Are you kidding me? Triathlon is for maniacs who have nothing to do but train. I have a life and other things I like to do. Triathlon training takes too much time."

"It doesn't take *that* much time. You can do it!"

"Naw, I've seen how much you train. I have to eat, sleep and work. Furthermore, I'm not giving up _____." (Fill in the blank with one or more of the following: aerobics classes, kickboxing, softball, golf, water-skiing, spending time with family and friends, or fill in your own choice.)

"You don't need to train as much as I do."

"How much would I need to train?"

Good question.

## PROFILE

Okay, busy person, this chapter is designed to help a never-ever triathlete complete his or her first event. The training recommendations are for someone who has minimal time to devote to triathlon training.

Your athletic profile begins with swimming. You know how to swim, but it has been a long time since once-fit arms and legs have actually propelled your body through water. In other words, you lack swimming endurance.

As for cycling, you might ride a bicycle now and again, mostly noodling around the neighborhood. On occasion, you might ride a stationary bicycle at the health club while waiting for aerobics to begin or to warm up before weight lifting. As with swimming, you have no real endurance on the bike.

Finally, running. The running you do is mostly short duration, like running bases in softball. Maybe you chase a ball in racquetball. You might have even run a 5K once.

So your multisport profile for endurance sports is not great, but you are not sitting around channel surfing either. This plan assumes you are currently active in sport three to six times per week. The specific sport is not as important as the fact that you are active doing something. If you are not currently active and decide to use this plan to get back into shape, of course, be sure to consult a physician before beginning.

One of the most common mistakes made by people just beginning to train for a triathlon, or any other endurance event, is doing too much too soon. Early enthusiasm can lead to injury or overtraining. A 12-week plan to get you through your first triathlon is shown in Table 4.1 on page 62-63. It gently builds aerobic endurance in all three sports.

## GOAL

Precisely, the goal will be to go from a current state of no swimming, minimal cycling and no running to completing a 450- to 500-yard swim, 11- to 15-mile bike and about a 3-mile run, consecutively—your first triathlon.

## SWIM

The plan assumes you are capable of swimming 50 yards or meters without stopping. It may not be Olympic speed, but you can do it. This particular plan does not utilize the swim workout chapter (Chapter 18); rather the workouts are listed on pages 64 to 66.

All you need for the swim is a comfortable swimming suit and goggles. For the women, if you decide to go with a two-piece suit, be certain it is one designed for sport and not sunbathing. For the guys, if you are uncomfortable in a small Speedo-style suit, trunks will work fine.

As for goggles, everyone's face is different. Go to a sporting goods store where the salesperson is willing to let you try on several different styles and give tips on proper fit. The nosepiece should not dig into the bridge of the nose. The foam on goggle cups should cover your eye socket, forming a waterproof seal. It is not necessary to pull the strap over your head to get an idea of proper fit.

If you wear glasses, it is possible to get prescription goggles. Unless one is really optically impaired, it is possible to get by without special goggles until triathlon becomes an addiction. Most of the timers-per-lap counters at a pool triathlon are willing to hold glasses, or you can position a person to hand up eyewear at the exit of an open-water swim.

## TABLE 4.1: SPRINT DISTANCE FOR LIMITED TIME AND FITNESS PLAN

| Week | Monday | Tuesday | Wednesday | Thursday |
|------|--------|---------|-----------|----------|
| 1 | Day off | Swim Workout #1 00:30 | Run E1 00:05 | Bike E1 00:20 |
| 2 | Day off | Swim Workout #2 00:30 | Run E1 00:09 | Bike E1 00:30 |
| 3 | Day off | Swim Workout #3 00:30 | Run E1 00:13 | Bike—accels 4–6 x 30 sec (1' 30") 00:30 |
| 4 | Day off | Swim Workout #4 00:30 | Run E1 00:17 | Bike—accels 4–6 x 30 sec (1' 30") 00:30 |
| 5 | Day off | Swim Workout #5 00:30 | Run E1 00:23 | Bike E1 00:30 |
| 6 | Day off | Swim Workout #6 00:30 | Run E1 00:10 | Bike or day off E1 00:30 |
| 7 | Day off | Swim Workout #7 00:30 | Run E1 00:30 | Bike—accels 10–20–30–30–20–10 (1'30") 00:30 |
| 8 | Day off | Swim Workout #8 00:30 | Run—accels 4–6 x 20 sec (1' 30") 00:30 | Bike—accels 6 x 30 sec (1' 30") 00:30 |
| 9 | Day off | Swim Workout #9 00:30 | Run—accels 6–8 x 20 sec (1' 30") 00:30 | Bike—accels 10–15–20–25–30–25–20–15–10 (1'30") 00:45 |
| 10 | Day off | Swim Workout #10 00:30 | Run E1 00:15 | Bike or day off E1 00:30 |
| 11 | Day off | Swim Workout #11 00:30 | Run E1 00:30 | Bike—accels 6–8 x 10 sec (1'50") 00:30 |
| 12 | Day off | Swim Workout #12 00:30 | Run E1 00:10 | Bike—accels 3 x 10 sec (1'50") 00:20 |

An antidote for foggy goggles is shampoo—seriously. A concoction of 50-percent no-tears shampoo and 50 percent water will do the trick. A handy way to carry the mixture is in a clean, empty eye-drop container. Pry the top off and put the no-fog goop in the bottle. Just before swimming, put a

| Friday | Saturday | Sunday | Weekly Total Workout Time |
|---|---|---|---|
| Repeat Tuesday | Run E2 | Bike E1 | |
| 00:30 | 00:07 | 00:30 | 02:02 |
| Repeat Tuesday | Run E2 | Bike E2 | |
| 00:30 | 00:11 | 00:45 | 02:35 |
| Repeat Tuesday | Run E2 | Bike E2 | |
| 00:30 | 00:15 | 01:00 | 02:58 |
| Repeat Tuesday | Run E2 | Bike E2 | |
| 00:30 | 00:20 | 01:15 | 03:22 |
| Repeat Tuesday | Run E2 | Bike E2 | |
| 00:30 | 00:26 | 01:30 | 03:49 |
| Repeat Tuesday | Run E2 | Bike E3 | |
| 00:30 | 00:30 | 00:45 | 02:55 |
| Repeat Tuesday | Run E2 | Bike E3 | |
| 00:30 | 00:35 | 01:30 | 04:05 |
| Repeat Tuesday | Run E2 | Bike E3 | |
| 00:30 | 00:40 | 01:45 | 04:25 |
| Swim at the lake or repeat Tuesday | Run E2 | Brick Bike—E3, 1:15 Run—E2, 0:15 | |
| 00:30 | 00:30 | 01:30 | 04:15 |
| Swim at the lake or repeat Tuesday | Day off | Brick Bike—E2, 1:30 Run—E3, 0:15 | |
| 00:30 | | 01:30 | 03:15 |
| Swim at the lake or repeat Tuesday | Bike E1 | Brick Bike 1:00, Run 0:30 Both fartlek | |
| 00:30 | 00:30 | 01:30 | 04:00 |
| Bike or day off E1 | Day off | Race Day! 500 meter swim, 15-mile bike, 5km run, all zones 1–3 | |
| 00:30 | | | |

drop or two in each lens of your goggles and smear it around. Be sure your fingers are clean and don't have lotion on them. Rinse the excess out by giving the goggles a couple of dips in the pool or dousing them with some clean water from a water bottle. When you are swimming, if the water in the goggles bothers your eye, you didn't rinse well enough. If the goggles fog, you rinsed too well. Definitely try this prior to race day.

### Swim Workouts

During weeks one through six, the swim workout on Friday is a repeat of Tuesday's workout. The goal on Friday is to put less effort into the swim than you did on Tuesday. Keep all swimming in weeks one through six at a RPE in zones 1 to 2. Try to relax when you swim, getting the most distance out of each stroke with the least amount of effort. Each swim workout is numbered. The details of the swims won't fit into the small squares in Table 4.1, so here they are:

*Workout No. 1:* This plan assumes you can swim down and back (50 yards or meters) in a standard pool. Although "yards" is used in each description, yards and meters are exchangeable. The first workout is simply swimming 10 x 50 yards, resting about 45 seconds between each 50. You may have to rest a whole minute between each 50; that is okay. Until we add a warm-up and cool-down to swimming, make the first couple and last couple of 50s very easy. The workout may take some of you less than 30 minutes: that's fine; just get out of the pool when you are done with the 500 yards of swimming.

*Workout No. 2:* Swim 10 x 50 yards, taking 30 to 45 seconds of rest between each 50 yards.

*Workout No. 3:* Swim 10 x 50 yards, taking 20 to 30 seconds of rest between each 50 yards.

*Workout No. 4:* We will bump the distance up a bit to 8 x 75 yards, with 30 seconds between each 75 yards. By now, you are building some endurance in the pool. If you would like to swim a bit longer, do a few yards of warm-up before the 8 x 75 and/or do a few yards after the assigned set. In the weeks to come, you can add warm-up, cool-down and a few yards of kicking to any day when you have the time and energy to do so. Do not swim over the assigned time—usually 30 minutes.

*Workout No. 5:* Swim 8 x 75 yards, taking 20 seconds of rest between each 75 yards.

*Workout No. 6:* Swim 8 x 75 yards, taking 10 seconds of rest between each 75 yards. You can do additional swimming, up to 30 minutes, if you have the time and energy.

For weeks seven through 12, we begin to speed up the Tuesday workouts. Make the swim intensity (RPE) on Tuesday in Zones 1 to 3 and the intensity on Friday in Zones 1 to 2.

*Workout No. 7:* Swim 5 x 100 yards, taking 20 seconds or rest between each 100 yards. You can do additional swimming, up to 30 minutes, if you have the time and energy.

*Workout No. 8:* Swim 5 x 100 yards, taking 10 seconds of rest between each 100 yards. You can do additional swimming, up to 30 minutes, if you have the time and energy.

*Workout No. 9:* Swim 500 yards, nonstop! Notice how much time it takes you to swim 500 yards. This time will improve with training. Swim as much as 30 minutes, if you have the desire. For the second workout this week, if the race will be in open water, make an effort to get to a swim beach with a lifeguard. Inform the lifeguard you are practicing for your first triathlon, and ask him or her to keep an eye on you. Swim about the same amount of time in open water that has been normal in each workout. Feel free to take your time. Swim to a buoy that is around 25 yards out (if possible) then swim back. Feel free to rest as much as you need between each "outing." If you will not be swimming in open water or do not have access to a safe open-water swimming situation, the swim workout on Friday is a repeat of Tuesday's workout.

*Workout No. 10:* Swim 3 x 200 yards, taking 15 seconds of rest between each 200 yards. Swim up to 30 minutes. On Friday, swim about 15 to 30 minutes in open water or repeat Tuesday's workout.

*Workout No. 11:* Swim 500 yards nonstop. Make the odd-numbered 25-yard segments very easy and the even-numbered 25-yard segments a bit faster. For Friday, repeat Tuesday's workout or swim up to 30 minutes in open water.

*Workout No. 12:* Swim 500 yards nonstop. Make the first 100 yards very easy; try to relax your arms on the out-of-water portion (recovery) of the second 100 yards; focus on a strong hand pull on the third 100 yards; relax your arms on the recovery of the fourth 100 yards; and make each 25 yards a bit faster on the final 100 yards. This is how you will swim your race.

## BIKE

Any style of bicycle will work. A road bike will be more efficient, but if your only velo is a mountain bike, it will do.

To reduce injury, be certain the bike is correctly set up for you. Bike set-up will not be covered in this book, so you'll need to ask the people at your local bike shop for help or consult one of the recommended reading books, such as Chapter 3 of my book, *The Female Cyclist: Gearing up a Level.* If you do business with the local bike shop, they should be willing to help you with proper fit. A final note on bike set-up: a seat that is too high or too low can cause numbness in toes or genitals. Do not assume this is common; alleviate the problem.

A good pair of cycling shorts will make training much more enjoyable. The seam that typically creates the crotch on any pair of shorts or pants can be a point of discomfort when located between your body weight and a bicycle seat. For longer rides, a layer of petroleum jelly, Body Glide or Sport Slick between you and your cycling shorts can help prevent saddle sores. Also, never wear dirty cycling shorts; launder them between each use.

If you do not have a helmet, get one. Most races require the use of a helmet. Any helmets that have the ANSI approval on the inside will work.

Unless you plan on walking the bike home during some point in training or racing, learn how to change a flat tire. Carry a spare tube and a pump or a $CO_2$ cartridge and tire-inflation device with you.

Most of the bike workouts in the first few weeks are in Zones 1 to 2. As the plan progresses, there is more Zone 3 work. There are a couple of workouts listed in Table 4.1 that say "accels 4–6 x 30 sec (1' 30")." This is shorthand for, do four to six times 30-second efforts, building speed throughout the 30 seconds. These are not all-out sprints, but rather a bit of speed-play, allowing you to go fast without sending you into deep oxygen debt. Take 1 minute and 30 seconds of easy spinning between each acceleration. Be sure to warm up before and cool down after the accelerations.

The longest ride is in week 8 and is 1 hour and 45 minutes long. For the bike rides that designate Zone 3 riding, you can ride a rolling course and allow your exertion to be as much as Zone 3 on the uphills and as low as Zone 1 on the way down. Do not feel compelled to make the entire ride in Zone 3.

## RUN

Invest in a good pair of running shoes. Do not run in your aerobics, softball, weight-training or lawn-mowing shoes. Once you purchase running shoes, use them for that purpose only. Go to a running store and tell the sales person about your exercise history and why you need new running shoes. They should let you try on several shoes. Do a bit of jogging in each shoe before making the final choice.

The run workouts gently build in time, because the assumption is you have not run in awhile and we want to minimize the risk of injury. In general, the Wednesday runs are all Zone 1 throughout the first 6 weeks, and the Saturday runs can be in Zones 1 and 2. When Zone 2 is designated, it means you can be anywhere in Zones 1 or 2.

When the runs begin to open into Zone 3 intensity, as with the bike, do not feel compelled to make the whole run in Zone 3. Some Wednesday runs begin to add accelerations, similar to the bike accelerations. These are not all-out sprints, but rather a gentle building of speed.

## General

The first column of the plan has the week number (on the Sunday of week 12 is when you will complete your race). The next seven columns are the days of the week, and the last column is the total training time for each week.

Where the row containing the week numbers intersects the columns with the day labels, you will see which sport you should be doing, a workout code or number and the total time for the workout. For example, on Wednesday of Week 1, you will be doing a run, in training Zone 1, and the total time will be five minutes—yes, only 5 minutes. Do not panic and think it is not enough. Notice that by the end of week 6, you will be running 30 minutes.

## BRICK

A "brick" workout is a bike ride immediately followed by a run. You will do three brick workouts prior to your race. Use these to figure out how to make your bike-to-run clothes or shoe changes as fast as possible. That change time is included in your overall race time.

One of the bricks uses a workout term called "fartlek" which means speed-play. For your brick, it means do most of the workout in Zones 1 to 3, but add a few 20- to 30-second accelerations, with rest periods (easy spinning on the bike or easy jogging) around two minutes long.

## RACE DAY

Prior to race day, get a map of the course from the race director. Drive the course so you know what to expect.

On race morning, get to the transition area with time to spare. Get your transition area set up, being cautious not to be a rack-hog. Then take a few moments to orient yourself. Find a landmark near your bike, so you can locate the transition space when exiting the swim area. Note the entrance and exit to the transition area.

On the swim leg of the race, swim it exactly as you did on the Tuesday prior to the race. On the bike leg of the race, ride no faster than you have in training—this goes for the run as well.

Most of all, relax, have fun and enjoy the experience. If you trained right and raced conservatively, this race should leave you with a desire to do more triathlons. Then, focus on that water- and land-speed record that crossed your mind.

# CHAPTER FIVE

# Olympic Distance
## *for Limited Preparation Time*

> *One of the toughest aspects of my training is knowing which races I am ready for and which ones I should save for next year.*
>
> —*Adam Book,*
> *Loveland, Colorado, age 21*

There is an Olympic-distance triathlon (swim 1500 meters, bike 24.8 miles, run 6.2 miles) in a nearby city. The event is only six weeks away: is there enough time to make your triathlon debut? While I usually encourage first-timers to try a sprint distance event before moving to Olympic status, a reasonably fit person can be ready to race in five to six weeks. Want to tri?

## PROFILE

The plan shown on Table 5.1 on page 72 outlines the path to race day. This particular plan is designed for athletes who maintain their health and are most likely fit all year round. Their fitness might include some combination of running, spin classes or outdoor biking. They may currently swim a few laps or have swimming experience from past years, and they might be involved in other sports. Their current regimen gives them the capability to run for about 30 minutes, twice per week. They can bike comfortably for about an hour. Since most Olympic distance triathlons are held in open water, this athlete needs to be comfortable swimming with wildlife—and that is not only the fish.

| | | | | | | | | |
|---|---|---|---|---|---|---|---|---|
| **TABLE 5.1. OLYMPIC DISTANCE FOR LIMITED PREPARATION TIME PLAN** | | | | | | | | |
| **Week** | **Sport** | **Mon** | **Tues** | **Wed** | **Thurs** | **Fri** | **Sat** | **Sun** |
| 1 | Brick Swim Bike Run | Day off | Workout #1 | 00:30 | 00:45 | Workout #2 | Brick | 1:00– 1:30 |
| 2 | Brick Swim Bike Run | Day off | Workout #3 | 00:30 | 00:45 | Workout #4 | Brick | 1:30– 2:00 |
| 3 | Brick Swim Bike Run | Day off | Workout #5 | 00:30 | 00:45 | Workout #6 | Brick | 2:00– 2:30 |
| 4 | Brick Swim Bike Run | Day off | Workout #7 | 00:30 | 00:45 | Workout #8 | Brick | 2:30– 3:00 |
| 5 | Brick Swim Bike Run | Day off | Workout #9 | 00:30 | 00:45 | Workout #10 | Brick | 2:30– 3:00 |
| 6 | Brick Swim Bike Run | Day off | Workout #11 | 00:20 | 00:45 | | Brick | RACE! |

## GOAL

Given the assumptions in the last paragraph, the goal is to complete an Olympic distance triathlon in about six weeks, with a race finish time between three and four hours. The estimated finish time comes from assuming a two- to three-minute pace per 100 meters for the 1500-meter swim. This puts total swim time between 30 and 45 minutes. If you are capable of riding a bike for about 25 miles, averaging 15 to 18 miles per hour, the bike leg of the race will take around 1:22 to 1:40. Finally the run, averaging 10- to 12-minute miles, will take 1:02 to 1:15. Throw in a few minutes for transition time and the event will total some three to four hours on a Sunday morning. If this sounds like something you would like to tri, let us move on.

## THE SWIM

The plan lists swim workouts by number. Specifics for each numbered workout are listed in the text following this paragraph. More than likely, if you are using this plan, you do not own a heart rate monitor nor do you have a good idea about what kind of pace to hold in training and in the race. Assuming that statement is true, use your breathing and the Borg scale (Rating of Perceived Exertion) chart in Table 1.1, page 7, to gauge training and racing intensity. To simplify, I will refer to training zones listed in the chart and we will use those zones for all three sports.

Back to swimming. The speed or intensity of the Tuesday swims should be pretty easy—Zone 1 or 2. The Friday swim can begin with moderate 100s, in Zone 1 or 2, and progress to Zone 3 for the 50s. The detail for each workout follows:

*Swim 1. 10 x 50 meters, resting 15 to 30 seconds between each 50.*

*Swim 2. 4 x 100 meters, resting 15 to 30 seconds between each 100. Rest one to two minutes, then swim 6 x 50, resting about 10 seconds between each 50.*

*Swim 3. 12 x 50 meters, resting 15 to 30 seconds between each 50.*

*Swim 4. 6 x 100 meters, resting 15 to 30 seconds between each 100. Rest one to two minutes, then swim 6 x 50, resting about 10 seconds between each 50.*

*Swim 5. 14 x 50 meters, resting 15 to 20 seconds between each 50.*

*Swim 6. 8 x 100 meters, resting 15 to 20 seconds between each 100. Rest one to two minutes, then swim 8 x 50, resting about 10 seconds between each 50.*

*Swim 7. 16 x 50 meters, resting 15 to 20 seconds between each 50.*

*Swim 8. 10 x 100 meters, resting 15 to 20 seconds between each 100. Rest one to two minutes, then swim 8 x 50, resting about 10 seconds between each 50.*

*Swim 9. 18 x 50 meters, resting 15 to 20 seconds between each 50.*

*Swim 10. 10 x 100 meters, resting 15 seconds between each 100. Rest one to two minutes, then swim 10 x 50, resting about 10 seconds between each 50.*

*Swim 11. 15 x 50 meters, resting 15 to 20 seconds between each 50.*

The Tuesday swims are intentionally shorter than the Friday sessions. The longer swim day builds endurance so you are eventually doing a 1500-meter broken swim with minimal rest. This will be enough to get you through the event, without having to do long, boring, continuous swims in training. If it has been a while since you have swum in open water, it would be good to take a dip at a swim beach with a lifeguard on duty. An open-water swim can be substituted for one of the Tuesday or Friday workouts.

A practice open-water swim refreshes the memory that the water is probably dark, creepy-feeling and colder than the pool. There might be floating, mysterious objects that will brush against your arms and legs; these are generally harmless, but can raise your heart rate to sonic speed. A practice swim can help calm the nerves, and unless you can swim a remarkably straight line, it is good to practice lifting your head every few strokes to sight landmarks to keep on course. There are no black lines to follow on the bottom of a lake or ocean.

## BIKE AND BRICK

The swim portion of training and racing will take the least amount of time; cycling will take the most. The plan is designed so that overall endurance is built on the bike to minimize the risk of injury. This assumes you are riding a bicycle that fits correctly. If there is any doubt, drop into a qualified bike shop and ask them to help you get set up.

The first ride of each week is on Thursday. It is intended to be an easy spin, mostly in Zone 1. To improve leg speed and coordination, throw in a few 30-second accelerations, building speed throughout the 30 seconds. Take two to three minutes of rest between accelerations. When ramping up the speed, try to relax your shoulders and toes. Go as fast as possible, not allowing your butt to bounce off the bike seat. Although 45-minute sessions are shown on the plan, the ride can be as short as 30 or as long as 60 minutes.

On Saturdays, you will do a "brick," which means a bike ride immediately followed by a run. This combination workout helps build running endurance, while minimizing injury risk—because the first part of the workout is cycling. The session also prepares legs for that strange feeling of running after they have just been spinning in circles. While you are at it, practice transitions in the garage (a.k.a. transition area) so it becomes easy to lay out all your gear in a small area and keep it organized.

The first three bricks, in weeks 1, 2 and 3, are performed in Zones 1 to 2 for both sports. The bricks in weeks four and five can be done anywhere in Zones 1 to 3. It is not necessary to maximize time in the upper zone. A range of running time is provided for the bricks to accommodate individual differences in fitness. If you decide to train on the low end, not to worry: it will work fine.

A range of workout times is also shown for the Sunday bike rides. The first two long rides are in Zones 1 to 2 and the last three rides can be in Zones 1 to 3. Use the nutrition guidelines in Chapter 3 to stay well hydrated and fueled. Testing the routine on long rides will hone in on the appropriate macronutrient values. Start practicing this routine on the long Sunday rides in week 1 and use the routine you have tested on race day.

## RUN

Since you have already been running, it is assumed a good pair of running-only shoes is in your wardrobe. Run twice per week. One of the run workouts was covered within the brick description; the other run workout is on Wednesday. Make Wednesday a form run that includes four to six repetitions of 20-second accelerations. Build speed throughout the acceleration to about 5K race pace. Take easy, two- to three-minute jogs between each acceleration. The remainder of that run is in Zones 1 to 2.

## TAPER AND RACE

At the beginning of this chapter, I mentioned you could be race ready in five to six weeks. If pressed for time, you could eliminate week 5 and go right from week 4 to week 6 Eliminating week 5 will mean eliminating a long swim practice that simulates race distance and overall endurance, but the race is still doable.

In either case, whether you choose five or six weeks of training, the last week on the schedule is a rest week. It is designed to have you feeling fresh for race day. Gather all the self-control you have to keep from doing more activity that week. Rest and visualize how much fun race day will be.

When race morning arrives, get to the transition area with

plenty of time to spare. Keep your eating and drinking schedule the same as it has been for all Sunday long rides. Get your equipment set up and look for the perfect route into and out of the transition area. Know where your trusty velo is racked.

As you line up for the swim, unless you are very experienced in open-water swimming, position yourself on the outside and near the rear of the pack. Sometimes the swim can get rough with people thrashing about (remember that wildlife I mentioned?). So unless you are a very competent swimmer, place yourself away from the crowd. When swimming, recall good stroke form and the strong workouts you had in the pool. Try to relax and get into a rhythm.

After the swim and a fast transition, it is off on the bike course. On the bike as well as the run, try to control pace so it is not beyond what you have practiced in workouts. Be certain to hydrate and fuel on both the bike and the run. After the ride, the second transition should be easy, because you have been practicing this one. After the second transition, start the run with a focus on relaxed shoulders and smooth, comfortable breathing. One strategy might be to walk through all the run aid stations to consume fluids and give yourself a break. A few seconds of walking will not extend your race time very much. At the end of the run, be sure to smile when crossing the finish line. You made it through the first of many triathlons.

# Cyclist *to* *Duathlete*

*Before we met and began our training program together, my training consisted of hard training almost all the time. I can remember riding with another racer and commenting about a "good hard ride"—that was the norm for me. Whenever I rode, I was always in Zone 3, 4 or 5—never in Zone 1 or 2. Now training in the lower zones makes all the sense in the world. It's a building-block approach to training and racing. To train smart, it's the relative quality that counts, not how hard you are always riding."*

*—Jeff Fryer,*
*Wolcott, Connecticut, age 56*

**M**any athletes arrive at multisport from a single-sport background. Without planning, a first duathlon—run, bike, run—can be frustrating. Typically, the move to duathlon for a cyclist is more difficult than for a runner. I know a cyclist (not Jeff from the quote) who showed up on race day with no previous run training. "After all," he responded, "everyone knows how to run and I have loads of fitness from cycling. How hard can this possibly be?"

He began the first run in his domestic-chore shoes and felt pretty cocky. Not a great finish, but he didn't clock a snail's pace either. He jumped on his noble steed and passed countless people on the bike—time trialing was his strength. "Man, this multisport stuff is great and easy! I am going to place for sure; I'm hot today," he said.

In the second transition, his trusty grass-stained shoes waited for that second run. Oh, that second run. The Tin Man

| | | | | | | | | | |
|---|---|---|---|---|---|---|---|---|---|
| **TABLE 6.1. CYCLIST-TO-DUATHLETE PLAN** | | | | | | | | | |
| **Week** | **Sport** | **Mon Time** | **Tues Time** | **Tues Code** | **Wed Time** | **Wed Code** | **Thurs Time** | **Thurs Code** | **Fri Time** |
| 1 | | Day off | | | | | | | Day Off |
| | Run | | 00:05 | E1 | | | 00:10 | E1 | |
| | Bike | | 01:00 | E2 | 00:45 | S3(4–6) | 01:00 | M1(15) | |
| 2 | | Day off | | | | | | | |
| | Run | | 00:10 | E1 | | | 00:15 | E1 | |
| | Bike | | 00:45 | E2 | 00:45 | S3(4–6) | 00:40 | M1(15) | 01:00 |
| 3 | | Day off | | | | | | | |
| | Run | | 00:15 | E1 | | | 00:20 | E1 | |
| | Bike | | 00:40 | E2 | 00:45 | S3(4–6) | 00:35 | M1(20) | 01:00 |
| 4 | Brick | Day off | | | Day Off | | Brick | | |
| | Run | | 00:10 | E1 | | | 00:10 | E1 | |
| | Bike | | 00:45 | E2 | | | 00:45 | E2 | 00:45 |
| 5 | | Day off | | | | | | | |
| | Run | | 00:15 | E1 | | | 00:15 | E2 | |
| | Bike | | 00:30 | E2 | 01:00 | S3(4–6) | 00:45 | M5(15) | 01:00 |
| 6 | | Day off | | | | | Brick | | |
| | Run | | 00:20 | E1 | | | 00:20 | E2 | |
| | Bike | | 00:30 | E2 | 01:00 | S3(4–6) | 00:45 | M5(20) | 01:00 |
| 7 | | Day off | | | | | | | |
| | Run | | 00:15 | E1 | | | 00:30 | S2 | |
| | Bike | | 00:30 | E2 | 01:00 | S3(4–6) | 00:45 | M5(20) | 01:00 |
| 8 | | Day off | | | Day off | | | | |
| | Run | | 00:15 | E1 | | | 00:15 | E1 | |
| | Bike | | 00:45 | E2 | | | 00:45 | S4 | 01:00 |
| 9 | | Day off | | | | | | | Day off |
| | Run | | 00:20 | E1 | | | 00:20 | S2 | |
| | Bike | | 00:30 | E2 | 01:00 | E2 | 00:30 | S4 | |
| 10 | | Day off | | | Day off | | | | Day off |
| | Run | | 00:10 | E1 | | | 00:10 | E1 | |
| | Bike | | 00:50 | E2 | | | 00:50 | S4 | |

from Oz could have moved faster out of the transition area and would probably have had better form as well.

"What the heck happened?" he wondered. His legs seemed filled with cement and his shins were killing him. "It seemed like such an easy transition to make—from cyclist to duathlete."

| Fri Code | Sat Time | Sat Code | Sun Time | Sun Code | Training Hours | Training Hours by Sport | |
|---|---|---|---|---|---|---|---|
| | 00:15 | E1 | | | | Run | 00:30 |
| | 01:00 | E2 | 02:00 | E3 | 06:15 | Bike | 05:45 |
| | 00:20 | E1 | | | | Run | 00:45 |
| E2 | 00:35 | E2 | 02:00 | E3 | 06:30 | Bike | 05:45 |
| | 00:25 | E2 | | | | Run | 01:00 |
| E2 | 00:30 | E2 | 02:00 | E3 | 06:30 | Bike | 05:30 |
| | 00:30 | E2 | | | | Run | 00:50 |
| S3(4–6) | | | 01:00 | T2 | 04:05 | Bike | 03:15 |
| | 00:35 | E2 | | | | Run | 01:05 |
| E2 | | | 02:00 | E4 | 06:20 | Bike | 05:15 |
| | 00:45 | E3 | | | | Run | 01:25 |
| E2 | | | 02:00 | E4 | 06:40 | Bike | 05:15 |
| | 00:45 | E2 | | | | Run | 01:30 |
| E2 | | | 02:00 | E4 | 06:45 | Bike | 05:15 |
| | Day off | | Brick 00:20 | E3 | | Run | 00:50 |
| E2 | | | 01:00 | M5(20) | 04:20 | Bike | 03:30 |
| | | | Race sim 00:40 | split | | Run | 01:20 |
| | 01:30 | E2 | 00:40 | M5(15) | 05:30 | Bike | 04:10 |
| | | | Race! | | | Run | 00:20 |
| | 00:30 | S4 | | | 02:30 | Bike | 02:10 |

Making the transition from training for one sport to training for two can be easier with a little planning. The plan in this chapter is for a cyclist preparing for a first duathlon.

## PROFILE

This plan is for a person who is primarily a cyclist who wants to try something new this season—a duathlon. This athlete has a good base in cycling and currently trains around 6 hours per week.

## GOAL

At the end of 10 weeks, complete a duathlon consisting of a 5K run, a 30K bike and a second 5K run.

## THE PLAN

Table 6.1 on page 80-81 is a 10-week plan that transforms a cyclist into a duathlete. The plan minimizes risk by slowly building total weekly run time from 30 minutes to a maximum of 1:20. Daily run time builds from five minutes (yes, I want you to run only 5 minutes) to between 45 and 60 minutes. In general, the run training contains less intensity than the bike training does.

The coded workout descriptions in the plan (such as E1, M5, and so on) are in Chapters 19 and 20. Some more specific instruction for various workouts follows in the remaining paragraphs of this chapter.

On Tuesday of the first week of the plan, you will run for

# Key Points—Cyclist To Duathlete

- Invest in a good pair of running shoes to decrease injury risk.
- The early weeks of short runs immediately followed by a bike (reverse bricks) will help transition training.
- The long run can be slowly built to around one hour.
- There is room in the plan for three bricks (a bike ride immediately followed by a run). Use these workouts to practice smooth and speedy transitions.
- The race simulation day will allow you to work the bugs out of the transitions and get the "feel" of the event.

five minutes and immediately jump on the bike for an hour ride. Wednesday of that week is a form workout, cycling only. All Wednesday bike rides can last anywhere from 45 to 60 minutes.

Thursday of the first week is a 10-minute run, immediately followed by an hour bike. This particular ride has a short tempo section in it. Friday is a day off and Saturday is again a run immediately followed by a bike ride. These "reverse bricks"—run, bike—has you run when your legs are fresh, allows overall training endurance to be maintained, and is early practice for the first transition.

The Sunday bike ride assumes you have been comfortably riding a hilly course in previous weeks. If this is not the case, reduce the intensity of these rides.

Week 2 is very similar to week 1, only the run time builds and a Friday workout is added. The Friday ride can be 45 to 60 minutes, although 60 minutes is typically shown on the plan. The only unusual item is the Thursday reverse brick, because the tempo segment should be in the last 25 minutes of the ride.

Up to week 4, all combination workouts are reverse bricks. On Thursday of week 4, you will do your first "brick"—the bike is immediately followed by the run. All combination days remain reverse bricks, unless "brick" is specifically shown for that day, such as in week 6 and week 8. The last workout in week 4 is a time trial. After a good warm-up, ride as fast as possible and record the time for a distance between five and eight miles. This time can be used later in training to benchmark improvements.

Training continues along a similar pattern described for weeks 1 to 4, up to week 9. At the end of week 9 is a race simulation. Begin the workout with a 20-minute E2 run. Dash into your garage (a.k.a. transition area) and hop on the bike for a 40-minute ride, including a 15-minute tempo section. After the bike, back into the garage to transform back into a runner for a 20-minute E3 run. Good job, you are ready to go!

Week 10 is a rest week of reduced volume to prepare you for the event. You can go into the race confident, strong and ready to play the game.

# CHAPTER SEVEN

# RUNNER *to* *Duathlete*

*Even if I couldn't make any money, I'd still be running around the mountains and challenging myself athletically.*
—Michael Tobin, 1999 XTERRA series winner,
14-time Powerman victor, two-time overall
Powerman series winner, quoted from
Inside Triathlon *magazine, September 1999*

I t's like riding a bike: Once you learn, you never forget." Ever heard that old saw? It is true, once one learns how, it is fairly easy to get back on a bike, pedal and keep the rubber side down. Riding a bike is something nearly everyone knows how to do, even "runners." Runners, like their cyclist counterparts in Chapter 6, figure participation in a duathlon should be easy. After all, they have been running for quite a while, are in good shape and have decent endurance. Just pop a little bike in the middle and voilà—duathlete.

Although it is frequently easier for a runner to become a duathlete than it is for a cyclist, a runner should not underestimate the transition. Rene commented on her first duathlon, "You should have seen me on that first 5km, I killed 'em. My first transition was fast and I headed out on Fred's bike." Race day was the second time she had ever ridden this bike. She continued, "I felt pretty good on the bike, really hauling—even passed a few people! Then, on the second run, my shoulders cramped, my knees were killing me and my legs were all rubbery. It felt like I didn't know how to run. I was

| Week | Sport | Mon Time | Tues Time | Tues Code | Wed Time | Wed Code | Thurs Time | Thurs Code | Fri Time |
|---|---|---|---|---|---|---|---|---|---|
| 1 | | Day off | | | | | | | Day off or |
| | Run | | 00:30 | E2 | 00:45 | M1(15) | 00:30 | E1 | 00:30 |
| | Bike | | | | | | 00:30 | E1 | |
| 2 | | Day off | | | | | | | Day off or |
| | Run | | 00:30 | E2 | 00:45 | M1(20) | 00:30 | E1 | 00:30 |
| | Bike | | 00:30 | E1 | | | 00:30 | E2 | |
| 3 | | Day off | | | | | | | Day off or |
| | Run | | 00:30 | E2 | 00:45 | M1(20) | 00:30 | E1 | 00:30 |
| | Bike | | 00:30 | E1 | | | 00:30 | E2 | |
| 4 | Brick | Day off | | | Day off | | | | Day off |
| | Run | | 00:30 | E2 | | | 00:30 | E1 | |
| | Bike | | | | | | 00:30 | E2 | |
| 5 | | Day off | | | | | | | Day off or |
| | Run | | 00:30 | E2 | 00:45 | M5(15) | 00:15 | E1 | 00:30 |
| | Bike | | 00:30 | E2 | | | 00:45 | S3(4–6) | |
| 6 | | Day off | | | | | | | Day off or |
| | Run | | 00:30 | E2 | 00:45 | M5(20) | 00:15 | E1 | 00:30 |
| | Bike | | 00:45 | E2 | | | 00:45 | S3(4–6) | |
| 7 | | Day off | | | | | | | Day off or |
| | Run | | 00:30 | E2 | 00:45 | M5(20) | 00:15 | E1 | 00:30 |
| | Bike | | 00:45 | E2 | | | 00:45 | S3(4–6) | |
| 8 | | Day off | | | Day off | | | | Day off |
| | Run | | | | | | 00:30 | E1 | |
| | Bike | | 00:30 | E1 | | | 00:30 | E2 | |
| 9 | | Day off | | | | | | | |
| | Run | | 00:30 | E2 | 00:45 | M5(20) | 00:15 | E1 | 00:30 |
| | Bike | | 00:45 | E2 | | | 00:45 | S3(4–6) | |
| 10 | | Day off | | | | | | | Day off |
| | Run | | 00:30 | E2 | 00:30 | S2 | 00:15 | E1 | |
| | Bike | | 00:30 | E1 | | | 00:30 | S4 | |

**TABLE 7. 1. RUNNER-TO-DUATHLETE PLAN**

reduced to a pathetic walk for the second 5km and my knees were sore for a week."

Rene failed to realize that riding a bike and racing a bike are two different things. She underestimated the importance of proper bike fit—not only to make her a more economical

| Fri Code | Sat Time | Sat Code | Sun Time | Sun Code | Weekly Training Hours | Weekly Training Hours by Sport | | %Hours by Sport | |
|---|---|---|---|---|---|---|---|---|---|
| E2 | 00:45 | E2 | 01:15 | E3 | 04:45 | Run Bike | 03:30 01:15 | Run Bike | 0.74 0.26 |
| E2 | 00:45 | E2 | 01:15 | E3 | 05:15 | Run Bike | 03:30 01:45 | Run Bike | 0.67 0.33 |
| E2 | 01:00 | E2 | 01:15 | E3 | 05:30 | Run Bike | 03:30 02:00 | Run Bike | 0.64 0.36 |
| | 01:00 | S3(4–6) | 01:00 | TT | 03:30 | Run Bike | 02:00 01:30 | Run Bike | 0.57 0.43 |
| E2 | 01:15 | E3 | 01:15 | S2 | 05:45 | Run Bike | 03:15 02:30 | Run Bike | 0.57 0.43 |
| E2 | 01:30 | E3 | 01:15 | S2 | 06:15 | Run Bike | 03:15 03:00 | Run Bike | 0.52 0.48 |
| E2 | 01:45 | E3 | 01:15 | S2 | 06:30 | Run Bike | 03:15 03:15 | Run Bike | 0.50 0.50 |
| | 01:00 | S4 | Brick 00:20 01:00 | S4 E3 | 03:50 | Run Bike | 01:50 02:00 | Run Bike | 0.48 0.52 |
| E2 | 01:10 | E2 | Race sim 00:40 00:40 | split M5(15) | 06:00 | Run Bike | 02:40 03:20 | Run Bike | 0.44 0.56 |
| | 00:10 00:20 | E2 E2 | Race! | | 02:45 | Run Bike | 01:25 01:20 | Run Bike | 0.52 0.48 |

# Key Points—Runner to Duathlete

- Train on the bike you will use in the race. This seems obvious, but many people have made last-minute switches because someone was willing to loan them a "trick" bike. All gains that might have been gained by technology were lost because legs cramped from being in a new position.
- Have the local bike shop help you get your position correct. Many studies have shown reduced oxygen consumption at a given workload when cycling positioning was optimized. Keep in mind you need to be comfortable in any optimal aerodynamic position.
- "Spin" in smaller gears. When riding, try to spin between 85 to 120 rpm on the flats and 65 to 80 rpm on the hills.
- Ride a straight line. This also seems obvious, but many people put their heads down and just hammer on the cranks. Meanwhile, they weave dangerously, wasting energy.

rider, but to prevent injury as well. She also underestimated the need to train on the bike so her muscles would be adapted to the motion necessary for cycling. The 10-week plan shown in Table 7.1 would have helped Rene prepare for her first duathlon. Is this a plan for you?

## PROFILE

Table 7.1 is a game plan for a runner to participate in a first duathlon. This athlete is currently actively training as a runner, logging some six hours of training each week and running four to five days per week. This athlete is currently doing some speedwork into at least Zone 3, perhaps including an occasional 5km or 10km race into training.

## GOAL

At the end of 10 weeks, complete a duathlon consisting of a 5km run, a 30km bike and a second 5km run.

## THE PLAN

For a runner, it would not be unusual for half of the duathlon race time to be spent on the bike. For this reason, the model on Table 7.1 builds endurance on the bike so that a long ride of about 1:45 is possible in week 7. Overall weekly cycling time also builds from about 1:15 in the first week to 3:20 in week 9. This gentle build in time spent on the bike reduces risk of injury and helps a runner be more economical on the bike. For additional tips, see the sidebar on page 88. The codes used in Table 7.1 (such as E2, S4, and so on) are explained in Chapters 19 and 20.

Let us look at week 1 in more detail. Monday is a day off, as are all Mondays on this plan. If it works better for you to have different day off, go ahead and shift the schedule to accommodate personal needs. Tuesday of week 1 is a 30-minute E2 run. Wednesday is a 45-minute run, including 15 minutes in Zone 3. Thursday is the first combination workout, beginning with a 30-minute easy E1 run, immediately followed by a 30-minute easy E1 bike ride. A run immediately followed by a bike is called a "brick."

In week 1, the Friday workout is optional and all Friday workouts will remain optional throughout the 10-week plan. If you do decide to work out, make it a 30- to 45-minute run. Saturday of week 1 is a 45-minute E2 bike. An E3 run on Sunday finishes out week 1. Although 1:15 is shown for the Sunday run, this long run can go up to 1:30 depending on your personal fitness.

The pattern described for week 1 is very similar for the remaining 10-week schedule, with two exceptions described in the next paragraphs. In this particular plan, any time a bike and a run workout are shown on the same day, bike first, then run immediately after—do a brick. If you would like to practice the first transition in duathlon, make some of the Tuesday workouts "reverse bricks"—run first, then bike.

One of the workouts needing a bit more description is the time trial at the end of week 4. This can be a self-administered time trial at the track, or a 5km race. If you decide to run at the track, run as fast as possible for 3 miles. At the track or in a race, record splits (the time for each mile), heart rate, weather conditions and how you felt in a journal. This time trial can serve as a benchmark for future improvements.

The only other workout that deserves special mention is the race simulation at the end of week 9. Begin the workout with a 20-minute E2 run. Dash into your garage (a.k.a. transition area) and hop on the bike for a 40-minute ride, including a 15-minute tempo section. After the bike, it's back into the garage to transform to a runner for a 20-minute E3 run. This race simulation is the end of the major portion of your preparation. The few days leading up to the race are for rest. Enjoy your race day.

# CHAPTER EIGHT

# Thirteen Weeks to *Half-Ironman for Those with Limited Training Time*

*I nearly went crazy in week five with three days off! I was lost with nothing to do. Later in the plan I loved Mondays and Fridays though. The last few weeks, fear, anxiety and doubt began to creep into my psyche. After a long ride, it was difficult just to run one 10-minute mile—how could I do a half-marathon? The last couple of weeks I realized I had paid my dues, completed the miles and stayed with The Plan. Regrets? I think I could have pushed harder because I sprinted to the finish with "gas in the tank." Oh, I had some tough miles, but I tasted the fruits of my efforts...awesome!*
*—Mike Poplin, Winston-Salem,*
*North Carolina, age 48*

The scene: your reading chair. Flip...flip...flip...flip through the pages of a triathlon magazine. A thought-bubble floats up: "A half-Ironman...wow, that would be fun. Ah, one on the schedule, but it is less than three months away. Can I be ready for a race of this distance given about 13 weeks to train and six to eleven training hours per week?"

Yes! The plan in this chapter prepares a seasoned triathlete to complete a half-Ironman event, while minimizing training. Speed is not an issue; rather, minimizing training hours and injury risk and increasing the odds of having fun are key.

## PROFILE

You are an experienced triathlete and have completed sprint- and Olympic-distance races. Either by choice or circumstance, you have only 13 weeks available to train for a half-Ironman. Before beginning this plan, you are capable of swimming three times per week for around an hour. Holding a 1:45 to 2:00 pace, per 100 yards for the 1.2-mile swim seems possible (total swim time of 38 to 43 minutes). You are currently able to cycle comfortably for an hour and a half or so. You guess that you average somewhere between 15 and 18 mph for 56 miles (total bike time between 3:07 and 3:45). Your long run is currently around 1:15 and a marathon pace of 10- to 11-minute miles is not unreasonable (total run time between 2:07 and 2:30). Up to this point, you have been training around six to nine hours each week, which is very comfortable.

Your typical training week needs to be fairly light during the week, due to a long list of commitments; however, weekends are open for long training hours. At least one day per week must be a rest day, with no training, as this keeps you healthy and in good spirits.

## GOAL

Complete a half-Ironman race in six to seven hours. If necessary, you are willing to walk to keep healthy and comfortable.

## PLAN DESCRIPTION

Table 8.1 on page 94-95 is a 13-week plan to get you ready for the half-Ironman, while minimizing injury and training hours. When looking at the first week of the training plan, you should be thinking, "Wow, that is too easy." On the other hand, if you are thinking the first week will be a struggle, more training time is necessary before embarking on this journey.

With that said, let us take a broad look at the plan. Weekly training hours have a pattern of building for three weeks, then reducing for a week or two. This pattern allows the body to be stressed, to prepare for the event, and rest, to make physical repairs and gains. Do not be tempted to increase training hours during any rest week, no matter how good you feel. Notice the weekly volume pattern does not change much between weeks 1 to 3 and 9 to 11. The change is a volume shift to the two weekend days. By week 11, the Saturday and Sunday combined training hours equal seven—about the total estimated finish time for the event. Overall intensity begins in heart rate Zones 1 to 2 and builds to Zone 3 for all three sports.

Swimming time stays between 45 minutes and 1:00. If you have the time and energy to do so, Saturday swims can be up

## TABLE 8.1: THIRTEEN WEEKS TO HALF-IRONMAN PLAN

| Week | Sport | Mon Time | Tues Time | Tues Code | Wed Time | Wed Code | Thurs Time | Thurs Code |
|------|-------|----------|-----------|-----------|----------|----------|------------|------------|
| 1 | Swim | Day off | 00:45 | Form | | | 01:00 | E3 |
| | Bike | | | | 01:00 | Form | | |
| | Run | | 00:30 | E2 | | | 00:30 | Form |
| 2 | Swim | Day off | 00:45 | Form | | | 01:00 | E3 |
| | Bike | | | | 01:00 | Form | | |
| | Run | | 00:30 | E2 | | | 00:45 | Form |
| 3 | Swim | Day off | 00:45 | Form | | | 01:00 | E3 |
| | Bike | | | | 01:00 | Form | | |
| | Run | | 00:45 | E2 | | | 01:00 | Form |
| 4 | Brick | | | | | | | |
| | Swim | Day off | 00:45 | Form | | | 00:45 | E3 |
| | Bike | | | | | | 00:30 | Form |
| | Run | | 00:30 | E2 | 00:30 | Form | | |
| 5 | Swim | Day off | 00:45 | Form | Day off | | 00:30 | E1 |
| | Bike | | | | | | 01:00 | Form |
| | Run | | 00:30 | E2 | | | | |
| 6 | Swim | Day off | 00:45 | Form | | | 01:00 | E3 |
| | Bike | | | | 01:00 | Form | | |
| | Run | | | | | | 00:45 | Form |
| 7 | Swim | Day off | 00:45 | Form | | | 01:00 | E3 |
| | Bike | | | | 01:00 | Form | | |
| | Run | | 00:15 | E2 | | | 01:00 | Form |
| 8 | Brick | | | | | | | |
| | Swim | Day off | 00:45 | Form | | | 01:00 | E3 |
| | Bike | | | | | | | |
| | Run | | | | 01:00 | E2 | | |
| 9 | Brick | | | | | | 01:00 | |
| | Swim | Day off | 00:45 | Form | | | | |
| | Bike | | 00:30 | E1 | | | 00:30 | E2 |
| | Run | | | | 00:15 | E1 | 00:30 | E2 |
| 10 | Swim | Day off | 00:45 | Form | | | 01:00 | E2 |
| | Bike | | | | 01:00 | E2 | | |
| | Run | | | | | | 00:30 | E2 |
| 11 | Swim | Day off | 00:45 | E2 | | | 00:30 | E1 |
| | Bike | | | | 01:00 | Form | | |
| | Run | | 00:30 | E1 | | | 00:45 | Form |
| 12 | Brick | | | | | | | |
| | Swim | Day off | 00:45 | Form | | | 01:00 | E3 |
| | Bike | | | | 01:00 | Form | | |
| | Run | | | | | | | |
| 13 | Brick | | | | | | | |
| | Swim | Day off | | | | | 00:30 | Form |
| | Bike | | | | 00:45 | Form | | |
| | Run | | 00:30 | Form | | | | |

| Fri Time | Fri Code | Sat Time | Sat Code | Sun Time | Sun Code | Weekly Training Hours | Weekly Hours by Sport | |
|---|---|---|---|---|---|---|---|---|
| | | 01:00 | E2 | | | | Swim | 02:45 |
| 00:45 | E1 | 01:30 | E2 | | | | Bike | 03:15 |
| | | | | 01:00 | E2 | 08:00 | Run | 02:00 |
| | | 01:00 | E2 | | | | Swim | 02:45 |
| 01:00 | E1 | 02:00 | E2 | | | | Bike | 04:00 |
| | | | | 01:15 | E2 | 09:15 | Run | 02:30 |
| | | 01:00 | E2 | | | | Swim | 02:45 |
| 01:00 | E1 | 02:15 | E2 | | | | Bike | 04:15 |
| | | | | 01:15 | E2 | 10:00 | Run | 03:00 |
| | | 02:00 | Text | | | | | |
| | | | | Day off | | | Swim | 01:30 |
| 01:00 | E1 | 01:30 | | | | | Bike | 03:00 |
| | | 00:30 | | | | 06:00 | Run | 01:30 |
| Day off | | 01:00 | E2 | | | | Swim | 02:15 |
| | | 02:30 | E2 | | | | Bike | 03:30 |
| | | | | 01:30 | E3 | 07:45 | Run | 02:00 |
| Day off | | 01:00 | E2 | | | | Swim | 02:45 |
| | | 03:00 | E3 | | | | Bike | 04:00 |
| | | | | 01:30 | E2 | 09:00 | Run | 02:15 |
| Day off | | 01:00 | E2 | | | | Swim | 02:45 |
| | | 03:15 | E2 | | | | Bike | 04:15 |
| | | | | 01:45 | E3 | 10:00 | Run | 03:00 |
| | | 02:15 | | | | | | |
| | | | | Day off | | | Swim | 01:45 |
| 01:00 | E1 | 01:30 | Form | | | | Bike | 02:30 |
| | | 00:45 | Form | | | 06:00 | Run | 01:45 |
| Day off | | 01:00 | E3 | | | | Swim | 01:45 |
| | | 03:15 | E2 | | | | Bike | 04:15 |
| | | | | 01:45 | E2 | 08:30 | Run | 02:30 |
| Day off | | 01:00 | E3 | | | | Swim | 02:45 |
| | | 03:30 | E3 | | | | Bike | 04:30 |
| | | | | 02:00 | E3 | 09:45 | Run | 02:30 |
| Day off | | 01:00 | Form | | | | Swim | 02:15 |
| | | 04:00 | E2 | | | | Bike | 05:00 |
| | | | | 02:00 | E2 | 10:30 | Run | 03:15 |
| | | 01:30 | Text | | | | | |
| | | | | | | | Swim | 01:45 |
| | | 01:00 | | 00:45 | E1 | | Bike | 02:45 |
| 01:00 | E2 | 00:30 | | | | 06:00 | Run | 01:30 |
| | | 00:30 | | Race! | | | | |
| Day off | | | | 6–7 | | | Swim | 00:30 |
| | | 00:20 | E2 | hours | | Race plus | Bike | 01:05 |
| | | 00:10 | E2 | | | 02:15 | Run | 00:40 |

to 1:15. The weekend long bike ride builds from 1:30 to 4:00 and the long runs build to 2:00.

For all three sports, training and racing will stay well below lactate threshold heart rate—the heart rate typically held for Olympic-distance races. It will be desirable to minimize the time spent in Zone 4 and higher during the half-Ironman race. (Hint: Try not to choose a hilly course for your first event.)

The coded workout descriptions for cycling and running are in Chapters 19 and 20. If the plan calls for a "form" workout, use "speed" drills. For swimming, a "form" workout includes several drills during the warm-up and a focus on good form throughout the session. Speed is less important than good technique.

Some of the workouts within Table 8.1 need a bit more instruction, specifically on swimming workouts and the bricks. First, I will give more information on swimming.

## SWIMMING DETAILS

**WEEKS 1 TO 4:** Include at least one 800- to 1000-yard steady swim or a broken set with rest intervals no greater than 10 seconds. On Saturdays, make the main set of the swim workout in the 1000- to 1500-yard range.

**WEEKS 5 TO 8:** Include at least one 800- to 1000-yard steady swim (or a broken swim with rest intervals no greater than 10 seconds), rest 2 to 3 minutes and immediately swim another 400 to 600 yards. On Saturdays, make the main set of the swim workout in the 1500- to 2000-yard range.

**WEEKS 9 TO 11:** Include at least one steady swim set, with minimal rest of 60 seconds or less, totaling 30 to 40 minutes. On Saturdays, make the main set of the swim workout in the 2000-yard range.

## BRICKS

The total brick workout time is shown in the top row of any week containing a brick. The breakdown of the brick is shown in the bike and run row details.

**WEEK 4:** Cycle for a 1:30 total time, with the first 60 minutes in Zones 1 to 2 and the last 30 minutes all in Zone 3. Go right to the run, allowing heart rate to be anywhere in Zones 1 to 3. If you feel great, spend more time in Zone 3.

**WEEK 12:** Ride the bike for an hour, with the first 40 minutes in Zones 1 to 2 and the last 20 minutes all in Zone 3. Go right to the 30-minute run, with the first 15 minutes in Zones 1 to 2 and the last 15 minutes all in Zone 3.

## QUESTIONS?

**Q:** There is a great group ride Wednesday night. They typically ride 1:15 to 1:30, and it is blazing fast. Can this ride be included in the plan?

**A:** If you have the time and energy to complete the 1:15 to 1:30 ride, it will work. My concern is "blazing fast." Allowing others to dictate your training usually leads to illness, injury or failure to meet personal goals.

**Q:** I would like to cycle a bit on Friday, will that ruin the plan?

**A:** A ride of 30 to 60 minutes, E1, E2 or form, will be fine.

**Q:** I have more running fitness than the plan shows. Can I add more time?

**A:** Adding around 15 minutes to each week of weeks 1 to 7 is fine. It is not necessary to run over 2:00.

**Q:** What is the shortest that my long run can be?

**A:** A long run of about 1:30 will be enough to get most people comfortably through the event.

Note: The Q and A section for Chapter 9 may be helpful for this chapter as well.

## GOING THE DISTANCE IN TRAINING AND ON RACE DAY

As you progress through the training plan, remember to refuel and keep hydrated as described in Chapter 3. Rest, recovery and refueling will go a long way to keep you on track to reach the goal.

On race day, wear a heart rate monitor and stay in mostly in Zones 1 to 3. One of the biggest mistakes made when triathletes step up to a longer race distance is to begin the event at a pace as though the race is Olympic-distance. Relax and control your speed during the swim and bike. Be willing to take walking bouts during long training runs, as well as during the race.

Practice using the Rating of Perceived Exertion, in addition to the heart rate monitor, as a guide for pace during training. This will be helpful in the event of a heart rate monitor malfunction. Another trick is to imagine anything that might go amiss during the race and plan strategies to solve problems before race day. These mental tools will help you be cool, calm and relaxed on race day—enjoy!

# CHAPTER NINE

# Thirteen Weeks, Thirteen Hours to *Ironman* for *Those with Limited Training Time*

*You are my new hero. I followed your article "13 Weeks to a 13-Hour Ironman." As a 195-pound 50-year-old I had no real idea it would get me anywhere near the 13-hour mark—like most Ironman virgins I just wanted to finish and not hurt some part of my body. But it did work! I did an easy 12:55 at Florida Ironman, 20 minutes ahead of a man my age who trained at least twice as hard and long and who e-mailed you when he first read your article to tell you it wouldn't work! Thank you Coach Gale—I will talk about you and your article the rest of my life, and will use it when I enter Ironman Hawaii at age 60.*
*—Brian Dowling, attorney, Dothan, Alabama*
*(age 51 by the time of the event)*

So, been racing awhile, have you? Doing the same races year after year? Looking for a new challenge? Would like to do an Ironman, but jeeeeeeze, there is just too much training involved—or is there?

If you are contemplating an Ironman-distance race, do not have much time and simply want to complete the event without illness or injury (the world-record performance comes next year), this chapter is for you. It is certainly not for beginner athletes, but it is for beginning Ironwomen and Ironmen. The plan is a 13-week training plan that culminates in completing your first Ironman race in about 12 to 14 hours. Since you do not have much time to train, the largest training week will be about 13 hours; other weeks are less.

## PROFILE

You are an experienced triathlete. You have completed sprint- and Olympic-distance races. Life, however, has your clock in a stranglehold and training time is at a premium. Before beginning this plan, you are capable of swimming three times per week for around an hour. You estimate you could hold a 1:45 to 2-minute pace per 100 yards for the 2.4-mile swim (total swim time of 1:14 to 1:25). You are currently able to cycle comfortably for an hour and a half or so. It is possible you average somewhere between 15 and 18 mph for 112 miles (total bike time between 6:15 and 7:30). Your long run is currently in the 1:15 to 1:30 range. You think a marathon pace of 10- to 11-minute miles is possible (total run time between 4:15 and 5:00). Up to this point, you have been training around eight to 10 hours each week, which is very comfortable.

Your typical training week is fairly light during the week, due to a long list of commitments; however, weekends are open for long training hours. You need at least one day totally off from training each week, because it keeps you healthy and in good spirits.

## GOAL

Your goal is to complete an Ironman-distance race in between 12 and 14 hours. If necessary, you are willing to walk to comfortably complete the race. What this means is that even if you are on the top end, estimating finish time at 14 hours, there is still a 3-hour buffer in order to complete the race under the 17-hour cut-off imposed by many races.

## PLAN DESCRIPTION

Table 9.1 on page 104-105 is a 13-week plan to get you ready for your first Ironman, while minimizing injury and training hours. When looking at the first week of the training plan, you should be thinking, "Wow, that's too easy." On the other hand, if you are thinking the first week will be a struggle, more training time is necessary before embarking on this journey.

With that said, let us look at the plan in general. Notice that the Saturday and Sunday training hours build throughout the 13 weeks. Weekend cycling begins at 1:30 and builds to 5:00, two weeks prior to the race. The long run begins at 1:30, building to 3:00 in week 11. Swimming begins at 1:00 and builds to 1:30—not as much growth as cycling and running.

In the first four weeks of the plan, midweek workouts and weekend workouts increase to build overall endurance. Intensity stays fairly low. In the second four weeks of the plan, the weekend volume continues to grow, not missing a beat after the rest week, number 4. Because weekend workouts will be the main focus, there are more days of rest during weeks 5,

# TABLE 9.1: THIRTEEN WEEKS TO IRONMAN PLAN

| Week | Sport | Mon Time | Tues Time | Tues Code | Wed Time | Wed Code | Thurs Time | Thurs Code |
|---|---|---|---|---|---|---|---|---|
| 1 | Swim | Day off | 01:00 | Form | | | 01:00 | E3 |
| | Bike | | | | 01:00 | Form | | |
| | Run | | 00:30 | E2 | | | 00:30 | Form |
| 2 | Swim | Day off | 01:00 | Form | | | 01:15 | E3 |
| | Bike | | | | 01:15 | Form | | |
| | Run | | 00:30 | E2 | | | 00:45 | Form |
| 3 | Swim | Day off | 01:15 | Form | | | 01:15 | E3 |
| | Bike | | | | 01:30 | Form | | |
| | Run | | 00:45 | E2 | | | 01:00 | Form |
| 4 | Brick | | | | | | | |
| | Swim | Day off | 00:45 | Form | | | 01:00 | E3 |
| | Bike | | | | | | 00:30 | Form |
| | Run | | 00:30 | E2 | 00:30 | Form | | |
| 5 | Swim | Day off | 01:00 | Form | Day off | | 00:30 | E1 |
| | Bike | | | | | | 01:00 | Form |
| | Run | | 00:30 | E2 | | | | |
| 6 | Swim | Day off | 01:00 | Form | | | 01:00 | E3 |
| | Bike | | | | 01:15 | Form | | |
| | Run | | | | | | 00:45 | Form |
| 7 | Swim | Day off | 01:00 | Form | | | 01:00 | E3 |
| | Bike | | | | 01:15 | Form | | |
| | Run | | 00:15 | E2 | | | 01:00 | Form |
| 8 | Brick | | | | | | | |
| | Swim | Day off | 01:00 | Form | | | 01:00 | E3 |
| | Bike | | | | | | | |
| | Run | | | | 01:00 | E2 | | |
| 9 | Brick | | | | | | 01:00 | |
| | Swim | Day off | 01:00 | Form | | | | |
| | Bike | | 00:30 | E1 | | | 00:30 | E2 |
| | Run | | | | 00:15 | E1 | 00:30 | E2 |
| 10 | Swim | Day off | 01:00 | Form | | | 01:00 | E2 |
| | Bike | | | | 01:00 | E2 | | |
| | Run | | | | | | 00:30 | E2 |
| 11 | Swim | Day off | 01:00 | E2 | | | 00:30 | E1 |
| | Bike | | | | 01:00 | Form | | |
| | Run | | 00:30 | E1 | | | 00:45 | Form |
| 12 | Brick | | | | | | | |
| | Swim | Day off | 01:00 | Form | | | 01:00 | E3 |
| | Bike | | | | 01:00 | Form | | |
| | Run | | | | | | | |
| 13 | Brick | | | | | | | |
| | Swim | Day off | | | | | 00:30 | Form |
| | Bike | | | | 00:45 | Form | | |
| | Run | | 00:30 | Form | | | | |

| Fri Time | Fri Code | Sat Time | Sat Code | Sun Time | Sun Code | Weekly Training Hours | Weekly Training Hours by Sport | |
|---|---|---|---|---|---|---|---|---|
| 00:45 | E1 | 01:00 01:30 | E2 E2 | 01:30 | E2 | 08:45 | Swim Bike Run | 03:00 03:15 02:30 |
| 01:00 | E1 | 01:15 02:00 | E2 E2 | 01:45 | E2 | 10:45 | Swim Bike Run | 03:30 04:15 03:00 |
| 00:30 | E1 | 01:15 02:30 | E2 E2 | 02:00 | E2 | 12:00 | Swim Bike Run | 03:45 04:30 03:45 |
| 01:00 | E1 | 02:00 01:30 00:30 | Text | Day off | | 06:15 | Swim Bike Run | 01:45 03:00 01:30 |
| Day off | | 01:15 03:00 | E2 E2 | 02:15 | E3 | 09:30 | Swim Bike Run | 02:45 04:00 02:45 |
| Day off | | 01:15 03:30 | E2 E3 | 02:30 | E2 | 11:15 | Swim Bike Run | 03:15 04:45 03:15 |
| Day off | | 01:15 04:00 | E2 E2 | 02:45 | E3 | 12:30 | Swim Bike Run | 03:15 05:15 04:00 |
| 01:00 | E1 | 02:15 01:30 00:45 | Form Form | Day off | | 06:15 | Swim Bike Run | 02:00 02:30 01:45 |
| Day off | | 01:00 04:00 | E3 E2 | 02:15 | E2 | 10:00 | Swim Bike Run | 02:00 05:00 03:00 |
| Day off | | 01:30 04:30 | E3 E3 | 02:30 | E3 | 12:00 | Swim Bike Run | 03:30 05:30 03:00 |
| Day off | | 01:30 05:00 | Form E2 | 03:00 | E2 | 13:15 | Swim Bike Run | 03:00 06:00 04:15 |
| 01:00 | E2 | 01:30 01:00 00:30 | Text | 00:45 | E1 | 06:15 | Swim Bike Run | 02:00 02:45 01:30 |
| Day off | | 00:30 00:20 00:10 | E2 E2 | Race! 12–14 hours | | Race plus 02:15 | Swim Bike Run | 00:30 01:05 00:40 |

6 and 7 to allow for recovery. By the end of week 7, you'll train a total of eight hours over the two weekend days.

The weekend hours continue to build, to about nine and a half by the end of week 11. The long run on Sunday of week 11 will be your last long workout before reducing training volume and resting. Weeks 12 and 13 are designed to allow you to recover and chock your muscles full of glycogen. Short workouts with short accelerations are designed to keep arms and legs feeling fresh. WARNING! WARNING! Do not be tempted to increase training volume during weeks 12 and 13.

For all three sports, we will stay well below lactate threshold heart rate—the heart rate you have held for Olympic-distance races. Being an experienced Olympic-distance racer, you know you've produced heart rates in Zones 4 and low-5 during training and races. You will want to avoid those zones during your Ironman race. (Hint: Try not to choose a hilly Ironman course for your first event.)

Most of the coded workout descriptions are in Chapters 18 through 20. Some of the workouts within Table 9.1 need more detailed instructions, specifically the bricks and the swimming. Those descriptions are in the text following this paragraph. The total brick workout time is shown in the top row of any week containing a brick. The breakdown of the brick is shown in the bike and run row details.

## BRICKS

**WEEK 4:** Ride your bike for a 1:30 total time, with the first 60 minutes in Zones 1 to 2 and the last 30 minutes all in Zone

3. Go right to the run, allowing heart rate to be anywhere in Zones 1 to 3. If you feel great, spend more time in Zone 3.

**WEEK 12:** Ride the bike for an hour, with the first 40 minutes in Zones 1 to 2 and the last 20 minutes all in Zone 3. Go right to the 30-minute run, with the first 15 minutes in Zones 1 to 2 and the last 15 minutes all in Zone 3.

## SWIMMING DETAILS

**WEEKS 1 TO 4:** Include at least one 1000-yard steady swim or a 1000-yard broken set with rest intervals no greater than 10 seconds. On Saturdays, make the main set of the swim workout in the 1000- to 1500-yard range.

**WEEKS 5 TO 8:** Include at least one 1650-yard steady swim (or a 1000-yard broken set with rest intervals no greater than 10 seconds), rest 2 to 3 minutes and immediately swim another 500 to 800 yards. On Saturdays, make the main set of the swim workout in the 1500- to 2500-yard range.

**WEEKS 9 TO 11:** Include at least one steady swim set, with minimal rest of 60 seconds or less, totaling 45 to 60 minutes. On Saturdays, make the main set of the swim workout in the 2000- to 3000-yard range.

## QUESTIONS?

**Q:** If I find I'm getting tired, what can I do to make some modifications without killing the plan?

**A:** It is okay to:

- Totally skip an E1 workout and rest instead.
- Reduce the Saturday bike by up to 30 minutes or the

Sunday run by 15 minutes.

• Do an entire E2 workout with your heart rate in Zone 1.

**Q:** What is the absolute minimum number of hours I can do and still complete the Ironman race?

**A:** There is no standard answer for this. The plan shown here, along with the modifiers already suggested, is along the lines of a minimal plan. The answer really depends on each individual athlete. The more you cut training hours, the longer and more torturous the race will be and the greater the risk for injury.

**Q:** Can I do some Zone 3 intervals (M2 [3Z]) on an "E3" day?

**A:** Yes, try to keep the work-to-rest ratio at 3 or 4 to 1 and slowly build up the Zone 3 work time, beginning at about 20 minutes total.

**Q:** What will happen to me if I get into Zone 4 heart rate during training and racing? Will I flame-out and die?

**A:** The plan is intended to keep you burning fuel at an aerobic rate. During training, you are trying to teach the body to be an efficient fat-burning machine. When getting into the heart rate zones near lactate threshold, the body prefers to use more glycogen as a fuel—as opposed to fat and oxygen. At the same time, short bouts into Zone 4 will not send you into flameout status. Although heart rate monitoring is a good tool, it is not a precise measure of aerobic metabolism. A few beats either side of the zones will not be a problem.

**Q:** I have more bike fitness than the plan shows. Can I increase the bike time?

**A:** Yes, you can modify all weeks and build the longest ride to about 6 hours if you have the time.

## GOING THE DISTANCE IN TRAINING AND ON RACE DAY

As you progress through the training plan, remember to refuel and keep hydrated as described in Chapter 3. Rest, recovery and refueling will go a long way to keep you on track to reach your goal.

On race day, wear your heart rate monitor and stay in Zones 1 to 3. One of the biggest mistakes beginning Ironman racers make is to begin the event at an Olympic-distance pace. Relax, control your speed and be willing to take walking bouts during long training runs and the race. If your heart rate monitor malfunctions, use RPE as your guide for pacing. Most of all, look around, have fun and enjoy your incredible fitness!

# PART III

The plans in Part III are 11 to 24 weeks in length. There are a wide variety of plans in this part to accommodate serious racers and serious fitness buffs. There are plans for increasing speed in short- to long-distance triathlon and a plan for duathlon. Chapter 16 is an outline for multisport athletes who include sports other than swimming, cycling or running in their routine.

Because these plans can span several months, each chapter includes a brief overview that displays the number of weeks in the plan, a suggested month to begin training, the phase of training for that month and the total training hours each week. Any special instructions for each training phase are detailed in the chapter text.

These plans are for "Level II" athletes, or those who are not beginners in sport. Intentionally, the plans are not carbon copies of one another, but show various patterns and workouts to achieve athletic goals. It may also be helpful to review the text in each of the plans in Parts I and II because sundry helpful tips are included with each of those plans.

# CHAPTER TEN

# Faster
# *Sprint Distance Performance*

*I do more before 9 a.m. than most people
do before noon.*
—*Triathlete Abe Rogers,
Burlington, Vermont, age 26*

I f simply completing a triathlon was intoxicating, how much joy will gush out of every body cell when speed is increased? Go faster! The quest for speed can be a nasty addiction. Yep, if a little is good, a lot simply must be better—yes?

The quote for this chapter is from National Team member Abe Rogers, who spent several seasons battling injuries. He has learned the hard way that "more" can be trouble. The end result may be no racing at all. Fortunately, Abe has learned to temper his training and is now experiencing success.

This chapter helps time-crunched athletes prepare to race faster. Weekly training hours range from 1:45 to 5:00, so training remains manageable with a hectic lifestyle.

## PROFILE

This plan is built for a summer triathlete. Triathlon training is seasonal for you, but you are physically active all year. You may or may not be an experienced triathlete. Either way, you are looking to do a sprint-distance triathlon at the end of the summer, after about 15 weeks of training. You know how to swim and can comfortably get through about 30 minutes in the pool. A 30-minute bike ride or run is easy.

## GOAL

Your goal is to complete a sprint-distance event at a fast pace, perhaps faster than last summer.

## PLAN DESCRIPTION

Table 10.1 on page 115 lists 15 training weeks, a column for months, a column designating the training period and the weekly training hours leading up to the race. The months are there for example only and the first week can begin on Monday of any month. Athletes in the Southern Hemisphere will certainly have different training months than those in the Northern Hemisphere.

In this plan, faster racing is accomplished by structuring a progression of workouts. Training hours need not be extravagant. In general, the first few weeks build overall training volume and increase endurance. Once weekly training volume is built to five hours, more intensity or longer-interval speed work is added. Every third week is a rest week to allow for recovery. Some athletes find this three-week rotation of training is a good way to rest and manage stress.

Table 10.2 on page 116-117 displays the plan in detail. Every Monday is a day of rest. Tuesday and Thursday are swimming days. Wednesday and Saturday are cycling days, with Saturday the day to build overall cycling endurance. Friday and Sunday are running days; longer runs are completed on Sunday. The sched-

| TABLE 10.1. PLAN OVERVIEW | | | |
|---|---|---|---|
| Week # | Month | Period | Weekly Planned Hours |
| 1 | May | Base 1 | 02:50 |
| 2 | May | Base 1 | 03:30 |
| 3 | May | Base 1 | 01:45 |
| 4 | May | Base 2 | 03:45 |
| 5 | May/June | Base 2 | 04:00 |
| 6 | June | Base 2 | 02:30 |
| 7 | June | Base 3 | 04:30 |
| 8 | June | Base 3 | 05:00 |
| 9 | June/July | Base 3 | 02:15 |
| 10 | July | Build 1 | 05:00 |
| 11 | July | Build 1 | 05:00 |
| 12 | July | Build 1 | 02:15 |
| 13 | July | Build 2 | 04:30 |
| 14 | July/August | Build 2 | 04:00 |
| 15 | August | Race | 01:35 |

ule can be rearranged to meet personal needs; however, try to alternate sports and not train two days in a row for the same sport. Workout codes are explained in Chapters 18, 19 and 20.

## Base 1

The training during this block is mostly low-intensity aerobic activity and form work. Overall swim descriptions are in Chapter 18, and more ideas for short swim workouts can be found in Chapters 8 and 9. Some of the workouts in the reference chapters may be longer than necessary for this plan. Those workouts can be reduced in volume, but you should keep the major theme of the workout the same. In other words, if you are using a workout designed for improving 1500-meter swimming and your race distance is 800 meters, the main set can be cut down by 25 to 50 percent.

## TABLE 10.2. FASTER SPRINT DISTANCE PERFORMANCE PLAN

| Week | Sport | Mon Time | Tues Time | Tues Code | Wed Time | Wed Code | Thurs Time | Thurs Code | Fri Time |
|---|---|---|---|---|---|---|---|---|---|
| 1 | Brick | Day off | | | | | | | |
| | Swim | | 00:30 | E2 | | | 00:30 | E(Form) | |
| | Bike | | | | 00:30 | S2 | | | |
| | Run | | | | | | | | 00:20 |
| 2 | Brick | Day off | | | | | | | |
| | Swim | | 00:30 | E2 | | | 00:30 | E(Speed) | |
| | Bike | | | | 00:30 | S2 | | | |
| | Run | | | | | | | | 00:30 |
| 3 | Brick | Day off | | | Day off | | 00:30 | | Day off |
| | Swim | | 00:30 | T1a | | | | | |
| | Bike | | | | | | 00:15 | E1 | |
| | Run | | | | | | 00:15 | E1 | |
| 4 | Brick | Day off | | | | | | | |
| | Swim | | 00:30 | E3 | | | 00:30 | E(Form) | |
| | Bike | | | | 00:30 | S1 | | | |
| | Run | | | | | | | | 00:30 |
| 5 | Brick | Day off | | | | | | | |
| | Swim | | 00:30 | E3 | | | 00:30 | E(Speed) | |
| | Bike | | | | 00:30 | S1 | | | |
| | Run | | | | | | | | 00:30 |
| 6 | Brick | Day off | | | Day off | | 00:45 | | Day off |
| | Swim | | 00:30 | E3 | | | | | |
| | Bike | | | | | | 00:30 | S4 | |
| | Run | | | | | | 00:15 | S2 | |
| 7 | Brick | Day off | | | | | | | |
| | Swim | | 00:30 | M | | | 00:30 | E(Form) | |
| | Bike | | | | 00:45 | E2 | | | |
| | Run | | | | | | | | 00:30 |
| 8 | Brick | Day off | | | | | | | |
| | Swim | | 00:30 | M | | | 00:30 | E(Speed) | |
| | Bike | | | | 01:00 | E4 | | | |
| | Run | | | | | | | | 00:30 |
| 9 | Brick | Day off | | | Day off | | 00:45 | | Day off |
| | Swim | | 00:30 | T1a | | | | | |
| | Bike | | | | | | 00:30 | S4 | |
| | Run | | | | | | 00:15 | S2 | |
| 10 | Brick | Day off | | | | | | | |
| | Swim | | 00:30 | M | | | 00:30 | E(Form) | |
| | Bike | | | | 01:00 | M2(4–5a) | | | |
| | Run | | | | | | | | 00:30 |
| 11 | Brick | Day off | | | | | | | |
| | Swim | | 00:30 | A | | | 00:30 | E(Speed) | |
| | Bike | | | | 01:00 | M2(4–5a) | | | |
| | Run | | | | | | | | 00:30 |
| 12 | Brick | Day off | | | Day off | | 00:45 | | Day off |
| | Swim | | 00:30 | M(Speed) | | | | | |
| | Bike | | | | | | 00:30 | S4 | |
| | Run | | | | | | 00:15 | S2 | |
| 13 | Brick | Day off | | | | | | | |
| | Swim | | 00:30 | A | | | 00:30 | EOW | |
| | Bike | | | | 01:00 | S4 | | | |
| | Run | | | | | | | | 00:30 |
| 14 | Brick | Day off | | | | | | | |
| | Swim | | 00:30 | A | | | 00:30 | EOW | |
| | Bike | | | | 01:00 | A7 | | | |
| | Run | | | | | | | | 00:30 |
| 15 | Brick | Day off | | | 00:30 | | Day off | | |
| | Swim | | 00:20 | E(Speed) | | | | | |
| | Bike | | | | 00:20 | E2 | | | 00:30 |
| | Run | | | | 00:10 | E2 | | | |

| Fri Code | Sat Time | Sat Code | Sun Time | Sun Code | Weekly Training Hours | Weekly Training Hours By Sport | |
|---|---|---|---|---|---|---|---|
| | | | | | | Brick | 00:00 |
| | | | | | | Swim | 01:00 |
| | 00:30 | E2 | | | | Bike | 01:00 |
| E1 | | | 00:30 | E2 | 02:50 | Run | 00:50 |
| | | | | | | Brick | 00:00 |
| | | | | | | Swim | 01:00 |
| | 00:45 | E2 | | | | Bike | 01:15 |
| E1 | | | 00:45 | E2 | 03:30 | Run | 01:15 |
| | 00:45 | | Day off | | | Brick | 01:15 |
| | | | | | | Swim | 00:30 |
| | 00:30 | E2 | | | | Bike | 00:45 |
| | 00:15 | E2 | | | 01:45 | Run | 00:30 |
| | | | | | | Brick | 00:00 |
| | | | | | | Swim | 01:00 |
| | 01:00 | E3 | | | | Bike | 01:30 |
| S2 | | | 00:45 | E3 | 03:45 | Run | 01:15 |
| | | | | | | Brick | 00:00 |
| | | | | | | Swim | 01:00 |
| | 01:15 | E3 | | | | Bike | 01:45 |
| S2 | | | 00:45 | E3 | 04:00 | Run | 01:15 |
| | 01:15 | | Day off | | | Brick | 02:00 |
| | | | | | | Swim | 00:30 |
| | 00:45 | text | | | | Bike | 01:15 |
| | 00:30 | text | | | 02:30 | Run | 00:45 |
| | | | | | | Brick | 00:00 |
| | | | | | | Swim | 01:00 |
| | 01:15 | E4 | | | | Bike | 02:00 |
| M5(15) | | | 01:00 | E2 | 04:30 | Run | 01:30 |
| | | | | | | Brick | 00:00 |
| | | | | | | Swim | 01:00 |
| | 01:30 | E2 | | | | Bike | 02:30 |
| S2 | | | 01:00 | M2(4–5a) | 05:00 | Run | 01:30 |
| | 01:30 | | Day off | | | Brick | 02:15 |
| | | | | | | Swim | 00:30 |
| | 01:00 | text | | | | Bike | 01:30 |
| | 00:30 | text | | | 02:15 | Run | 00:15 |
| | | | | | | Brick | 00:00 |
| | | | | | | Swim | 01:00 |
| | 01:30 | E2 | | | | Bike | 02:30 |
| S2 | | | 01:00 | A2*(5bZ) | 05:00 | Run | 01:30 |
| | | | | | | Brick | 00:00 |
| | | | | | | Swim | 01:00 |
| | 01:30 | E2 | | | | Bike | 02:30 |
| S2 | | | 01:00 | A2*(5bZ) | 05:00 | Run | 01:30 |
| | 01:30 | | Day off | | | Brick | 02:15 |
| | | | | | | Swim | 00:30 |
| | 01:00 | text | | | | Bike | 01:30 |
| | 00:30 | text | | | 02:15 | Run | 00:15 |
| | | | | | | Brick | 00:00 |
| | | | | | | Swim | 01:00 |
| | 01:15 | text | | | | Bike | 02:15 |
| S2 | | | 00:45 | text | 04:30 | Run | 01:15 |
| | | | 01:00 | | | Brick | 01:00 |
| | | | | | | Swim | 01:00 |
| | 00:30 | E1 | 00:45 | text | | Bike | 02:15 |
| S2 | | | 00:15 | text | 04:00 | Run | 00:45 |
| | | | Race! | | | Brick | 00:30 |
| | | | | | | Swim | 00:20 |
| S4 | | | | | | Bike | 00:50 |
| | 00:15 | S2 | | | 01:35 | Run | 00:25 |

A swimming time trial is in the first rest week. After a day of rest, an easy brick is on Wednesday and a second brick is on Saturday. One swim and two bricks are the pattern for all subsequent rest weeks.

## Base 2

Tuesday swim workouts become a bit faster during this block. Endurance is still important; however, speed is slightly increased. The distance of long weekend workouts continues to build and speed is increased here as well. The speed increases are subtle; high speeds are reserved for later training blocks.

The brick on Saturday of week 6 totals 1:15. It begins with a 45-minute bike and ends with a 30-minute run. Both bike and run segments begin in Zones 1 to 2 for the first half of the time. The second half of each one ends in Zones 2 to 3. Finishing the second half of each workout faster than the first is called a "negative split."

## Base 3

This training block adds hill work on the bike to increase strength. Allow the hills to drive heart rates into higher training zones, but no higher than 5a. These combination workouts not only improve strength, they improve lactate threshold speed as well.

For running, Friday week 7 includes a short tempo run of 15 minutes. Sunday of week 8 includes cruise intervals. Specifically, M2(4 to 5a): 4 to 5 x 4' (1' RI), increasing heart rate into Zones 4 to 5a. Take 1 minute of easy jogging between run intervals.

The rest week (week 9) begins with a retest of the swimming time trial. The brick on Saturday of the rest week is 1:30, beginning with a 60-minute bike and ending with a 30-minute run. Both bike and run segments begin in Zones 1 to 2 and both finish with 15 minutes in Zones 4 to 5a. This is called a tempo finish.

### Build 1

In this block, swimming has a mix of muscular endurance work and anaerobic endurance work and cycling moves to cruise intervals, specifically: in Wednesday of week 10, ride 4 to 6 x 3' (1" RI), increasing heart rate into Zones 4 to 5a; and on Wednesday of week 11, ride 4 to 6 x 4' (1' RI), increasing heart rate into Zones 4 to 5a. The Sunday run in both weeks 10 and 11 includes anaerobic intervals. For both days, do A2(5b): 4 to 5 x 3' (3' RI), increasing heart rate into Zone 5b.

This block ends with a 1:30 brick on Saturday of week 12. The bike is 1 hour and the run is 30 minutes. Both workouts are negative split, using an out-and-back course. Go out at intensities in Zones 1 and 2; bring it home in Zones 4 to 5a. The second half of each workout should be faster. How fast can you go while keeping heart rate as low as possible?

### Build 2

In this block, training is very fast or easy. Tuesday main-set swims are anaerobic. Thursday swims are either in open water—in a safe situation only—or in the pool at an easy pace.

The bike on Saturday of week 13 includes a good 40-minute warm-up, followed by 30 minutes at race pace, or speeds eliciting heart rates in Zones 4 to 5b. Spin an easy 5 minutes (or more) at the end. Be sure to stretch well.

The run on Sunday of week 13 is 20 minutes in the lower zones and 20 minutes at race pace, or heart rates in Zones 4 to 5b. Jog an easy 5 minutes at the end and perhaps add some walking as well.

On Wednesday of week 14, the bike ride includes 4 x 90 seconds, building heart rate into Zones 4 to 5a with 3-minute easy-spinning recovery intervals. The brick that week is a negative split workout, with both the bike and the run beginning in Zones 1 to 2. At the turnaround, bring both home at race pace.

### Race

The few days preceding the race have reduced volume and include some segments of short speed work. The brick on Wednesday is to loosen the legs, but also to check equipment. Be sure that all race equipment is in working order and ready for Sunday. If repairs are necessary, you have a few days to get problems taken care of.

On race day, recall all the successful workouts you had in the past 15 weeks. Today is the day to enjoy the harvest of your hard work, a day to relax and have fun. Use strategies you found useful in training to keep calm, motivated and focused. Going fast is a blast!

# CHAPTER ELEVEN

# Improved Performance for

# *Olympic Distance Triathlon:*

# Six-Month Plan

*Consistency, planning and rest are the keys to successful training.*

—*Alexander Durst, Boulder, CO, age 29*

P erhaps it was a New Year's resolution or the lingering memory of how much fun that triathlon was last summer—for any number of reasons, it would be fun to do an Olympic distance triathlon and try to race faster. The plan in this chapter is designed to help you do just that.

Table 11.1 on page 122 gives an overview of the plan. The first column shows a plan length of 24 weeks, and the fourth column reveals weekly training hours ranging from 6:15 to a maximum of 13:00. The plan begins on the first Monday in January and ends with a race in June, but could just as eas-

| TABLE 11.1. PLAN OVERVIEW | | | |
|---|---|---|---|
| Week # | Month | Period | Weekly Planned Hours |
| 1 | January | Preparation | 07:30 |
| 2 | January | Preparation | 07:30 |
| 3 | January | Preparation | 07:30 |
| 4 | January | Preparation | 06:15 |
| 5 | January/February | Base 1 | 08:45 |
| 6 | February | Base 1 | 10:45 |
| 7 | February | Base 1 | 12:00 |
| 8 | February | Base 1 | 06:15 |
| 9 | February/March | Base 2 | 09:30 |
| 10 | March | Base 2 | 11:15 |
| 11 | March | Base 2 | 12:30 |
| 12 | March | Base 2 | 06:15 |
| 13 | March/April | Base 3 | 10:00 |
| 14 | April | Base 3 | 12:00 |
| 15 | April | Base 3 | 13:00 |
| 16 | April | Base 3 | 06:15 |
| 17 | April/May | Build 1 | 11:15 |
| 18 | May | Build 1 | 11:15 |
| 19 | May | Build 1 | 06:15 |
| 20 | May | Build 2 | 10:45 |
| 21 | May | Build 2 | 10:45 |
| 22 | May/June | Peak/Taper | 09:30 |
| 23 | June | Peak/Taper | 07:30 |
| 24 | June | Race | 3:00 + Race |

ily start on the first Monday in February, with a race in July. In other words, the months are shown as examples. Finally, the third column indicates which training period corresponds to each week.

If this plan looks manageable, read on.

## PROFILE

You may or may not be an experienced triathlete. Either way, you are looking to do an Olympic-distance triathlon about six months in the future. You know how to swim and can comfortably get through about 30 minutes in the pool. An hour bike ride or an hour run is not a stretch for you. Your total weekly training hours are around six prior to beginning the plan.

## GOAL

Your goal is to complete an Olympic-distance event that is about six months away. You want more than simple survival. You want to race at a fast pace.

## PLAN DESCRIPTION

Table 11.2 on page 124-129 outlines the journey to a faster-paced Olympic-distance race. It begins with a Preparation period, an overall conditioning phase. Base 1 emphasizes strength training and begins to build overall training volume. Base 2 reduces heavy strength training and adds more hills to cycling and running. Base 3 begins lactate threshold training. Build 1 and 2 have spicy days of anaerobic threshold training. Finally, in Peak and Taper, a reduction of overall training volume and some fast workouts in the mix each week bring you to a fast race with a well-rested body. Let us look at each period in more detail.

## PREPARATION

This period prepares the body for future stresses by introducing strength training and an opportunity to establish a routine. Week 1 has a time trial in each sport, used as baseline measure for fitness. The rest of the Preparation block contains a good deal of form and speed work in all three sports. Form work is included throughout the entire plan to emphasize good technique—its goal being "free" speed. That is, efficient form can reduce the effort it takes to travel at any given pace, while inefficient form can rob an athlete of precious energy.

There are numerous types of speed work, all intended to get you going faster. Short segments of speed, like those in the Preparation period, help train the neuromuscular system to go fast, without a huge tax on the aerobic system. The

## TABLE 11.2. OLYMPIC DISTANCE TRIATHLON PLAN

| Week | Sport | Mon Time | Mon Code | Tues Time | Tues Code | Wed Time | Wed Code | Thurs Time | Thurs Code |
|------|-------|----------|----------|-----------|-----------|----------|----------|------------|------------|
| 1 | Strength | 01:15 | AA | | | 01:15 | AA | | |
| | Swim | | | 00:30 | E2 | | | 00:45 | T1 |
| | Bike | | | | | | | 00:45 | S1 |
| | Run | | | 00:30 | E1 | | | 00:30 | S2 |
| 2 | Strength | 01:15 | AA | | | 01:15 | AA | | |
| | Swim | | | 00:30 | E2 | | | 00:45 | E(Form) |
| | Bike | | | | | | | | |
| | Run | | | 00:30 | E1 | | | 00:30 | S2 |
| 3 | Strength | 01:15 | AA | | | 01:15 | AA | | |
| | Swim | | | 00:30 | E2 | | | 00:45 | E(Form) |
| | Bike | | | | | | | | |
| | Run | | | 00:30 | E1 | | | 00:30 | S2 |
| 4 | Strength | 01:15 | AA | | | 01:15 | AA | | |
| | Swim | | | 00:30 | E2 | | | 00:30 | E(Speed) |
| | Bike | | | | | | | | |
| | Run | | | 00:30 | E1 | | | | |
| 5 | Strength | 01:30 | MS | | | 01:30 | MS | | |
| | Swim | | | 00:45 | E(Form) | | | 00:45 | E3 |
| | Bike | | | | | | | | |
| | Run | | | 00:30 | E1 | | | 00:30 | S1 |
| 6 | Strength | 01:30 | MS | | | 01:30 | MS | | |
| | Swim | | | 01:00 | E(Speed) | | | 01:00 | E3 |
| | Bike | | | | | | | | |
| | Run | | | 00:30 | E1 | | | 00:30 | S2 |
| 7 | Strength | 01:30 | MS | | | 01:30 | MS | | |
| | Swim | | | 01:00 | E(Form) | | | 01:00 | E3 |
| | Bike | | | | | | | | |
| | Run | | | 00:30 | E1 | | | 00:45 | S1 |
| 8 | Strength | 01:00 | MS | | | 01:00 | MS | | |
| | Swim | | | 00:30 | E(Speed) | | | 00:30 | T1 |
| | Bike | | | | | | | 00:45 | S3 |
| | Run | | | 00:30 | S2 | | | | |
| 9 | Strength | 01:15 | PE | | | 01:15 | PE | | |
| | Swim | | | 01:00 | Force | | | 00:45 | E2 |
| | Bike | | | | | | | | |
| | Run | | | 00:30 | E2 | | | 00:30 | S2 |
| 10 | Strength | 01:15 | PE | | | 01:15 | PE | | |
| | Swim | | | 01:00 | Force | | | 01:00 | E2 |
| | Bike | | | | | | | | |
| | Run | | | 00:30 | E2 | | | 00:30 | S2 |

| Fri Time | Fri Code | Sat Time | Sat Code | Sun Time | Sun Code | Weekly Training Hours | Weekly Training Hours By Sport | |
|---|---|---|---|---|---|---|---|---|
| | | | | | | | Strength | 02:30 |
| | | | | | | | Swim | 01:15 |
| | | 01:00 | T1 | | | | Bike | 01:45 |
| | | 01:00 | T1 | | | 07:30 | Run | 02:00 |
| | | | | | | | Strength | 02:30 |
| | | | | | | | Swim | 01:15 |
| 00:30 | S2 | | | 01:15 | E2 | | Bike | 01:45 |
| | | 01:00 | E2 | | | 07:30 | Run | 02:00 |
| | | | | | | | Strength | 02:30 |
| | | | | | | | Swim | 01:15 |
| 00:30 | S1 | | | 01:15 | E2 | | Bike | 01:45 |
| | | 01:00 | E2 | | | 07:30 | Run | 02:00 |
| | | | | | | | Strength | 02:30 |
| | | | | | | | Swim | 01:00 |
| 00:30 | S2 | | | 01:00 | E2 | | Bike | 01:30 |
| | | 00:45 | S1 | | | 06:15 | Run | 01:15 |
| | | | | | | | Strength | 03:00 |
| | | | | | | | Swim | 01:30 |
| 00:45 | S1 | | | 01:30 | E3 | | Bike | 02:15 |
| | | 01:00 | S2 | | | 08:45 | Run | 02:00 |
| | | | | | | | Strength | 03:00 |
| | | 00:30 | E1 | | | | Swim | 02:30 |
| 01:00 | S2 | | | 02:00 | E2 | | Bike | 03:00 |
| | | 01:15 | E3 | | | 10:45 | Run | 02:15 |
| | | | | | | | Strength | 03:00 |
| | | 00:45 | E1 | | | | Swim | 02:45 |
| 01:00 | S1 | | | 02:30 | E3 | | Bike | 03:30 |
| | | 01:30 | E2 | | | 12:00 | Run | 02:45 |
| Day off | | | | | | | Strength | 02:00 |
| | | | | | | | Swim | 01:00 |
| | | | | 01:00 | T1 | | Bike | 01:45 |
| | | 01:00 | T1 | | | 06:15 | Run | 01:30 |
| | | | | | | | Strength | 02:30 |
| | | 01:00 | E(Form) | | | | Swim | 02:45 |
| 00:30 | S1 | | | 01:45 | E4 | | Bike | 02:15 |
| | | 01:00 | E2 | | | 09:30 | Run | 02:00 |
| | | | | | | | Strength | 02:30 |
| | | 01:15 | M | | | | Swim | 03:15 |
| 01:00 | S5 | | | 02:15 | E2 | | Bike | 03:15 |
| | | 01:15 | E4 | | | 11:15 | Run | 02:15 |

TABLE 11.2. OLYMPIC DISTANCE TRIATHLON PLAN (CONTINUED)

| Week | Sport | Mon Time | Mon Code | Tues Time | Tues Code | Wed Time | Wed Code | Thurs Time | Thurs Code |
|------|-------|----------|----------|-----------|-----------|----------|----------|------------|------------|
| 11 | Strength | 01:15 | PE | | | 01:15 | PE | | |
| | Swim | | | 01:00 | Force | | | 01:00 | E2 |
| | Bike | | | | | | | | |
| | Run | | | 00:30 | E2 | | | 00:45 | S2 |
| 12 | Strength | 01:00 | PE | | | 01:00 | PE | | |
| | Swim | | | 00:30 | E(Form) | | | 00:30 | T1 |
| | Bike | | | | | | | 00:45 | S3 |
| | Run | | | 00:30 | S2 | | | | |
| 13 | Strength | 01:00 | SM | | | | | | |
| | Swim | | | 01:00 | | | | 00:45 | M(Form) |
| | Bike | | | | | 01:00 | M2(4-5a) | | |
| | Run | | | 00:30 | S1 | | | 00:30 | E2 |
| 14 | Strength | 01:00 | SM | | | | | | |
| | Swim | | | 01:00 | | | | 01:15 | M(Speed) |
| | Bike | | | | | 01:00 | M2(4-5a) | | |
| | Run | | | 00:30 | S2 | | | 01:00 | M2(4-5a) |
| 15 | Strength | 01:00 | SM | | | | | | |
| | Swim | | | 01:15 | | | | 01:15 | M(Form) |
| | Bike | | | | | 01:30 | E2 | | |
| | Run | | | 00:30 | S1 | | | 01:00 | M2(4-5a) |
| 16 | Strength | 01:00 | SM | | | | | | |
| | Swim | | | 00:45 | | | | 00:45 | E2 |
| | Bike | | | | | 01:00 | S5 | | |
| | Run | | | | | | | 00:30 | S2 |
| 17 | Strength | 01:00 | SM | | | | | | |
| | Swim | | | 01:00 | E2 | | | 01:00 | A |
| | Bike | | | | | 01:00 | S5 | | |
| | Run | | | 01:00 | A2(5bZ) | | | 00:30 | E1 |
| 18 | Strength | 01:00 | SM | | | | | | |
| | Swim | | | 01:00 | E2 | | | 01:00 | A |
| | Bike | | | | | 01:00 | M4(20) | | |
| | Run | | | 01:00 | E2 | | | 00:30 | S1 |
| 19 | Strength | 01:00 | SM | | | | | | |
| | Swim | | | 01:00 | E1 | | | 01:00 | M(Speed) |
| | Bike | | | | | | | | |
| | Run | | | | | 00:45 | E2 | | |
| 20 | Strength | 01:00 | SM | | | | | | |
| | Swim | | | 01:00 | E2 | | | 01:00 | A |
| | Bike | | | | | 01:00 | M5(20) | | |
| | Run | | | 00:45 | E2 | | | 00:30 | S2 |

| Fri Time | Fri Code | Sat Time | Sat Code | Sun Time | Sun Code | Weekly Training Hours | Weekly Training Hours By Sport | |
|---|---|---|---|---|---|---|---|---|
| | | 01:15 | E1 | | | | Strength | 02:30 |
| | | | | | | | Swim | 03:15 |
| 01:15 | S1 | | | 02:45 | E4 | | Bike | 04:00 |
| | | 01:30 | E4 | | | 12:30 | Run | 02:45 |
| Day off | | | | | | | Strength | 02:00 |
| | | | | | | | Swim | 01:00 |
| | | | | 01:00 | T1 | | Bike | 01:45 |
| | | 01:00 | T1 | | | 06:15 | Run | 01:30 |
| | | 01:00 | E2 | | | | Strength | 01:00 |
| | | | | | | | Swim | 02:45 |
| 01:00 | S5 | | | 02:15 | E2 | | Bike | 04:15 |
| | | 01:00 | M2(4-5a) | | | 10:00 | Run | 02:00 |
| | | 01:15 | E1 | | | | Strength | 01:00 |
| | | | | | | | Swim | 03:30 |
| 01:15 | E1 | | | 02:30 | E4 | | Bike | 04:45 |
| | | 01:15 | E2 | | | 12:00 | Run | 02:45 |
| | | 01:15 | E1 | | | | Strength | 01:00 |
| | | | | | | | Swim | 03:45 |
| 01:00 | M2(4-5a) | | | 03:00 | E4 | | Bike | 05:30 |
| | | 01:15 | E2 | | | 13:00 | Run | 02:45 |
| Day off | | | | | | | Strength | 01:00 |
| | | | | | | | Swim | 01:30 |
| | | | | 01:15 | E2 | | Bike | 02:15 |
| | | 01:00 | A1c | | | 06:15 | Run | 01:30 |
| | | 01:00 | E1 | | | | Strength | 01:00 |
| | | | | | | | Swim | 03:00 |
| 00:45 | E2 | | | 03:00 | A1c | | Bike | 04:45 |
| | | 01:00 | S2 | | | 11:15 | Run | 02:30 |
| | | | | Brick | | | Strength | 01:00 |
| | | 01:15 | E1 | | | | Swim | 03:15 |
| 01:00 | E1 | | | 02:00 | E2 | | Bike | 04:00 |
| | | 01:00 | A1c | 00:30 | E2 | 11:15 | Run | 03:00 |
| Day off | | | | Brick | | | Strength | 01:00 |
| | | | | | | | Swim | 02:00 |
| | | 01:00 | T2 | 01:00 | S4 | | Bike | 02:00 |
| | | | | 00:30 | S2 | 06:15 | Run | 01:15 |
| | | 01:00 | E(Speed) | | | | Strength | 01:00 |
| | | | | | | | Swim | 03:00 |
| 01:00 | S5 | | | 02:30 | A1c | | Bike | 04:30 |
| | | 01:00 | A1c | | | 10:45 | Run | 02:15 |

TABLE 11.2. OLYMPIC DISTANCE TRIATHLON PLAN (CONTINUED)

| Week | Sport | Mon Time | Mon Code | Tues Time | Tues Code | Wed Time | Wed Code | Thurs Time | Thurs Code |
|---|---|---|---|---|---|---|---|---|---|
| 21 | Strength | 01:00 | SM | | | | | | |
| | Swim | | | 01:00 | E2 | | | 01:00 | A |
| | Bike | | | | | 01:00 | M5(25-30) | | |
| | Run | | | 00:45 | E2 | | | 00:30 | S2 |
| 22 | Strength | 01:00 | SM | | | | | | |
| | Swim | | | 01:00 | M | | | 01:00 | E2 |
| | Bike | | | | | 01:00 | M5(30-35) | | |
| | Run | | | 00:30 | E2 | | | 00:30 | S2 |
| 23 | Strength | 01:00 | SM | | | | | | |
| | Swim | | | 00:45 | M | | | | |
| | Bike | | | | | 01:00 | M2(4-5a) | | |
| | Run | | | 00:30 | E2 | | | 00:45 | A7 |
| 24 | Strength | | | | | | | | |
| | Swim | | | 00:45 | E(Form) | | | 00:30 | E(Speed) |
| | Bike | 00:45 | A7 | | | | | | |
| | Run | | | | | 00:30 | S1 | | |

energy system needed for this type of speed is anaerobic, but the workouts are not intended to produce piles of lactate that the body must labor to process. This type of speed work, in addition to form work, is ideally continued throughout the season.

## Base 1

This block of training begins the delicate balancing act of increasing volume and intensity. Certain workouts are intended to stress the body so that when followed by a period of rest, the body is stronger and/or faster. These stressful workouts are called "breakthrough" or BT workouts. As a general rule of thumb, a single week should not include more than four BT workouts total, in all three sports; usually two or three BTs per week is a better idea. How the BT sessions are scheduled within a week depends on the intended bene-

| Fri Time | Fri Code | Sat Time | Sat Code | Sun Time | Sun Code | Weekly Training Hours | Weekly Training Hours By Sport | |
|---|---|---|---|---|---|---|---|---|
| | | 01:00 | E1 | | | | Strength | 01:00 |
| 01:00 | S2 | | | 02:30 | A1c | | Swim | 03:00 |
| | | | | | | | Bike | 04:30 |
| | | 01:00 | A2(5bZ) | | | 10:45 | Run | 02:15 |
| | | | | Brick | | | Strength | 01:00 |
| | | 01:00 | E(Form) | | | | Swim | 03:00 |
| 01:15 | S1 | | | 01:30 | text | | Bike | 03:45 |
| | | 00:45 | E1 | :30 | text | 09:30 | Run | 01:45 |
| Day off | | | | Brick | | | Strength | 01:00 |
| | | 01:00 | E(Speed) | | | | Swim | 01:45 |
| | | 01:00 | E2 | 01:30 | text | | Bike | 03:30 |
| | | | | :30 | text | 07:30 | Run | 01:15 |
| Day off | | Brick | | Race! | | | Strength | 00:00 |
| | | | | | | | Swim | 01:15 |
| | | 00:20 | S4 | | | | Bike | 01:05 |
| | | 00:10 | S2 | | | 03:00 | Run | 00:40 |

fit. If it becomes necessary to rearrange the daily schedule shown on the plan, be conscious of stacking stressful workouts together. Give thought to what you are doing and why.

For Base 1, an MS workout (see Chapter 21) is considered a BT session. If done correctly, this phase of strength training yields excellent results on the bike. Because this type of strength training involves building muscle, some athletes will gain small amounts of weight (two to five pounds), and will notice their legs feel heavy while running and on the bike. Hang in there: this is normal, and positive changes—like fast and powerful feeling legs—emerge as training progresses.

Low-end lactate threshold work begins in all three sports by spending time in Zone 3. Do not make it a goal to see how much time you can spend in Zone 3, rather, allow hills, wind and strong arms or legs to dictate the amount of time spent in this higher zone.

## Base 2

Strength was built in the weight room in Base 1. Now we can apply that strength directly to each sport by adding paddles to swimming and more aggressive hills to cycling and running. If your city is pancake-flat, use the wind, a treadmill or higher gears on the bike to simulate hills.

Paddles in the pool and more challenging terrain for cycling and running also provide a natural opportunity for lactate threshold training. Specific-sport strength and lactate threshold training are combined in a single workout for each sport. For swimming, this is the Tuesday workout, and in running and cycling, it is one or both weekend workouts. It is important to be rested for those workouts.

## Base 3

Strength training in Base 3, and for the rest of the plan, goes into a maintenance mode. Gains in the weight room (adding more plates to the stack), are no longer expected. Strength is simply maintained in the gym.

The energy that once went into weights is now going into sport. Lactate threshold intervals are scheduled in all three sports. During this training block, volume is still increasing, so be very conscientious about overextending yourself. Here is more detail on the lactate threshold workouts in this training block:

### Bike

On Wednesday of week 13, 5 to 6 x 3 minutes into Zones 4 to 5a, with 1-minute rest intervals; on Wednesday of week 14, 4 to 6 x 4 minutes into Zones 4 to 5a, with 1-minute rest intervals; and in week 15, on Friday, 4 to 5 x 5 minutes into Zones 4 to 5a, with 2-minute rest intervals.

### Run

On Saturday of week 13, 5 to 6 x 3 minutes into Zones 4 to 5a, with 1-minute rest intervals; on Thursday of week 14, 4 to 6 x 4 minutes into Zones 4 to 5a, with 1-minute rest intervals; and on Thursday of week 15, 4 to 5 x 5 minutes into Zones 4 to 5a, with 2-minute rest intervals.

At the end of the rest week in this block, a 10K race or fast group run can be used as a new benchmark for progress.

### Build 1

For the remainder of the plan, training is either very fast or very easy. Avoid spending large amounts of training time in Zone 3 during this period. It is important for you to be well rested before workouts where top speed is important. The remainder of the workouts are for maintenance purposes, to aid in recovery and to continue to work on form.

This training block includes two bricks. The first brick is endurance-based and trains legs to run right after a bike ride. The second brick adds some short speed work.

### Build 2

In this block of training, some athletes may need to modify the training plan due to fatigue. If you are struggling to recover and constantly feel fatigued, the intensity of the Wednesday or the Sunday bike ride may need to change to an E2 ride.

### Peak/Taper

As you taper for the big race, strange feelings may appear. Not all athletes experience the same feelings, but some of the typical "taper blues" include:

- *When beginning to taper volume, some say they feel more tired than when they were putting in lots of training hours.*
- *As the taper continues, some athletes notice they are slightly grouchy—or their friends and family members notice it.*
- *Others report little aches and pains they never noticed before. The pains show up for no apparent reason. In other words, there were no "incidents" to cause a sore knee, so where did that come from?*
- *The last week before the race, some athletes begin feeling slightly blue or depressed. Others feel they have so much energy, they want to go work out or they will go nuts. Hang on....*
- *Within one to two days of the race, most athletes feel darn good. They are typically ready to go and want race day to be here—right now!*

The short intervals done before the race should help legs and arms remain "fast" and feel strong. Here's some more detail on the fast workouts:

### Bike

On Wednesday of week 23, repeat one of the muscular endurance interval sessions listed in Base 3.

## Bricks

On Sunday of week 22, begin with a 1:30 bike ride in which the first hour of the ride is mostly in Zones 1 to 2 and the last 30 minutes of the ride is at race pace, or Zones 4 to 5a. The run following the bike is 30 minutes on an out-and-back course. The first 15 minutes of the run are in Zones 1 to 2—try to relax your shoulders and face. The last 15 minutes are at race pace or Zones 4 to 5a.

On Sunday of week 23, begin with a 1-hour bike ride in which the first 30 minutes of the ride is mostly in Zones 1 to 2 and the last 30 minutes of the ride is at race pace, or Zones 4 to 5a. The run following the bike is 30 minutes on an out-and-back course. The first 15 minutes of the run are in Zones 1 to 2—try to relax your shoulders and face. The last 15 minutes are at race pace, or Zones 4 to 5a.

## RACE WEEK

Calm your nerves and resist temptation to do more training. The work is complete, now it is time to relax and enjoy the experience. Expect to feel good and go fast.

# CHAPTER TWELVE

# Faster *Duathlon Performance*

*In an Ironman race I got a flat tire 15 miles into the bike after having a good swim and feeling great to boot. I was all thumbs trying to change the tire and ran into problems. I lost almost an hour. My race goals out the window, I started feeling sorry for myself. Then, I had a thought: "Find Norton Davey, the 81-year-old Ironman, and keep him company on his run." I found Norton and had one of the best experiences of my life, keeping him company during his marathon. I was thrilled to be able to run, walk and talk with this legend.*

—*Tom Manzi,*
*Point Pleasant, New Jersey*

The duathlon plans in Part I were for single-sport athletes making the change to multisport. This plan is for athletes who already have a good base in running and cycling and want to get faster in both sports, but are not sure what path to take.

## PROFILE

The athlete this plan is designed for is quite comfortable running three times per week for 30, 40 and 60 minutes per session, before beginning the plan. You are also comfortable cycling three days per week. Two of the cycling sessions are around 45 minutes long, with the third session at 90 minutes. From Chapter 1, you have determined that most of your training, before entering this plan, has been in Zones 1 to 3.

You want to get faster but without adding much more training time to your current routine. Also, your body responds best to only two stressful, or breakthrough (BT), workouts each week. A third BT day each week is too much.

## GOAL

At the end of 11 weeks of training, complete a duathlon consisting of a 5km run, a 30km bike and a second 5km run—at a fast clip.

| TABLE 12.1. PLAN OVERVIEW | | | |
|---|---|---|---|
| Week # | Month | Period | Weekly Planned Hours |
| 1 | May | Base 3 | 05:15 |
| 2 | May | Base 3 | 05:45 |
| 3 | May | Base 3 | 06:15 |
| 4 | May | Base 3 | 02:45 |
| 5 | May/June | Build 1 | 05:45 |
| 6 | June | Build 1 | 05:45 |
| 7 | June | Build 1 | 02:45 |
| 8 | June | Build 2 | 05:45 |
| 9 | June/July | Build 2 | 05:45 |
| 10 | July | Build 2 | 05:05 |
| 11 | July | Race | 1:45 + Race |

## PLAN DESCRIPTION

Table 12.1 gives an overall snapshot of the plan, showing weekly training hours ranging from 2:24 to 6:15. As with all the plans in this book, the month names are given for example only. Table 12.2 on page 138-139 shows the plan in detail. Following this program requires running three days per week and cycling three days per week. The plan shows Monday as a day off; however, it could be used as a strength training day if that is already part of your routine.

If you have the time and energy to do so, each training day could be increased by 15 minutes. It is not necessary to increase all the days; for example, only increasing the Wednesday bike rides by 15 minutes is an option. Read on to examine the plan in more detail.

### Base 3

The workouts needing special explanation in this period are the Thursday runs and the brick in week 4. All other workouts are available in Part V, separated into chapters by sport. For the Thursday run workouts in this block, do week 1 with 4 to 6 x 3' (1' RI); week 2 with 4 to 5 x 4' (1' RI); and week 3 with 2 to 3 x 6' (2' RI). All these intervals should be into Zones 4 to 5a.

For the brick scheduled on Saturday of week 4: Bike one hour and immediately transition to a 30-minute run. Both workouts are negative-split. Split each workout time in half and go out at an intensity in Zones 1 to 2. Come back in Zones 4 to 5a.

### Build 1

This block is three weeks long, and the two fast workouts are shown on Saturday and Sunday. Some athletes are better served to separate the fast training days. If this is the case

| Week | Sport | Mon Time | Tues Time | Tues Code | Wed Time | Wed Code | Thurs Time | Thurs Code |
|---|---|---|---|---|---|---|---|---|
| 1 | | Day off | | | | | | |
| | Run | | 00:30 | S2 | | | 00:45 | M2(4–5a) |
| | Bike | | | | 00:45 | S2 | | |
| 2 | | Day off | | | | | | |
| | Run | | 00:30 | S2 | | | 00:45 | M2(4–5a) |
| | Bike | | | | 00:45 | S3 | | |
| 3 | | Day off | | | | | | |
| | Run | | 00:30 | S2 | | | 00:45 | M2(4–5a) |
| | Bike | | | | 00:45 | S2 | | |
| 4 | Brick | Day off | | | Day off | | | |
| | Run | | 00:30 | S2 | | | | |
| | Bike | | | | | | 00:45 | S3 |
| 5 | | Day off | | | | | | |
| | Run | | 00:30 | S2 | | | 00:45 | E2 |
| | Bike | | | | 00:45 | S3 | | |
| 6 | | Day off | | | | | | |
| | Run | | 00:30 | S2 | | | 00:45 | E2 |
| | Bike | | | | 00:45 | S5 | | |
| 7 | Race Sim. | | Day off | | Day off | | | |
| | Run | | 00:30 | S2 | | | | |
| | Bike | | | | | | 00:45 | S3 |
| 8 | | Day off | | | | | | |
| | Run | | 00:30 | S2 | | | 00:45 | E2 |
| | Bike | | | | 00:45 | S3 | | |
| 9 | | Day off | | | | | | |
| | Run | | 00:30 | S2 | | | 00:45 | E2 |
| | Bike | | | | 00:45 | S5 | | |
| 10 | Race Sim. | | Day off | | | | | |
| | Run | | 00:30 | S2 | | | 00:45 | E2 |
| | Bike | | | | 00:45 | S3 | | |
| 11 | Brick | Day off | | | Day off | | Brick | |
| | Run | | 00:30 | S2 | | | 00:30 | A7 |
| | Bike | | | | | | 00:15 | A7 |

for you, do the fast run on Thursday and make Saturday the E2 run.

Special instructions for Saturday run workouts in this block of training are to do 3 to 4 x 3' (3' RI) in week 5 and 4 to 5 x 3' (3' RI) in week 6. These are both into Zone 5b.

| Fri Time | Fri Code | Sat Time | Sat Code | Sun Time | Sun Code | Weekly Training Hours | Weekly Training Hours By Sport | |
|---|---|---|---|---|---|---|---|---|
| | | 01:00 | E2 | | | | Run | 02:15 |
| 00:45 | E2 | | | 01:30 | E4 | 05:15 | Bike | 03:00 |
| | | 01:15 | E2 | | | | Run | 02:30 |
| 00:45 | E2 | | | 01:45 | E4 | 05:45 | Bike | 03:15 |
| | | 01:30 | E2 | | | | Run | 02:45 |
| 00:45 | E2 | | | 02:00 | E4 | 06:15 | Bike | 03:30 |
| Day off | | Brick | | Day off | | | | |
| | | 00:30 | text | | | | Run | 01:00 |
| | | 01:00 | text | | | 02:45 | Bike | 01:45 |
| | | 01:00 | A2(5b) | | | | Run | 02:15 |
| 00:45 | E2 | | | 02:00 | M5(20-25) | 05:45 | Bike | 03:30 |
| | | 01:00 | A2(5b) | | | | Run | 02:15 |
| 00:45 | E2 | | | 02:00 | M2(4–5a) | 05:45 | Bike | 03:30 |
| Day off | | Race | Day off | | | | | |
| | | 00:30 | Sim. | | | | Run | 01:00 |
| | | 01:00 | | | | 02:45 | Bike | 01:45 |
| | | 01:00 | text | | | | Run | 02:15 |
| 00:45 | E2 | | | 02:00 | M2(4–5a) | 05:45 | Bike | 03:30 |
| | | 01:00 | text | | | | Run | 02:15 |
| 00:45 | E2 | | | 02:00 | M2(4–5a) | 05:45 | Bike | 03:30 |
| | | Race Sim. | | | | | | |
| | | 00:50 | | | | | Run | 02:05 |
| 00:45 | S5 | 01:00 | | 00:30 | E1 | 05:05 | Bike | 03:00 |
| Day off | | | | Race! | | | | |
| | | | | | | | Run | 01:00 |
| | | 00:30 | S3 | | | 01:45 | Bike | 00:45 |

There are also special instructions for one of the bike workouts: in week 6, on Sunday, do 4 to 5 x 6' (2' RI) into Zones 4 to 5a.

This training block has the first race-simulation workout, in week 7. Total run time is shown as 30 minutes, but is split as follows: Begin the workout by running for 15 minutes in Zones 1 to 2. Move right to a bike ride of 1:00, including a 20-minute segment in Zones 4 to 5a near the end of the ride. Transition back to a run. The last run is 15 minutes and builds speed throughout the entire run. Begin in Zone 1 and gently increase the speed throughout the 15 minutes so the last three to five minutes is in Zone 5a.

### Build 2

This block is three weeks long, and the two fast workouts are shown on Saturday and Sunday. As with Build 1, some athletes are better served to separate the fast training days. If this is the case for you, complete the fast run on Thursday and make Saturday the E2 run.

The special run workouts in this block are both at the track. First, on Saturday in week 8, warm up and include a few 20- to 30-second accelerations. Then:

- *Run 2 x 880 yards, checking pace at each 440. The goal is to run at your current 10K race pace plus 1 to 5 seconds. For example, if your current 10K pace is 8 minutes per mile, half-mile pace (880 yards) is 4 minutes and quarter-mile pace (440 yards) is 2 minutes. In the example, this set would be run at a 2:01 to 2:05 pace per 440 yards. Jog easy in Zone 1 to recover for time equal to the run time. After the last recovery interval go right into the next run.*

- *Run 2 x 660 yards at the current 10K race pace. Jog easy in Zone 1 to recover, for time equal to the run time.*

*After the last recovery interval go right into the next run.*

- *Run 2 x 440 yards, with each 440 at the current 10K race pace, minus 1 to 5 seconds. (In other words, slightly faster than race pace.) Check pace at each 220 yards or half-lap. Jog easy in Zone 1 to recover for time equal to the run time. After the last recovery interval, go right into the next run.*

- *Run 2 x 220 yards, with each 220 at 1 to 5 seconds faster than you ran the 220s in the previous 440 set. Jog easy in Zone 1 to recover for time equal to the run time. Cool down with easy jogging for 5 to 10 minutes and stretch.*

In week 9, for the Saturday run, warm up and include a few 20- to 30-second accelerations. Then:

- *Run 3 x 880 yards, checking pace at each 440. The goal is to run at your current 10K race pace plus 1 to 5 seconds. This is just slightly slower than race pace. Jog easy in Zone 1 to recover for time equal to the run time. After the last recovery interval, go right into the next run.*

- *Run 3 x 660 yards at current 10K race pace. Jog easy in Zone 1 to recover for time equal to the run time. After the last recovery interval go right into the next run.*

- *Run 3 x 440 yards at current 10K race pace, minus 1 to 5 seconds. (In other words, slightly faster than race pace.) Check pace at each 220 yards or half-lap. Jog easy in Zone 1 to recover for a time equal to the run time. After*

*the last recovery interval go right into the next run.*
- *Run 3 x 220 yards, with each 220 at 1 to 5 seconds faster than you ran the 220s in the previous 440 set. Jog easy in Zone 1 to recover for a time equal to the run time. Cool down with easy jogging for 5 to 10 minutes and stretch.*

Two bike workouts need special instruction. In week 8, on Sunday, include 2 to 3 x 2 miles, raising heart rate into Zones 4 to 5a. Note the time it takes you to cover 2 miles and make the recovery interval, in Zone 1, one-quarter the time of the work interval.

In week 9, on Sunday, do 3 x 3 miles, raising heart rate into Zones 4 to 5a. Note the time it takes you to cover 3 miles and make the recovery interval, in Zone 1, one-quarter the time of the work interval.

For the race simulation workout on Saturday of week 10, begin with a 20-minute run in Zones 1 to 2. Transition to a 1:00 bike ride, beginning in Zones 1 to 2 and finishing the last 20 minutes at race pace, or roughly Zones 4 to 5a. Transition to a final run of 30 minutes, with 10 minutes in Zones 1 to 2 and the last 20 minutes at race pace.

## RACE

Week 11 is race week and you need to rest. The only workout needing special instructions is the brick. Begin the brick by cycling for 30 minutes, and include 3 x 90-second taper intervals. Follow the bike ride with a short run of 15 minutes, with 2 x 90-second taper intervals.

With rest and proper nutrition, race day is greeted with eager, energized legs. After setting your gear up in the transition area, take an easy jog of 5 to 10 minutes to warm up. When the race begins, be patient during the first run. Open at a pace that feels like Zone 1 to 2 intensity and make the run a negative-split effort. Transition to the bike and make the bike a negative-split effort as well.

The transition to the second run is always awkward; however, the beginning of the second run is at the pace at which you finished the first run. The second run is also a negative-split effort. The last half of the race should have a perceived exertion of being faster than the first half. This strategy will help you have a successful race experience. Try to relax and take pleasure from the experience!

# CHAPTER THIRTEEN

# Twenty-seven Week Plan to
# *Half-Ironman*

*During the race I try to keep my motivation up by saying, "Anything can happen to anyone, so it ain't over 'til it's over!" Again I remind myself to "RACE YOUR RACE." After the race I don't dwell too long on the events of the race, instead I try to draw on the experiences and lessons I learned from the race and move on to preparing myself for the next one.*
— Gail Laurence,
Manitou Springs, Colorado, age 36

The experienced triathlete using the half-Ironman plan in this chapter prefers a gentle increase in training hours. Weekly training hours during the early part of the year are somewhat limited by short days (and perhaps short desire). There is something about winter that turns normally enjoyable hours of endurance activities into arduous training.

The plan overview is shown on Table 13.1 on page 146. Although the plan begins on the first Monday in January, the weeks could easily slide forward a month or two to prepare

| Week # | Month | Period | Weekly Planned Hours |
|--------|-------|--------|----------------------|
| | TABLE 13.1. PLAN OVERVIEW | | |
| 1 | January | Base 1 | 09:30 |
| 2 | January | Base 1 | 09:45 |
| 3 | January | Base 1 | 09:45 |
| 4 | January | Base 1 | 07:15 |
| 5 | January/February | Base 2 | 10:30 |
| 6 | February | Base 2 | 10:30 |
| 7 | February | Base 2 | 10:30 |
| 8 | February | Base 2 | 06:45 |
| 9 | February/March | Base 3 | 11:00 |
| 10 | March | Base 3 | 11:00 |
| 11 | March | Base 3 | 11:00 |
| 12 | March | Base 3 | 06:45 |
| 13 | March/April | Base 2 | 10:15 |
| 14 | April | Base 2 | 11:45 |
| 15 | April | Base 2 | 12:45 |
| 16 | April | Base 2 | 07:00 |
| 17 | April/May | Base 3 | 11:45 |
| 18 | May | Base 3 | 13:30 |
| 19 | May | Base 3 | 14:15 |
| 20 | May | Base 3 | 07:00 |
| 21 | May | Base 4 | 12:45 |
| 22 | May/June | Base 4 | 14:30 |
| 23 | June | Base 4 | 15:30 |
| 24 | June | Base 4 | 07:00 |
| 25 | June | Peak/Taper | 12:15 |
| 26 | June/July | Peak/Taper | 08:15 |
| 27 | July | Race | 3:35+Race |

for a late July or August race. This plan is very similar to the Ironman plan in Chapter 14, and it may be helpful to read the instructions for that chapter as well. One of the major differences in format between the Ironman plan and this plan, besides volume, is the addition of a rest week at week 24 and a full three-week taper. Both methods work and the decision about which format to use depends on each individual athlete and the number of weeks available to train. Some athletes need that extra week of rest prior to a taper, while others prefer to head into a gentle tapering of volume after the largest training week.

## PROFILE

You are an experienced triathlete and maintain fitness throughout the year. Holiday commitments and a conscious decision to take a break have you training between seven and eight hours each week. This training has been consistent for at least four weeks. The training has consisted of swimming once or twice per week, running three times per week and cycling an hour on a trainer or in a spin class. You may have done a bit of cross training, such as hiking, cross-country skiing or snowshoeing. Week 1 on the first page of the detailed plan (Table 13.2), seems quite easy to accomplish. The long weekend workouts for the remainder of the plan, although challenging, seem doable.

## GOAL

Your goal is to complete a half-Ironman race in about six months.

## PLAN DESCRIPTION

The entire 27-week plan is shown on pages 148 to 153. In the first three months overall training time builds by four-week blocks, rather than weekly. Weekly training hours begin to build in late March as the days get warmer and longer. Those living in the Southern Hemisphere might begin week 1 in May. The longest training week on the plan is around 15:30, four weeks before race week. The structure of the plan typically puts long runs on Saturday and long bike rides on Sunday. One benefit of this kind of structure is that athletes run on relatively rested legs and reduce their risk for injury. Some would argue that legs are tired after a bike ride of 56 miles on race day, and that therefore the long bike in training should be on Saturday and the long run on Sunday. Either

TABLE 13.2. HALF-IRONMAN PERFORMANCE PLAN

| Week | Sport | Mon Time | Mon Code | Tues Time | Tues Code | Wed Time | Wed Code | Thurs Time | Thurs Code |
|---|---|---|---|---|---|---|---|---|---|
| 1 | Strength | 01:15 | AA | | | 01:15 | AA | | |
| | Swim | | | 01:00 | E2 | | | 01:00 | T1b |
| | Bike | | | | | | | | |
| | Run | | | 00:30 | S2 | | | 00:30 | E1* |
| 2 | Strength | 01:15 | AA | | | 01:15 | AA | | |
| | Swim | | | 01:00 | E2 | | | 01:00 | E(Speed) |
| | Bike | | | | | | | | |
| | Run | | | 00:45 | S2 | | | 00:30 | E1* |
| 3 | Strength | 01:15 | AA | | | 01:15 | AA | | |
| | Swim | | | 01:00 | E2 | | | 01:00 | E(Speed) |
| | Bike | | | | | | | | |
| | Run | | | 00:45 | S2 | | | 00:30 | E1* |
| 4 | Strength | 01:15 | AA | | | 01:15 | AA | | |
| | Swim | | | | | | | 01:00 | E(Speed) |
| | Bike | | | | | | | | |
| | Run | | | 00:45 | S2 | | | | |
| 5 | Strength | 01:15 | MS | | | 01:30 | MS | | |
| | Swim | | | 01:00 | E(Form) | | | 01:00 | E2 |
| | Bike | | | | | | | | |
| | Run | | | 00:45 | S2 | | | 00:30 | E1* |
| 6 | Strength | 01:15 | MS | | | 01:30 | MS | | |
| | Swim | | | 01:00 | E(Speed) | | | 01:00 | E2 |
| | Bike | | | | | | | | |
| | Run | | | 00:45 | S2 | | | 00:30 | E2 |
| 7 | Strength | 01:15 | MS | | | 01:30 | MS | | |
| | Swim | | | 01:00 | E(Form) | | | 01:00 | E2 |
| | Bike | | | | | | | | |
| | Run | | | 00:45 | S2 | | | 00:30 | E1* |
| 8 | Strength | 01:00 | MS | | | 01:00 | MS | | |
| | Swim | | | | | | | 01:00 | T1b |
| | Bike | | | | | | | | |
| | Run | | | 00:45 | S2 | | | | |
| 9 | Strength | 01:00 | PE | | | 01:15 | PE + Plyo#1 | | |
| | Swim | | | 01:00 | E(Speed) | | | 01:00 | M |
| | Bike | | | | | | | | |
| | Run | | | 00:45 | TM#1 or S2 | | | 00:30 | E2 |
| 10 | Strength | 01:00 | PE | | | 01:15 | PE + Plyo#2 | | |
| | Swim | | | 01:00 | Force | | | 01:00 | E2 |
| | Bike | | | | | | | | |
| | Run | | | 00:45 | TM#2 or S2 | | | 00:30 | E2 |

| Fri Time | Fri Code | Sat Time | Sat Code | Sun Time | Sun Code | Weekly Training Hours | Weekly Training Hours By Sport | |
|---|---|---|---|---|---|---|---|---|
| | | 01:00 | E(Form) | | | | Strength | 02:30 |
| 01:00 | S1 | | | 01:00 | T1(5) | | Swim | 03:00 |
| | | | | | | | Bike | 02:00 |
| | | 01:00 | T1(3) | | | 09:30 | Run | 02:00 |
| | | 01:00 | E(Form) | | | | Strength | 02:30 |
| 01:00 | S2 | | | 01:00 | E2* | | Swim | 03:00 |
| | | | | | | | Bike | 02:00 |
| | | 01:00 | E2 | | | 09:45 | Run | 02:15 |
| | | 01:00 | E(Form) | | | | Strength | 02:30 |
| 01:00 | S1 | | | 01:00 | E2* | | Swim | 03:00 |
| | | | | | | | Bike | 02:00 |
| | | 01:00 | E2 | | | 09:45 | Run | 02:15 |
| | | 00:45 | E(Form) | | | | Strength | 02:30 |
| 00:30 | S2 | | | 01:00 | S5 | | Swim | 01:45 |
| | | | | | | | Bike | 01:30 |
| | | 00:45 | S1 | | | 07:15 | Run | 01:30 |
| | | 01:15 | E3 | | | | Strength | 02:45 |
| 01:00 | S1 | | | 01:15 | E3 | | Swim | 03:15 |
| | | | | | | | Bike | 02:15 |
| | | 01:00 | E2 | | | 10:30 | Run | 02:15 |
| | | 01:15 | E3 | | | | Strength | 02:45 |
| 01:00 | S2 | | | 01:15 | E2* | Swim | 03:15 | |
| | | | | | | | Bike | 02:15 |
| | | 01:00 | E3 | | | 10:30 | Run | 02:15 |
| | | 01:15 | E3 | | | | Strength | 02:45 |
| 01:00 | S1 | | | 01:15 | E3 | | Swim | 03:15 |
| | | | | | | | Bike | 02:15 |
| | | 01:00 | E2 | | | 10:30 | Run | 02:15 |
| | | 00:45 | E(Form) | | | | Strength | 02:00 |
| 00:30 | S2 | | | 01:00 | T1(5) | | Swim | 01:45 |
| | | | | | | | Bike | 01:30 |
| | | 00:45 | T1(3) | | | 06:45 | Run | 01:30 |
| | | 01:15 | E2 | | | | Strength | 02:15 |
| 01:00 | S1 | | | 02:00 | E2 | | Swim | 03:15 |
| | | | | | | | Bike | 03:00 |
| | | 01:15 | E4 | | | 11:00 | Run | 02:30 |
| | | 01:15 | E2 | | | | Strength | 02:15 |
| 01:00 | S2 | | | 02:00 | E2* | | Swim | 03:15 |
| | | | | | | | Bike | 03:00 |
| | | 01:15 | E2 | | | 11:00 | Run | 02:30 |

TABLE 13.2. HALF-IRONMAN PERFORMANCE PLAN (CONTINUED)

| Week | Sport | Mon Time | Mon Code | Tues Time | Tues Code | Wed Time | Wed Code | Thurs Time | Thurs Code |
|---|---|---|---|---|---|---|---|---|---|
| 11 | Strength | 01:00 | PE | | | 01:15 | PE + Plyo#3 | | |
| | Swim | | | 01:00 | Force | | | 01:00 | M |
| | Bike | | | | | | | | |
| | Run | | | 00:45 | TM#3 or S2 | | | 00:30 | E2 |
| 12 | Strength | 01:00 | PE | | | 01:15 | PE + Plyo#4 | | |
| | Swim | | | | | | | 00:45 | M(Speed) |
| | Bike | | | | | | | | |
| | Run | | | 00:45 | TM#4 or S2 | | | 00:30 | E2 |
| 13 | Strength | 01:00 | SM | | | | | | |
| | Swim | | | 01:00 | E(Speed) | | | 01:00 | E2 |
| | Bike | | | | | 01:00 | M1(20) | | |
| | Run | | | 00:45 | S2 | | | 00:30 | E2 |
| 14 | Strength | 01:00 | SM | | | | | | |
| | Swim | | | 01:00 | E(Form) | | | 01:00 | E2 |
| | Bike | | | | | 01:00 | E2 | | |
| | Run | | | 00:45 | S1 | | | 01:00 | M2(3Z) |
| 15 | Strength | 01:00 | SM | | | | | | |
| | Swim | | | 01:00 | E(Speed) | | | 01:00 | E2 |
| | Bike | | | | | 01:30 | M1(30) | | |
| | Run | | | 00:30 | S2 | | | 01:00 | E2 |
| 16 | Strength | 01:00 | SM | | | | | | |
| | Swim | | | | | | | 01:00 | T1b |
| | Bike | | | | | 01:00 | S5 | | |
| | Run | | | 00:45 | S1 | | | | |
| 17 | Strength | 01:00 | SM | | | | | | |
| | Swim | | | 01:00 | E(Form) | | | 01:00 | E2 |
| | Bike | | | | | 00:45 | E2 | | |
| | Run | | | 00:30 | A2(5bZ) | | | 00:30 | E1 |
| 18 | Strength | 01:00 | SM | | | | | | |
| | Swim | | | 01:00 | E(Speed) | | | 01:15 | E3 |
| | Bike | | | | | 01:15 | M1(40) | | |
| | Run | | | 00:30 | E2 | | | 01:00 | E2 |
| 19 | Strength | 01:00 | SM | | | | | | |
| | Swim | | | 01:00 | E(Form) | | | 01:00 | E2 |
| | Bike | | | | | 01:15 | E2 | | |
| | Run | | | 01:00 | M2(3Z) | | | 00:30 | S2 |
| 20 | Strength | 01:00 | SM | | | | | | |
| | Swim | | | | | | | 01:00 | T1b |
| | Bike | | | | | 01:00 | S5 | | |
| | Run | | | 00:45 | S1 | | | | |

| Fri Time | Fri Code | Sat Time | Sat Code | Sun Time | Sun Code | Weekly Training Hours | Weekly Training Hours By Sport | |
|---|---|---|---|---|---|---|---|---|
| | | | | | | | Strength | 02:15 |
| | | 01:15 | E2 | | | | Swim | 03:15 |
| 01:00 | S1 | | | 02:00 | E2* | | Bike | 03:00 |
| | | 01:15 | E4 | | | 11:00 | Run | 02:30 |
| Day off | | | | | | | Strength | 02:15 |
| | | 00:45 | E(Form) | | | | Swim | 01:30 |
| | | | | 01:00 | S5 | | Bike | 01:00 |
| | | 00:45 | A1b | | | 06:45 | Run | 02:00 |
| | | | | | | | Strength | 01:00 |
| | | 01:00 | M | | | | Swim | 03:00 |
| 01:00 | E1 | | | 01:30 | E2 | | Bike | 03:30 |
| | | 01:30 | E3 | | | 10:15 | Run | 02:45 |
| | | Brick | | | | | Strength | 01:00 |
| | | 01:15 | E3 | | | | Swim | 03:15 |
| 01:15 | S4 | 01:00 | E2 | 02:00 | E3 | | Bike | 05:15 |
| | | 00:30 | E2 | | | 11:45 | Run | 02:15 |
| | | | | | | | Strength | 01:00 |
| | | 01:15 | E3 | | | | Swim | 03:15 |
| 01:30 | E1 | | | 02:30 | E2 | | Bike | 05:30 |
| | | 01:30 | E3 | | | 12:45 | Run | 03:00 |
| Day off | | | | | | | Strength | 01:00 |
| | | 01:00 | E(Form) | | | | Swim | 02:00 |
| | | | | 01:30 | T1(6–10) | | Bike | 02:30 |
| | | 00:45 | E2 | | | 07:00 | Run | 01:30 |
| | | | | | | | Strength | 01:00 |
| | | 01:15 | E3 | | | | Swim | 03:15 |
| 01:00 | S5 | | | 03:00 | E3 | | Bike | 04:45 |
| | | 01:45 | E3 | | | 11:45 | Run | 02:45 |
| | | Brick | | | | | Strength | 01:00 |
| | | 01:00 | E1 | | | | Swim | 03:15 |
| 01:15 | S4 | 01:00 | text | 03:30 | E2 | | Bike | 07:00 |
| | | 00:45 | text | | | 13:30 | Run | 02:15 |
| | | | | | | | Strength | 01:00 |
| | | 01:15 | E3 | | | | Swim | 03:15 |
| 01:30 | S4 | 01:45 | E2 | 04:00 | E3 | | Bike | 08:30 |
| | | | | | | 14:15 | Run | 01:30 |
| Day off | | | | | | | Strength | 01:00 |
| | | 01:00 | E(Form) | | | | Swim | 02:00 |
| | | | | 01:30 | E2 | | Bike | 02:30 |
| | | 00:45 | T1(3) | | | 07:00 | Run | 01:30 |

TABLE 13.2. HALF-IRONMAN PERFORMANCE PLAN (CONTINUED)

| Week | Sport | Mon Time | Mon Code | Tues Time | Tues Code | Wed Time | Wed Code | Thurs Time | Thurs Code |
|------|-------|----------|----------|-----------|-----------|----------|----------|------------|------------|
| 21 | Strength | 01:00 | SM | | | | | | |
| | Swim | | | 01:00 | E(Speed) | | | 01:00 | E2 |
| | Bike | | | | | 00:45 | E2 | | |
| | Run | | | 00:30 | E2 | | | 00:30 | E1 |
| 22 | Strength | 01:00 | SM | | | | | | |
| | Swim | | | 01:00 | E(Form) | | | 01:00 | E2 |
| | Bike | | | | | 01:30 | M1 | | |
| | Run | | | 01:00 | E2 | | (40-50) | 00:30 | E1 |
| 23 | Strength | 01:00 | SM | | | | | | |
| | Swim | | | 01:00 | E(Speed) | | | 01:00 | E2 |
| | Bike | | | | | 01:15 | E2 | | |
| | Run | | | 01:00 | E2 | | | 00:30 | E1 |
| 24 | Strength | 01:00 | SM | | | | | | |
| | Swim | | | | | | | 01:00 | T1b |
| | Bike | | | | | 01:00 | S5 | | |
| | Run | | | 00:45 | S1 | | | | |
| 25 | Strength | 01:00 | SM | | | | | | |
| | Swim | | | 01:00 | E(Form) | | | 01:00 | E2 |
| | Bike | | | | | 01:00 | E2 | | |
| | Run | | | 01:00 | S1 | | | 00:30 | E2 |
| 26 | Strength | 01:00 | SM | | | | | | |
| | Swim | | | 00:45 | E(Speed) | | | 00:45 | E2 |
| | Bike | | | | | 01:00 | S5 | | |
| | Run | | | 00:30 | E2 | | | 00:45 | E2 |
| 27 | Strength | | | | | | | | |
| | Swim | | | 00:45 | E(Speed) | | | | |
| | Bike | | | | | 00:45 | M1(15) | | |
| | Run | 00:45 | M1(20) | | | | | 00:30 | S2 |

way will work, so choose the format that suits your personal needs.

As you progress through the plan, notice that leg- and arm-speed drills are included throughout the 27 weeks. Too often athletes who train for a long event slog through endless, slow miles. While that strategy does build endurance, constantly swimming, cycling or running at a sauntering pace

| Fri Time | Fri Code | Sat Time | Sat Code | Sun Time | Sun Code | Weekly Training Hours | Weekly Training Hours By Sport |
|---|---|---|---|---|---|---|---|
| | | 01:00 | E3 | | | | Strength 01:00 |
| 01:00 | S2 | | | 04:00 | E3 | | Swim 03:00 |
| | | 02:00 | E3 | | | | Bike 05:45 |
| | | | | | | 12:45 | Run 03:00 |
| | | Brick | | | | | Strength 01:00 |
| | | 01:30 | E3 | | | | Swim 03:30 |
| 00:30 | S1 | 01:00 | text | 04:30 | E2 | | Bike 07:30 |
| | | 01:00 | text | | | 14:30 | Run 02:30 |
| | | 01:30 | E3 | | | | Strength 01:00 |
| 01:15 | S5 | | | 05:00 | E3 | | Swim 03:30 |
| | | 02:00 | E3 | | | | Bike 07:30 |
| | | | | | | 15:30 | Run 03:30 |
| Day off | | 01:00 | E(Form) | | | | Strength 01:00 |
| | | | | 01:30 | T1(6–10) | | Swim 02:00 |
| | | 00:45 | E2 | | | | Bike 02:30 |
| | | | | | | 07:00 | Run 01:30 |
| | | 01:15 | E3 | | | | Strength 01:00 |
| 01:00 | S4 | 02:15 | text | 01:00 | E1 | | Swim 03:15 |
| | | 01:15 | text | | | | Bike 05:15 |
| | | | | | | 12:15 | Run 02:45 |
| Day off | | Brick | | | | | Strength 01:00 |
| | | 01:00 | M | | | | Swim 02:30 |
| | | 01:00 | text | 01:00 | E1 | | Bike 03:00 |
| | | 00:30 | text | | | 08:15 | Run 01:45 |
| Day off | | Brick | | Race! | | | Strength 00:00 |
| | | 00:30 | E(Speed) | | | | Swim 01:15 |
| | | 00:20 | S4 | | | | Bike 01:05 |
| | | 00:10 | S2 | | | 03:45 | Run 01:25 |

teaches the body to function at that one speed. To enhance endurance training, form work is included, because it is neuromuscular in nature and is intended to improve economy. Form work sessions give you more gears, so to speak. The fast segments are high-speed movements, with good form, for short duration. After finishing a form session, you should feel fast and eager to do more, not exhausted.

## Swimming

For the first few weeks, include at least one 800- to 1000-yard main set. The swim can be continuous or broken. If broken, make the rest intervals no greater than 10 seconds. Slowly increase the distance of this main set over the course of several weeks to 1500 to 2000 yards. Some athletes may reach a main set of 2500 yards, but much over that is not necessary. If you have accomplished the main-set goals, add some Zone 3 intensity to segments of the main set to increase muscular endurance.

## Base 1

The first week of the plan includes a baseline time trial in each sport. It goes without saying that if you have not been training consistently, do not begin the plan—especially time trials—until some foundation conditioning has been achieved. That foundation is described in the Profile section (page 146).

This plan allows for crosstraining. A "*" beside the code of any workout, such as the run on Thursday of week 1, means cross-training is an option. Because heart rate ranges vary for different sports, use rating of perceived exertion (RPE) to determine the correct training zones. Some suggestions for cross-training include aerobics classes, circuit training, kickboxing, snowshoeing, cross-country skiing and hiking, to name a few.

Spin classes can also serve as excellent sources of winter training. A few words of caution—do not let the instructor or other students in the class determine the intensity of your session, but work out at your own pace.

For all Friday bike rides for weeks 1 through 12, ride time can be between 30 and 60 minutes.

### Base 2 (Weeks 5 to 8)

This first block of Base 2 training includes two maximum strength (MS) training days per week, which are particularly helpful to build strength for hilly bike courses. Some athletes find that two days of MS strength training are fatiguing for the legs and that they need to reduce the intensity of one of the weekend workouts. If this is the case for you, reduce the intensity of the sport that is already your strength.

### Base 3 (Weeks 9 to 12)

The first Base 3 block has several options. The first option is the Tuesday run. For experienced athletes, I recommend doing the treadmill workouts found in Appendix H. Choose the lower number of repetitions in each set. I have found no better training tool to improve running speed and pace perception than a treadmill. People who are uncomfortable getting on and off of a running treadmill are better off sticking to simple pick-ups.

The second option during this block is the plyometric workouts shown with the Wednesday strength training session and found in Appendix G. Chapter 21, which covers strength training, explains why plyometrics will enhance an endurance athlete's training program. If you are in the first season of plyometric work, select the lowest number of sets and repetitions.

Also, if in the first year of plyometrics, do plyo only once per week.

Both plyometrics and the treadmill sessions are not intended to be exceptionally difficult workouts. If you are exhausted or extremely sore after either workout, it is a message to back off on speed or intensity of the sessions.

This is the last block that includes optional cross-training.

### Base 2 (Weeks 13 to 16)

The second block of Base 2 is when weekly endurance volume begins to build and strength training is reduced to one day for strength maintenance (SM). The intensity of workouts remains in Zones 1 to 3, where most of a half-Ironman race will occur. Hilly races will solicit some time in Zone 4 and above, but keep this time very minimal.

Week 14 of the plan has a Zone 3 run on Thursday that should be 3 to 4 x 6' (2' RI). All Wednesday bike rides that do not include Zone 3 time should be considered optional. Cut the ride time down or eliminate the ride altogether if you are feeling excessive fatigue.

Saturday of week 14 has the first brick of the schedule, which can be done immediately after the swim or later in the day. Both bike and run segments are in Zones 1 and 2.

Once athletes begin to increase training volume, many find that more than two aerobic time trials within the rest week are too much. So, with that in mind, there are only two time trials in week 16; notice that the distance on the bike time trial is increased.

## Base 3 (Weeks 17 to 20)

Weekly volume continues to build during this block. This is a perfect opportunity to establish the eating and drinking format you will use on race day. Take the time to figure out a nutritional plan—in detail—and write it down. What will you eat and drink each 15 to 20 minutes of the entire race? Do not take this lightly: many Ironman races were spoiled by under- or overeating and/or drinking. Make a plan and practice it.

The workouts needing additional explanation during this block include the brick on Saturday of Week 18 and the run in Week 19. For the week 18 Saturday brick, both sports are controlled at Zones 1 to 2 for the first half of the assigned time. The second half of the time can go Zones 1 to 3. It is not a goal to maximize time in Zone 3. For the week 19 Tuesday run, do 3 to 5 x 6' (2' RI).

## Base 4

The most important workouts of weeks 21 through 23 are scheduled on the weekends. Other workouts during the week should be reduced, if necessary, to allow for full recovery for the weekend sessions. For the week 22 Saturday brick, both sports are controlled at Zones 1 to 2 for the first half of the assigned time. The second half of the time can go Zones 1 to 3. It is not a goal to maximize time in Zone 3.

## Peak/Taper and Race

All of the hard work is complete; it is time to enjoy. Weeks 25, 26 and 27 have reduced volume and some intensity to keep legs and arms feeling rested and fresh for race day. The bricks in weeks 25 and 26 are negative-split efforts, that is, the first half of time for the bike and run are at Zone 1 to 2. The second half are at Zone 1 to 3, and should be slightly faster. Two to three weeks prior to the race is a good time for a total bike tune-up. This allows enough time for new cables to stretch and any problems to appear so they can be addressed before the bike is racked in the transition area on race day.

On race day, pace yourself and recall all the practice sessions—long runs, long bike rides, long swims and bricks. Those workouts were all simply dress rehearsal for race day. Race pace is no faster than what was practiced in training. This can be difficult to control as surging adrenaline and a rested body wants to take off like a quarter horse coming out of the gate at the track.

To help control that quarter horse feeling, recall the negative split workouts where the first half of the session was done at a lower intensity than the second half of the workout. Try to make each individual sport, and the entire race, negative split. This means the swim will be at a lower rating of perceived exertion and relative speed than the last half of the run. Each leg of the race—swim, bike and run—should be split in half. The first half of each event is a bit slower, or at a lower intensity, than the second half. These increases in speed are subtle.

At the end of the race, celebrate—and do not make it subtle!

## QUESTION AND ANSWER

**Q.** Can I race—do a triathlon—instead of a brick?

**A.** Yes, but try to keep overall time and the goal of the scheduled workout in mind. Too much racing while training for a half- or full Ironman can get in the way of long training sessions or cause excessive fatigue.

# CHAPTER FOURTEEN

# Twenty-six Week Plan to *Ironman*

*I have loved training and racing in endurance sports, especially running, since I was fourteen. Long intense workouts were enjoyable, so hard work came naturally. However, constant injury disrupted my training continuity, causing regression and frustration. Training with a great coach is teaching me that part of discipline is training intelligently. Hard work alone can be a powerfully destructive force without a well-focused plan based on knowledge.*

*—Paul O'Brien,*
*Tucson, Arizona, age 43*

It is the post-holiday, northern-latitude Ironman who appreciates the plan in this chapter. Cold, short winter days keep bike rides at a two-hour limit on the indoor trainer. There are stories of people spending inhumane amounts of time on an indoor trainer watching multiple tapes of old Ironman races—but that is not for you, thank you.

The plan overview is shown on Table 14.1 on page 163. Although the plan begins on the first Monday in January, the weeks could easily slide forward a month or two to prepare for a late July or August race. The plan in this chapter is similar to the Chapter 13 plan for a half-Ironman; it may be beneficial to read that chapter.

## PROFILE

You are an experienced triathlete and maintain fitness throughout the year. Holiday commitments and a conscious decision to take a break have you training between seven-and-a-half and eight-and-a-half hours each week. This has been consistent for at least four weeks. Training has been swimming once or twice per week, running three times per week and cycling an hour on a trainer or in a spin class. You may have done a bit of cross-training, such as hiking, cross-country skiing or snowshoeing. Week 1 on the first page of the detailed plan (Table 14.2), seems easy to accomplish. The long weekend workouts for the remainder of the plan, although challenging, seem doable.

## GOAL

Your goal is to complete an Ironman-distance race in about six months.

## PLAN DESCRIPTION

The entire 26-week plan is shown on pages 164-169. In the first three months, overall training time does not build significantly. Weekly training hours begin to build in late March as the days get warmer and longer. The longest training week on the plan is around 18 hours; this is three weeks before race week. The structure of the plan typically puts long runs on Saturday and long bike rides on Sunday. One benefit of this kind of structure is that athletes run on relatively rested legs and reduce the risk for injury. Some would argue that Ironman athletes run on tired legs after a bike ride of 112 miles on race day, and that therefore the long bike in training should be on Saturday and the long run on Sunday. Either way will work.

As you progress through the plan, notice that leg- and arm-speed drills are included throughout the 26 weeks. Too often athletes training for an Ironman event slog through endless slow miles. It is critical to keep some form work included in training, as it is intended to improve economy, or the oxygen cost to produce any given speed. Do not be tempted to make a form session killer-hard, which is not the goal. The goal is to feel fast and light.

| TABLE 14.1. PLAN OVERVIEW | | | |
|---|---|---|---|
| Week # | Month | Period | Weekly Planned Hours |
| 1 | January | Base 1 | 09:30 |
| 2 | January | Base 1 | 10:30 |
| 3 | January | Base 1 | 11:15 |
| 4 | January | Base 1 | 07:30 |
| 5 | January/February | Base 2 | 12:30 |
| 6 | February | Base 2 | 12:45 |
| 7 | February | Base 2 | 12:45 |
| 8 | February | Base 2 | 07:30 |
| 9 | February/March | Base 3 | 12:15 |
| 10 | March | Base 3 | 12:15 |
| 11 | March | Base 3 | 12:15 |
| 12 | March | Base 3 | 08:00 |
| 13 | March/April | Base 2 | 12:45 |
| 14 | April | Base 2 | 14:45 |
| 15 | April | Base 2 | 16:00 |
| 16 | April | Base 2 | 08:30 |
| 17 | April/May | Base 3 | 13:30 |
| 18 | May | Base 3 | 16:00 |
| 19 | May | Base 3 | 17:00 |
| 20 | May | Base 3 | 08:30 |
| 21 | May | Base 4 | 14:45 |
| 22 | May/June | Base 4 | 16:30 |
| 23 | June | Base 4 | 18:15 |
| 24 | June | Peak/Taper | 14:30 |
| 25 | June | Peak/Taper | 10:30 |
| 26 | June/July | Race | 4:45+race |

## TABLE 14.2. IRONMAN PERFORMANCE PLAN

| Week | Sport | Mon Time | Mon Code | Tues Time | Tues Code | Wed Time | Wed Code | Thurs Time | Thurs Code |
|---|---|---|---|---|---|---|---|---|---|
| 1 | Strength | 01:15 | AA | | | 01:15 | AA | | |
| | Swim | | | 01:00 | E2 | | | 01:00 | T1b |
| | Bike | | | | | | | | |
| | Run | | | 00:30 | S2 | | | 00:30 | E1* |
| 2 | Strength | 01:15 | AA | | | 01:15 | AA | | |
| | Swim | | | 01:00 | E2 | | | 01:15 | E(Speed) |
| | Bike | | | | | | | | |
| | Run | | | 00:45 | S2 | | | 00:30 | E1* |
| 3 | Strength | 01:15 | AA | | | 01:15 | AA | | |
| | Swim | | | 01:15 | E2 | | | 01:15 | E(Speed) |
| | Bike | | | | | | | | |
| | Run | | | 00:45 | S2 | | | 00:30 | E1* |
| 4 | Strength | 01:15 | AA | | | 01:15 | AA | | |
| | Swim | | | | | | | 01:00 | E(Speed) |
| | Bike | | | | | | | | |
| | Run | | | 00:45 | S2 | | | | |
| 5 | Strength | 01:30 | MS | | | 01:30 | MS | | |
| | Swim | | | 01:15 | E(Form) | | | 01:00 | E2 |
| | Bike | | | | | | | | |
| | Run | | | 01:00 | S2 | | | 00:30 | E1* |
| 6 | Strength | 01:30 | MS | | | 01:30 | MS | | |
| | Swim | | | 01:15 | E(Speed) | | | 01:15 | E2 |
| | Bike | | | | | | | | |
| | Run | | | 01:00 | S2 | | | 00:30 | E2 |
| 7 | Strength | 01:30 | MS | | | 01:30 | MS | | |
| | Swim | | | 01:15 | E(Form) | | | 01:15 | E2 |
| | Bike | | | | | | | | |
| | Run | | | 01:00 | S2 | | | 00:30 | E1* |
| 8 | Strength | 01:00 | MS | | | 01:00 | MS | | |
| | Swim | | | | | | | 01:00 | T1b |
| | Bike | | | | | | | | |
| | Run | | | 01:00 | S2 | | | | |
| 9 | Strength | 01:00 | PE | | | 01:30 | PE + Plyo#1 | | |
| | Swim | | | 01:15 | E(Speed) | | | 01:15 | M |
| | Bike | | | | | | | | |
| | Run | | | 01:00 | TM#1 or S2 | | | 00:30 | E2 |
| 10 | Strength | 01:00 | PE | | | 01:30 | PE + Plyo#2 | | |
| | Swim | | | 01:15 | Force | | | 01:15 | E2 |
| | Bike | | | | | | | | |
| | Run | | | 01:00 | TM#2 or S2 | | | 00:30 | E2 |

| Fri Time | Fri Code | Sat Time | Sat Code | Sun Time | Sun Code | Weekly Training Hours | Weekly Training Hours By Sport | |
|---|---|---|---|---|---|---|---|---|
|  |  | 01:00 | E(Form) |  |  |  | Strength | 02:30 |
| 01:00 | S1 |  |  | 01:00 | T1(5) |  | Swim | 03:00 |
|  |  | 01:00 | T1(3) |  |  |  | Bike | 02:00 |
|  |  |  |  |  |  | 09:30 | Run | 02:00 |
|  |  | 01:00 | E(Form) |  |  |  | Strength | 02:30 |
| 01:00 | S2 |  |  | 01:15 | E2* |  | Swim | 03:15 |
|  |  | 01:15 | E2 |  |  |  | Bike | 02:15 |
|  |  |  |  |  |  | 10:30 | Run | 02:30 |
|  |  | 01:00 | E(Form) |  |  |  | Strength | 02:30 |
| 01:00 | S1 |  |  | 01:30 | E2* |  | Swim | 03:30 |
|  |  | 01:30 | E2 |  |  |  | Bike | 02:30 |
|  |  |  |  |  |  | 11:15 | Run | 02:45 |
|  |  | 01:00 | E(Form) |  |  |  | Strength | 02:30 |
| 00:30 | S2 |  |  | 01:00 | S5 |  | Swim | 02:00 |
|  |  | 00:45 | E2 |  |  |  | Bike | 01:30 |
|  |  |  |  |  |  | 07:30 | Run | 01:30 |
|  |  | 01:15 | E3 |  |  |  | Strength | 03:00 |
| 01:00 | S1 |  |  | 02:00 | E3 |  | Swim | 03:30 |
|  |  | 01:30 | E2 |  |  |  | Bike | 03:00 |
|  |  |  |  |  |  | 12:30 | Run | 03:00 |
|  |  | 01:15 | E3 |  |  |  | Strength | 03:00 |
| 01:00 | S2 |  |  | 02:00 | E2* |  | Swim | 03:45 |
|  |  | 01:30 | E3 |  |  |  | Bike | 03:00 |
|  |  |  |  |  |  | 12:45 | Run | 03:00 |
|  |  | 01:15 | E3 |  |  |  | Strength | 03:00 |
| 01:00 | S1 |  |  | 02:00 | E3 |  | Swim | 03:45 |
|  |  | 01:30 | E2 |  |  |  | Bike | 03:00 |
|  |  |  |  |  |  | 12:45 | Run | 03:00 |
|  |  | 01:00 | E(Form) |  |  |  | Strength | 02:00 |
| 00:30 | S2 |  |  | 01:00 | T1(5) |  | Swim | 02:00 |
|  |  | 01:00 | T1(3) |  |  |  | Bike | 01:30 |
|  |  |  |  |  |  | 07:30 | Run | 02:00 |
|  |  | 01:15 | E2 |  |  |  | Strength | 02:30 |
| 01:00 | S1 |  |  | 02:00 | E2 |  | Swim | 03:45 |
|  |  | 01:30 | E4 |  |  |  | Bike | 03:00 |
|  |  |  |  |  |  | 12:15 | Run | 03:00 |
|  |  | 01:15 | E2 |  |  |  | Strength | 02:30 |
| 01:00 | S2 |  |  | 02:00 | E2* |  | Swim | 03:45 |
|  |  | 01:30 | E2 |  |  |  | Bike | 03:00 |
|  |  |  |  |  |  | 12:15 | Run | 03:00 |

TABLE 14.2. IRONMAN PERFORMANCE PLAN (CONTINUED)

| Week | Sport | Mon Time | Mon Code | Tues Time | Tues Code | Wed Time | Wed Code | Thurs Time | Thurs Code |
|---|---|---|---|---|---|---|---|---|---|
| 11 | Strength | 01:00 | PE | | | 01:30 | PE + Plyo#3 | | |
| | Swim | | | 01:15 | Force | | | 01:15 | M |
| | Bike | | | | | | | | |
| | Run | | | 01:00 | TM#3 or S2 | | | 00:30 | E2 |
| 12 | Strength | 01:00 | PE | | | 01:30 | PE + Plyo#4 | | |
| | Swim | | | | | | | 01:00 | M(Speed) |
| | Bike | | | | | | | | |
| | Run | | | 01:00 | TM#4 or S2 | | | 00:30 | E2 |
| 13 | Strength | 01:00 | SM | | | | | | |
| | Swim | | | 01:15 | E(Speed) | | | 01:15 | E2 |
| | Bike | | | | | 01:00 | M1(20) | | |
| | Run | | | 00:45 | S2 | 00:30 | E1** | 00:30 | E2 |
| 14 | Strength | 01:00 | SM | | | | | | |
| | Swim | | | 01:15 | E(Form) | | | 01:15 | E2 |
| | Bike | | | | | 01:00 | E2 | | |
| | Run | | | 00:45 | S1 | 00:30 | E1** | 01:00 | M2(3Z) |
| 15 | Strength | 01:00 | SM | | | | | | |
| | Swim | | | 01:15 | E(Speed) | | | 01:15 | E2 |
| | Bike | | | | | 01:30 | M1(30) | | |
| | Run | | | 00:30 | S2 | 00:30 | E1** | 01:00 | E2 |
| 16 | Strength | 01:00 | SM | | | | | | |
| | Swim | | | | | | | 01:00 | T1b |
| | Bike | | | | | 01:00 | S5 | | |
| | Run | | | 00:45 | S1 | | | 00:30 | E1 |
| 17 | Strength | 01:00 | SM | | | | | | |
| | Swim | | | 01:00 | E(Form) | | | 01:00 | E2 |
| | Bike | | | | | 00:45 | E2 | | |
| | Run | | | 00:30 | A2(5bZ) | | | 00:30 | E1 |
| 18 | Strength | 01:00 | SM | | | | | | |
| | Swim | | | 01:00 | E(Speed) | | | 01:30 | E3 |
| | Bike | | | | | 01:30 | M1(40) | | |
| | Run | | | 01:00 | E2 | 00:30 | E2** | 01:00 | E2 |
| 19 | Strength | 01:00 | SM | | | | | | |
| | Swim | | | 01:15 | E(Form) | | | 01:15 | E2 |
| | Bike | | | | | 01:30 | E2 | | |
| | Run | | | 01:00 | M2(3Z) | | | 00:30 | S2 |
| 20 | Strength | 01:00 | SM | | | | | | |
| | Swim | | | | | | | 01:00 | T1b |
| | Bike | | | | | 01:00 | S5 | | |
| | Run | | | 00:45 | S1 | | | 00:30 | E2 |

| Fri Time | Fri Code | Sat Time | Sat Code | Sun Time | Sun Code | Weekly Training Hours | Weekly Training Hours By Sport | |
|---|---|---|---|---|---|---|---|---|
| | | 01:15 | E2 | | | | Strength | 02:30 |
| 01:00 | S1 | | | 02:00 | E2* | | Swim | 03:45 |
| | | | | | | | Bike | 03:00 |
| | | 01:30 | E4 | | | 12:15 | Run | 03:00 |
| Day off | | | | | | | Strength | 02:30 |
| | | 01:00 | E(Form) | | | | Swim | 02:00 |
| | | | | 01:00 | S5 | | Bike | 01:00 |
| | | 01:00 | A1b | | | 08:00 | Run | 02:30 |
| | | 01:15 | M | | | | Strength | 01:00 |
| 01:00 | E1 | | | 02:30 | E2 | | Swim | 03:45 |
| | | | | | | | Bike | 04:30 |
| | | 01:45 | E3 | | | 12:45 | Run | 03:30 |
| | | Brick | | | | | Strength | 01:00 |
| | | 01:30 | E3 | | | | Swim | 04:00 |
| 01:30 | S4 | 01:00 | E2 | 03:00 | E3 | | Bike | 06:30 |
| | | 01:00 | E2 | | | 14:45 | Run | 03:15 |
| | | | | | | | Strength | 01:00 |
| | | 01:30 | E3 | | | | Swim | 04:00 |
| 02:00 | E1 | | | 03:30 | E2 | | Bike | 07:00 |
| | | 02:00 | E3 | | | 16:00 | Run | 04:00 |
| Day off | | | | | | | Strength | 01:00 |
| | | 01:15 | E(Form) | | | | Swim | 02:15 |
| | | | | 02:00 | T1(6-10) | | Bike | 03:00 |
| | | 01:00 | E2 | | | 08:30 | Run | 02:15 |
| | | | | | | | Strength | 01:00 |
| | | 01:30 | E3 | | | | Swim | 03:30 |
| 01:00 | S5 | | | 04:00 | E3 | | Bike | 05:45 |
| | | 02:15 | E3 | | | 13:30 | Run | 03:15 |
| | | Brick | | | | | Strength | 01:00 |
| | | 01:00 | E1 | | | | Swim | 03:30 |
| 01:00 | S4 | 01:00 | text | 04:30 | E2 | | Bike | 08:00 |
| | | 01:00 | text | | | 16:00 | Run | 03:30 |
| | | | | | | | Strength | 01:00 |
| | | 01:30 | E3 | | | | Swim | 04:00 |
| 01:30 | S4 | 02:30 | E2 | 05:00 | E3 | | Bike | 10:30 |
| | | | | | | 17:00 | Run | 01:30 |
| Day off | | | | | | | Strength | 01:00 |
| | | 01:15 | E(Form) | | | | Swim | 02:15 |
| | | | | 02:00 | E2 | | Bike | 03:00 |
| | | 01:00 | T1(4–6) | | | 08:30 | Run | 02:15 |

TABLE 14.2. IRONMAN PERFORMANCE PLAN (CONTINUED)

| Week | Sport | Mon Time | Mon Code | Tues Time | Tues Code | Wed Time | Wed Code | Thurs Time | Thurs Code |
|---|---|---|---|---|---|---|---|---|---|
| 21 | Strength | 01:00 | SM | | | | | | |
| | Swim | | | 01:00 | E(Speed) | | | 01:00 | E2 |
| | Bike | | | | | 00:45 | E2 | | |
| | Run | | | 00:30 | E2 | | | 00:30 | E1 |
| 22 | Strength | 01:00 | SM | | | | | | |
| | Swim | | | 01:15 | E(Form) | | | 01:15 | E2 |
| | Bike | | | | | 01:30 | M1(40–50) | | |
| | Run | | | 01:00 | E2 | | | 00:30 | E1 |
| 23 | Strength | 01:00 | SM | | | | | | |
| | Swim | | | 01:15 | E(Speed) | | | 01:15 | E2 |
| | Bike | | | | | 01:15 | E2 | | |
| | Run | | | 01:00 | E2 | | | 00:30 | E1 |
| 24 | Strength | 01:00 | SM | | | | | | |
| | Swim | | | 01:15 | E(Form) | | | 01:15 | E2 |
| | Bike | | | | | 01:00 | E2 | | |
| | Run | | | 01:00 | S1 | | | 01:00 | E2 |
| 25 | Strength | 01:00 | SM | | | | | | |
| | Swim | | | 01:00 | E(Speed) | | | 00:45 | E2 |
| | Bike | | | | | 01:00 | S5 | | |
| | Run | | | 00:45 | E2 | | | 00:45 | E2 |
| 26 | Strength | | | | | | | | |
| | Swim | | | 00:45 | E(Speed) | | | | |
| | Bike | | | | | 01:00 | M1(15) | | |
| | Run | 01:00 | M1(20) | | | | | 00:30 | S2 |

## Swimming

For the first few weeks, include at least one 1000-yard main set. The swim can be continuous or broken. If broken, make the rest intervals no greater than 10 seconds. Slowly increase the distance of this main set over the course of several weeks to 2000 to 3000 yards. Some athletes may reach a main set of 2500 to 3500 yards. Look in *Workouts in a Box™ for Ironman Athletes* for specific, detailed swimming workouts designed for Ironman athletes. (Estimated release is early 2001.)

| Fri Time | Fri Code | Sat Time | Sat Code | Sun Time | Sun Code | Weekly Training Hours | Weekly Training Hours By Sport |
|---|---|---|---|---|---|---|---|
| | | 01:00 | E3 | | | | Strength 01:00 |
| 01:00 | S2 | | | 05:00 | E3 | | Swim 03:00 |
| | | 03:00 | E3 | | | | Bike 06:45 |
| | | | | | | 14:45 | Run 04:00 |
| | | Brick | | | | | Strength 01:00 |
| | | 01:30 | E3 | | | | Swim 04:00 |
| 00:30 | S1 | 01:00 | text | 05:30 | E2 | | Bike 08:30 |
| | | 01:30 | text | | | 16:30 | Run 03:00 |
| | | 01:30 | E3 | | | | Strength 01:00 |
| 01:30 | S5 | | | 06:00 | E3 | | Swim 04:00 |
| | | 03:00 | E3 | | | | Bike 08:45 |
| | | | | | | 18:15 | Run 04:30 |
| | | 01:30 | E3 | | | | Strength 01:00 |
| 01:00 | S4 | 03:00 | text | 01:00 | E1 | | Swim 04:00 |
| | | 01:30 | text | | | | Bike 06:00 |
| | | | | | | 14:30 | Run 03:30 |
| Day off | | Brick | | | | | Strength 01:00 |
| | | 01:15 | M | | | | Swim 03:00 |
| | | 02:00 | text | 01:00 | E1 | | Bike 04:00 |
| | | 01:00 | text | | | 10:30 | Run 02:30 |
| Day off | | Brick | | Race! | | | Strength 00:00 |
| 00:30 | E(Speed) | | | | | | Swim 01:15 |
| | | 00:45 | S4 | | | | Bike 01:45 |
| | | 00:15 | S2 | | | 04:45 | Run 01:45 |

## Base 1

The first week of the plan includes a baseline time trial in each sport. It goes without saying that if you have not been training consistently, do not begin the plan—especially these time trials—until some foundation conditioning has been achieved. That foundation is described in the Profile section.

This plan allows for cross training. A "*" beside the code of any workout, such as the run on Thursday of week 1, means cross-training is an option. Because heart rate ranges vary for different sports, use rating of perceived exertion

(RPE) to determine the correct training zones. Suggestions for cross-training include aerobics classes, circuit training, kickboxing, snowshoeing, cross-country skiing and hiking, to name a few.

Spin classes can also serve as excellent sources of winter training. A few words of caution: make the intensity of a spin class suit your personal goals. Some athletes have a difficult time controlling intensity and allow the instructor or others in the class to tempt them into a workout that becomes cough-up-a-lung hard. Have enough self-esteem to work out at your own pace.

### Base 2 (Weeks 5 to 8)

This first block of Base 2 training includes two maximum strength (MS) training days each week. This is particularly helpful for building strength for hilly bike courses. Some athletes find that two days of MS strength training is fatiguing for the legs and that they need to reduce the intensity of one of the weekend workouts. If this is the case for you, reduce the intensity of the sport that is already your strong suit.

### Base 3 (Weeks 9 to 12)

This block has several options. The first option is on the Tuesday runs. For experienced athletes, I recommend doing the treadmill workouts found in Appendix H. I have found no better training tool to improve form, running speed and pace perception than a treadmill. The Appendix H treadmill workouts are excellent for form. People who are uncomfortable getting on and off of a running treadmill are better off sticking to simple pick-ups.

The second option during this block is the plyometric workouts shown with the Wednesday strength training session and found in Appendix G. Chapter 21, which covers strength training, explains why plyometrics will enhance an endurance athlete's training program. If you are in the first season of plyometric work, do plyo only once per week and select the lowest number of sets and repetitions.

Both plyometrics and the treadmill sessions are not intended to be exceptionally difficult workouts. If you are exhausted or extremely sore after either workout, reduce the intensity of these sessions.

This is the last block that includes cross training.

## Base 2 (Weeks 13 to 16)

The second block of Base 2 training is when overall weekly volume begins to build and strength training is reduced to one day of strength maintenance. The intensity of workouts remains in Zones 1 to 3, where most of an Ironman race will occur. Hilly races may solicit some time in Zone 4 and above, but keep this time very minimal.

Week 14 of the plan has a Zone 3 run on Thursday that should be 3 to 4 x 6' (2' RI). Also beginning in week 14, any workout with a "**" is optional.

Saturday of Week 14 has the first brick of the schedule, which can be done immediately after the swim or later in the day. Both bike and run segments are in Zones 1 and 2.

There are four M1-type workouts scheduled on the bike in the remaining weeks. These workouts can be done as steady-state rides or broken into intervals with work-to-rest ratios of 3:1 or 4:1.

Once athletes begin to increase training volume, many find that more than two aerobic time trials within the rest week are too much. So, with that in mind, there are only two time trials in week 16. Notice that the distance on the bike time trial is increased.

### Base 3 (Weeks 17 to 20)

Weekly volume continues to build during this block. Now is a perfect opportunity to establish the eating and drinking format you will use on race day. Take the time to figure out a nutritional plan—in detail—and write it down. What will you eat and drink each 15 to 20 minutes of the entire race? Do not take this lightly, as many Ironman races are spoiled by under- or overeating and/or drinking. Make a plan, practice it, modify and continue to refine it until you find what works for you.

The workouts needing additional explanation during this block include the brick in week 18, a run in week 19 and the run time trial in week 20. For the week 18 Saturday brick, both sports are controlled at Zones 1 to 2 for the first half of the assigned time. The second half of the time can go Zones 1 to 3. It is not a goal to maximize time in Zone 3. For the week 18 Tuesday run, do 3 to 5 x 6' (2' RI) in Zone 3. For week 20 Saturday run time trial, notice the change in distance: anywhere between four and six miles is fine.

## Base 4

The most important workouts are scheduled on the weekend during this block. Other workouts during the week should be reduced, if necessary, to allow for full recovery for the weekend sessions. For week 22's Saturday brick, both sports are controlled at Zones 1 to 2 for the first half of the assigned time. The second half of the time can go Zones 1 to 3. It is not a goal to maximize time in Zone 3.

## Peak-Taper

All of the hard work is done; it is time to enjoy. Weeks 24, 25 and 26 have reduced volume and some intensity to keep legs and arms feeling rested and fresh for race day. The bricks shown in weeks 24 and 25 are done exactly like the brick in week 22. Bike and run out in Zones 1 and 2 for the first half of the assigned time. Bring it back home in Zones 1 to 3. Two to three weeks prior to the race is a good time for a total bike tune-up. When race day finally arrives, take a deep breath at the start line. You are ready. Relax any tight muscles, especially neck and shoulders, and plan to enjoy your health.

*I am finally getting the joke on pace. Controlling the pace within each sport, so I don't start too fast, is critical for Ironman training and racing—this goes for eating and drinking as well.*

> *—Paul O'Brien*

# CHAPTER FIFTEEN

# Mountain Bike
# *Triathlon*

*My favorite quote comes from the quotemeister, Dave French. It must be said with bloodshot, bleary eyes and dried, sleeve-smeared snot across your face. Dave frequently said, "I look bad, but I feel good."*
*—Rob Forister (a.k.a. Rocket Rob), triathlete and ultradistance runner, Sheridan, Wyoming*

Mountain bike multisport events are quickly rising in popularity. A couple of common events include those taking around an hour to two hours to complete and the mid-distance events commonly taking between two and four hours. There are also multiday stage races, such as Tinley's Dirty Adventures. This particular venue has the short-stage option and a long-stage option. There is nothing like a little dirt to make you feel young.

This chapter includes a 12-week plan to prepare for a single-day mountain event. Many multisport athletes heading into an off-road event don't have great mountain bike skills. If your mountain bike skills are marginal, try to begin with a course that is not technical. If nontechnical is not an option, there are other choices. For example, I coached an athlete who could ride a flat 40km bike leg in a triathlon in just over an hour. He decided to do a mountain bike event. After the first course preride he called to report the bad news: "This course is only 14 miles and it is just awful. It is rocky, technical, there are water crossings and it took me two-and-a-half hours to preride it. I will be out there forever!"

After talking awhile, I discovered a couple of things. First, he considered getting off the bike a major failure. His goal on the preride was to stay on his bike over the entire course. Second, when he did get off the bike to clear a difficult obstacle, he might remount the bike only to ride five yards and have to dismount again.

I suggested he consider viewing the bike portion of the event like a puzzle. There is nothing wrong with getting off the bike and running with it—in fact, depending on the particular obstacle, that might be the best strategy. Also, look ahead and decide if it is best to run 15 yards or more. The real question is "What is the fastest way to get through the course in one piece?"

After this discussion, he had a chance to preride the course two more times prior to race day. Each time he rode the course, he reduced the amount of time and energy it took him to complete the course. On race day, he completed the course in less than two hours and won his age group.

## PROFILE

This plan is for an athlete who can train about an hour each weekday and a couple of hours on one day of the weekend. The second weekend day will allow about an hour of training. Total training hours available each week is about seven. You are already training some in all three sports and prefer not to have a day without some type of activity. You are capable of swimming at least 20 to 30 minutes. A bike ride of two hours is not a challenge; however, you may not have expert mountain bike handling skills. An hour run is no problem.

By looking at the training zone charts in Chapter 1, you have determined that most of your training has been in Zones 1 and 2. You might have had a bit more intensity than that, but not much. Also, you would like to add some strength training to your routine, but are not sure where to start— especially with only 12 weeks until race day.

## GOAL

Complete an off-road triathlon after twelve weeks of preparation. Estimated race completion time is in the neighborhood of two hours. The swim will take between 15 and 30 minutes, depending on swim ability and the particular race distance. The bike portion of the race is anticipated to take around an hour and the run will likely take 30 to 45 minutes.

## THE PLAN

Table 15.1 shows a simplified overview of the 12-week plan. The first column lists the week number, the second the

| TABLE 15.1. PLAN OVERVIEW | | | |
|---|---|---|---|
| Week # | Month | Period | Weekly Planned Hours |
| 1 | May | Base 2 | 07:15 |
| 2 | May | Base 2 | 07:15 |
| 3 | May | Base 2 | 07:15 |
| 4 | May | Base 2 | 04:15 |
| 5 | May/June | Base 3 | 07:15 |
| 6 | June | Base 3 | 07:15 |
| 7 | June | Base 3 | 07:15 |
| 8 | June | Base 3 | 04:15 |
| 9 | June/July | Build 1 | 07:15 |
| 10 | July | Build 1 | 06:45 |
| 11 | July | Peak | 05:45 |
| 12 | July | Race | 2:55+race |

month each weeks falls in (if you start on the first Monday in January). The exact months are not important, they are simply used as examples—and could start in April for a race in June, for instance. The third column is the particular training period for each week. Weekly training hours are in the last column and vary between 5:45 and 7:15.

The detailed plan is in Table 15.2. Monday and Wednesday are typically swim days. Bike rides are on Wednesday, Friday and Sunday. Run days are Tuesday, Thursday and Saturday. On the days that a run and strength training are both scheduled, run first, then strength train. It is most time-efficient if the two activities can be done one after the other, but they can be split.

## Base 2

On the first Monday of the plan, the first swim is a time trial to establish baseline fitness. In general, all Mondays not in a rest week will include fast swimming. Most of the Wednesday swims will be easy, form workouts. There are only two exceptions, in weeks 5 and 9, where time trials are scheduled on a Wednesday.

Saturday runs in Base 2 should be on a trail if possible; this is indicated with the "Trail" note on the plan. If you have not been trail running, take it easy on the first few trail runs to allow tendons and ligaments to gain strength. It also takes time for body-awareness adjustments—judging obstacles that can be jumped over or stepped on and working on overall balance.

Sunday bike rides are also to be done off-road when indicated by "MTB" on the plan. The Friday M2 rides are best completed on the road and should include 4 to 6 x 4' (1' RI), in Zone 3. Because of the intensity of the Friday M2 ride, the Sunday ride that week will be easy and preferably on the road.

The fourth week is a rest week, when volume is reduced. The running time trial scheduled for that week should be done at the track. The cycling time trial is 5 miles long and is also best done on the road, unless you would like to track technical skill improvement as well as fitness improvement. In that case, find an off-road loop approximately 3 miles long to conduct the time trial. Record all time trial results in a journal.

### Base 3

A strength maintenance (SM) phase begins in Base 3. Although this plan does not follow the customary strength training progression of anatomical adaptation, maximum strength, power endurance, muscular endurance and strength maintenance gains can be made with some modifications.

Go ahead and follow the instructions for SM in Chapter 21, just be conservative when increasing weight on the last set. Legs need to be fresh for running and cycling. However, some athletes are able to slowly increase the weight of that last set over the course of several weeks, making strength gains.

The first week of Base 3, week 5, includes a swim time trial. Repeat the same distance covered in the first time trial.

## TABLE 15.2. MOUNTAIN BIKE TRIATHLON PLAN

| Week | Sport | Mon Time | Mon Code | Tues Time | Tues Code | Wed Time | Wed Code | Thurs Time | Thurs Code |
|------|-------|----------|----------|-----------|-----------|----------|----------|------------|------------|
| 1 | Strength | | | 00:45 | AA | | | | |
| | Swim | 00:30 | T1a | | | 00:30 | E(Speed) | | |
| | Bike | | | | | 00:30 | S3(4–5) | | |
| | Run | | | 00:30 | E2 | | | 00:30 | S2 |
| 2 | Strength | | | 00:45 | AA | | | | |
| | Swim | 00:30 | E3 | | | 00:30 | E(Form) | | |
| | Bike | | | | | 00:30 | S2 | | |
| | Run | | | 00:30 | E2 | | | 00:30 | S2 |
| 3 | Strength | | | 00:45 | AA | | | | |
| | Swim | 00:30 | E3 | | | 00:30 | E(Speed) | | |
| | Bike | | | | | 00:30 | S3(4–5) | | |
| | Run | | | 00:30 | E2 | | | 00:30 | S2 |
| 4 | Strength | | | 00:45 | AA | | | | |
| | Swim | 00:30 | E2 | | | | | | |
| | Bike | | | | | 00:30 | S2 | | |
| | Run | | | 00:30 | E2 | | | 00:30 | S2 |
| 5 | Strength | | | 00:30 | SM | | | | |
| | Swim | 00:30 | E(Form) | | | 00:30 | T1a | | |
| | Bike | | | | | 00:30 | S3(4–5) | | |
| | Run | | | 00:30 | E2 | | | 00:45 | S2 |
| 6 | Strength | | | 00:30 | SM | | | | |
| | Swim | 00:30 | M | | | 00:30 | E(Speed) | | |
| | Bike | | | | | 00:30 | S2 | | |
| | Run | | | 00:30 | E2 | | | 00:45 | M2(4–5a) |
| 7 | Strength | | | 00:30 | SM | | | | |
| | Swim | 00:30 | M | | | 00:30 | E(Form) | | |
| | Bike | | | | | 00:30 | S3(4–5) | | |
| | Run | | | 00:30 | E2 | | | 00:45 | S2 |
| 8 | Strength | | | 00:30 | SM | | | | |
| | Swim | 00:30 | E2 | | | | | | |
| | Bike | | | | | 00:30 | S2 | | |
| | Run | | | 00:30 | E2 | | | 00:30 | S2 |
| 9 | Strength | | | 00:30 | SM | | | | |
| | Swim | 00:30 | E2(Speed) | | | 00:30 | T1a | | |
| | Bike | | | | | 00:30 | S3(4–5) | | |
| | Run | | | 00:30 | E2 | | | 00:45 | S1 |
| 10 | Strength | | | 00:30 | SM | | | | |
| | Swim | 00:30 | A | | | 00:30 | E(Form) | | |
| | Bike | | | | | 00:30 | S2 | | |
| | Run | | | 00:30 | E2 | | | 00:45 | S1 |
| 11 | Strength | | | 00:30 | SM | | | | |
| | Swim | 00:30 | A | | | 00:30 | E(Form) | | |
| | Bike | | | | | 00:30 | E2 | | |
| | Run | | | 00:30 | E2 | | | 00:45 | S1 |
| 12 | Strength | | | | | | | | |
| | Swim | 00:30 | E(Speed) | | | | | | |
| | Bike | | | 00:45 | A7 | | | 00:30 | S5 |
| | Run | | | | | 00:30 | A7 | | |

| Fri Time | Fri Code | Sat Time | Sat Code | Sun Time | Sun Code | Weekly Training Hours | Weekly Training Hours By Sport | |
|---|---|---|---|---|---|---|---|---|
| 01:00 | E2 | | | 02:00 | MTB(E3) | | Strength | 00:45 |
| | | | | | | | Swim | 01:00 |
| | | | | | | | Bike | 03:30 |
| | | 01:00 | Trail-E3 | | | 07:15 | Run | 02:00 |
| 01:00 | M2(3z) | | | 02:00 | R(E2) | | Strength | 00:45 |
| | | | | | | | Swim | 01:00 |
| | | | | | | | Bike | 03:30 |
| | | 01:00 | Trail-E3 | | | 07:15 | Run | 02:00 |
| 01:00 | S5 | | | 02:00 | MTB(E3) | | Strength | 00:45 |
| | | | | | | | Swim | 01:00 |
| | | | | | | | Bike | 03:30 |
| | | 01:00 | Trail-E3 | | | 07:15 | Run | 02:00 |
| Day off | | | | | | | Strength | 00:45 |
| | | | | | | | Swim | 00:30 |
| | | | | 01:00 | T2(5) | | Bike | 01:30 |
| | | 00:30 | T1 | | | 04:15 | Run | 01:30 |
| 01:00 | M2(4–5a) | | | 02:00 | R(E2) | | Strength | 00:30 |
| | | | | | | | Swim | 01:00 |
| | | | | | | | Bike | 03:30 |
| | | 01:00 | Trail-E4 | | | 07:15 | Run | 02:15 |
| 01:00 | E2 | | | 02:00 | MTB(E4) | | Strength | 00:30 |
| | | | | | | | Swim | 01:00 |
| | | | | | | | Bike | 03:30 |
| | | 01:00 | E2 | | | 07:15 | Run | 02:15 |
| 01:00 | S5 | | | 02:00 | MTB(E4) | | Strength | 00:30 |
| | | | | | | | Swim | 01:00 |
| | | | | | | | Bike | 03:30 |
| | | 01:00 | Trail-E4 | | | 07:15 | Run | 02:15 |
| Day off | | | | | | | Strength | 00:30 |
| | | | | | | | Swim | 00:30 |
| | | | | 01:00 | T2(5) | | Bike | 01:30 |
| | | 00:30 | T1 | | | 04:00 | Run | 01:30 |
| 01:00 | E2 | | | 02:00 | MTB(E4) | | Strength | 00:30 |
| | | | | | | | Swim | 01:00 |
| | | | | | | | Bike | 03:30 |
| | | 01:00 | Trail-E4 | | | 07:15 | Run | 02:15 |
| | | | | Brick | | | Strength | 00:30 |
| | | | | | | | Swim | 01:00 |
| 01:00 | E1 | | | 01:30 | text | | Bike | 03:00 |
| | | 00:30 | E2 | 00:30 | text | 06:45 | Run | 02:15 |
| | | Day off | | Brick | | | Strength | 00:30 |
| | | | | | | | Swim | 01:00 |
| 01:00 | S3(6–8) | | | 01:00 | text | | Bike | 02:30 |
| | | | | 00:30 | text | 05:45 | Run | 01:45 |
| Day off | | Brick | | Race! | | | Strength | 00:00 |
| | | | | | | | Swim | 00:30 |
| | | 00:30 | E2 | | | | Bike | 01:45 |
| | | 00:10 | E2 | | | 02:55 | Run | 00:40 |

The Monday swims in weeks 6 and 7 are faster, muscular endurance swims.

Friday of week 5 is a road bike session, similar to the session in week 2. This session reaches for higher speeds: 4 to 6 x 4' (1' RI), into Zones 4 and 5a.

The second ride in week 5 should be an easy ride on the road. The Sunday rides in weeks 6 and 7 are off-road. Off-road running is scheduled on Saturday in weeks 5 and 7, allowing higher speed than in Base 2. One interval session is scheduled for running, in week 6. For the M2(4 to 5a) run, do 4 to 6 x 4' (1' RI). This is best done on a flat or slightly uphill course.

To complete Base 3, rest week 8 duplicates rest week 4 with running and cycling time trials.

## BUILD, PEAK AND RACE

The final four weeks heading into race day include workouts with higher speeds and decreasing volume. The pattern is similar to previous training blocks. Needing special instruction are: the Thursday runs in week 9, do 4 to 6 x 20" (1' 40") on a flat course; in week 10, do 4 to 6 x 20" (1' 40"), slightly downhill; in week 11, do 4 to 6 x 30" (1' 30"), slightly downhill.

### Bricks

The brick in week 10 is on the road, with the last 30 minutes of the bike and the last 15 minutes of the run in Zones 4 to 5a. The brick in week 11 can be done off-road with the last half of each sport at race pace.

## Race Week

Finally, in week 12, do the A7 bike with 4 x 90"(3'), and the A7 run with 3 x 90"(3'). The short brick on Saturday is mostly an equipment check. It is just enough exercise to loosen the legs without taking too much energy. On race day, have fun and get dirty.

## QUESTIONS AND ANSWERS

**Q.** What if my event will take longer, say around 3 hours. How do I modify this schedule?

**A.** Depending on the anticipated length of your swim, swim time may not need to be increased at all. Increase swim time if: a) you simply enjoy swimming; b) you think the swim will take longer than 30 minutes; or c) you are a competitive swimmer. If the swim is increased, increase the Monday workouts to about 45 minutes.

The Sunday long ride can be built to about 3 hours. If you are pressed for time, 2.5 hours will do the job. All other rides will be fine as shown on the schedule. If the run will take around an hour, the schedule shown will work. Increasing the run time beyond what is shown on the schedule may help build base, but I would not recommend going over 1.5 hours.

**Q.** If my event will only take an hour, how do I modify the schedule?

**A.** The swim days can be as short as 20 minutes. Friday bike rides can be reduced to as little as 30 minutes and Sunday rides can be reduced to around 1:15 or 1:30. Weekday runs can remain at 30 minutes, not building to 45 minutes. Saturday runs can remain at one hour or be reduced to 30 to 45 minutes. All interval segments will need to be reduced proportional to the running or cycling time reduction.

# CHAPTER SIXTEEN

# Multisport
# *Fitness Plan*

*Walking the wire in the circus we call triathlon.*
*—Michael Smedley, Buchanan, Michigan, age 26,*
*1999 runner-up ITU North American Championships,*
*USA Triathlon National Resident Team Member*

"How about a plan for an all-around athlete? Something that plans for participation in other sports like racquetball, handball, tennis, softball or soccer? At the same time, it would be nice to do a 5km or 10km or maybe a sprint triathlon. Heck, I don't plan on winning the race; I just want to have enough fitness to enjoy myself. I'd like to lift weights too. How do I blend everything together with limited training time and without doing the same boring routine for weeks on end? Oh yeah, one more thing, it would be fun to feel fast and strong for some of the workouts, races or sporting events."

If the paragraph above sounds like something you might ask, this chapter is specially designed to suit your needs. It has allowances for other sport and gives guidelines for change. It is designed for a lifestyle of fitness. That means being fit enough to participate in a shorter running race, a sprint distance triathlon or a team sport. There is even room for a weeklong summer vacation!

## PROFILE

This plan is designed for a person with a fitness lifestyle. You like to do a bit of something most every day, but no more than an hour on weekdays. Saturday or Sunday workouts can be up to two hours, but not more. You are active in other sports two days per week. That means sports other than swimming, cycling, running or weight training. The sport may change with the seasons, but the gang counts on your participation.

## GOALS

Your major goal is to stay fit and healthy. Subgoals include a couple of running races and one or two sprint triathlons. Perhaps you downplay competitiveness; however, secretly or not, you think kicking butt now and again is really fun.

## PLAN DESCRIPTION

Table 16.1 on page 187 lists 24 training weeks, a column for the month, and columns designating the training period and the weekly training hours. The final column is a list of possible activities. If there is no race or you decide not to race, other workout options are given for that day. The months are there for example only and the first week can begin on Monday of any month. At the beginning of each week of the plan, you need to decide which workouts will be fast, intense or long. These workouts are considered break-throughs or BTs. One of the dangers of being a fitness buff with a hint of competitive edge is the desire for all workouts to be fast or long or hard. You need to decide each week where to put maximum energy or effort. Notice the "Code" column next to Tuesday and Thursday on Table 16.2 is left blank. This is so you can pencil in "BT," "easy" or "form." As the plan progresses, if you decide to keep both sport days as BT workouts, another workout in swimming, cycling or running may have to change. The change can be shorter distance or lower speeds; the choice depends on your over-all goals.

### Base 1

Base 1 training is getting a routine estab-lished both in the weight room and in other sport activities. Table 16.2 shows sport participation on Tuesday and Thursday through-out the entire plan. If

| TABLE 16.1. PLAN OVERVIEW | | | | |
|---|---|---|---|---|
| Week # | Month | Period | Weekly Planned Hours | Activities |
| 1 | March | Base 1 | 06:00 | |
| 2 | March/April | Base 1 | 06:00 | |
| 3 | April | Base 1 | 06:00 | |
| 4 | April | Base 1 | 05:00 | |
| 5 | April | Base 2 | 06:20 | |
| 6 | April/May | Base 2 | 06:40 | |
| 7 | May | Base 2 | 06:45 | |
| 8 | May | Base 2 | 05:00 | |
| 9 | May | Base 3 | 06:45 | |
| 10 | May | Base 3 | 07:10 | |
| 11 | May/June | Base 3 | 07:30 | |
| 12 | June | Base 3 | 05:00 | |
| 13 | June | Build 1 | 07:30 | 10K |
| 14 | June | Build 1 | 07:30 | |
| 15 | June/July | Build 1 | 07:30 | |
| 16 | July | Build 1 | tbd | Vacation |
| 17 | July | Build 2 | 07:30 | |
| 18 | July | Build 2 | 08:00 | |
| 19 | July | Build 2 | 07:00 | Triathlon |
| 20 | July/August | Build 2 | 04:45 | 5K |
| 21 | August | Build 3 | 07:30 | |
| 22 | August | Build 3 | 07:30 | |
| 23 | August | Build 3 | 07:30 | |
| 24 | August/ September | Build 3 | 3:00+Race | Triathlon |

187

## TABLE 16.2. MULTISPORT PERFORMANCE PLAN

| Week | Sport | Mon Time | Mon Code | Tues Time | Tues Code | Wed Time | Wed Code | Thurs Time | Thurs Code |
|---|---|---|---|---|---|---|---|---|---|
| 1 | Strength | 01:00 | AA | | | 01:00 | AA | | |
| | Sport | | | 01:00 | | | | 01:00 | |
| | Swim | | | | | | | | |
| | Bike | | | | | | | | |
| | Run | | | | | | | | |
| 2 | Strength | 01:00 | AA | | | 01:00 | AA | | |
| | Sport | | | 01:00 | | | | 01:00 | |
| | Swim | | | | | | | | |
| | Bike | | | | | | | | |
| | Run | | | | | | | | |
| 3 | Strength | 01:00 | AA | | | 01:00 | AA | | |
| | Sport | | | 01:00 | | | | 01:00 | |
| | Swim | | | | | | | | |
| | Bike | | | | | | | | |
| | Run | | | | | | | | |
| 4 | Strength | 01:00 | AA | | | Day off | | | |
| | Sport | | | 01:00 | | | | 01:00 | |
| | Swim | | | | | | | | |
| | Bike | | | | | | | | |
| | Run | | | | | | | | |
| 5 | Strength | 01:00 | MS | | | 01:00 | MS | | |
| | Sport | | | 01:00 | | | | 01:00 | |
| | Swim | | | | | | | | |
| | Bike | | | | | | | | |
| | Run | | | | | | | | |
| 6 | Strength | 01:00 | MS | | | 01:00 | MS | | |
| | Sport | | | 01:00 | | | | 01:00 | |
| | Swim | | | | | | | | |
| | Bike | | | | | | | | |
| | Run | | | | | | | | |
| 7 | Strength | 01:00 | MS | | | 01:00 | MS | | |
| | Sport | | | 01:00 | | | | 01:00 | |
| | Swim | | | | | | | | |
| | Bike | | | | | | | | |
| | Run | | | | | | | | |
| 8 | Strength | 01:00 | MS | | | Day off | | | |
| | Sport | | | 01:00 | | | | 01:00 | |
| | Swim | | | | | | | | |
| | Bike | | | | | | | | |
| | Run | | | | | | | | |
| 9 | Strength | 01:00 | PE | | | | | | |
| | Sport | | | 01:00 | | | | 01:00 | |
| | Swim | | | | | 00:30 | E(Form) | | |
| | Bike | | | | | 00:30 | E1 | | |
| | Run | | | | | | | | |

| Fri Time | Fri Code | Sat Time | Sat Code | Sun Time | Sun Code | Weekly Training Hours | Weekly Training Hours By Sport | |
|---|---|---|---|---|---|---|---|---|
| | | | | | | | Strength | 02:00 |
| | | | | | | | Sport | 02:00 |
| 00:30 | T1a | | | | | | Swim | 00:30 |
| | | | | 01:00 | E2 | | Bike | 01:00 |
| | | 00:30 | E1 | | | 06:00 | Run | 00:30 |
| | | | | | | | Strength | 02:00 |
| | | | | | | | Sport | 02:00 |
| 00:30 | E2 | | | | | | Swim | 00:30 |
| | | | | 01:00 | E2 | | Bike | 01:00 |
| | | 00:30 | E1 | | | 06:00 | Run | 00:30 |
| | | | | | | | Strength | 02:00 |
| | | | | | | | Sport | 02:00 |
| 00:30 | E2 | | | | | | Swim | 00:30 |
| | | | | 01:00 | E2 | | Bike | 01:00 |
| | | 00:30 | E2 | | | 06:00 | Run | 00:30 |
| Day off | | | | | | | Strength | 01:00 |
| | | | | | | | Sport | 02:00 |
| | | 00:30 | E3 | | | | Swim | 00:30 |
| | | | | 01:00 | E2 | | Bike | 01:00 |
| | | 00:30 | E2 | | | 05:00 | Run | 00:30 |
| | | | | | | | Strength | 02:00 |
| | | | | | | | Sport | 02:00 |
| 00:30 | E2 | | | | | | Swim | 00:30 |
| | | | | 01:15 | E3 | | Bike | 01:15 |
| | | 00:35 | E2 | | | 06:20 | Run | 00:35 |
| | | | | | | | Strength | 02:00 |
| | | | | | | | Sport | 02:00 |
| 00:30 | E2 | | | | | | Swim | 00:30 |
| | | | | 01:30 | E3 | | Bike | 01:30 |
| | | 00:40 | S2 | | | 06:40 | Run | 00:40 |
| | | | | | | | Strength | 02:00 |
| | | | | | | | Sport | 02:00 |
| 00:30 | E2 | | | | | | Swim | 00:30 |
| | | | | 01:30 | E3 | | Bike | 01:30 |
| | | 00:45 | E2 | | | 06:45 | Run | 00:45 |
| Day off | | | | | | | Strength | 01:00 |
| | | | | | | | Sport | 02:00 |
| | | 00:30 | E2 | | | | Swim | 00:30 |
| | | | | 01:00 | S3 | | Bike | 01:00 |
| | | 00:30 | M1(15) | | | 05:00 | Run | 00:30 |
| | | | | | | | Strength | 01:00 |
| | | | | | | | Sport | 02:00 |
| 00:30 | T1a | | | | | | Swim | 01:00 |
| | | | | 01:30 | E2 | | Bike | 02:00 |
| | | 00:45 | E3 | | | 06:45 | Run | 00:45 |

TABLE 16.2. MULTISPORT PERFORMANCE PLAN (CONTINUED)

| Week | Sport | Mon Time | Mon Code | Tues Time | Tues Code | Wed Time | Wed Code | Thurs Time | Thurs Code |
|---|---|---|---|---|---|---|---|---|---|
| 10 | Strength | 01:00 | PE | | | | | | |
| | Sport | | | 01:00 | | | | 01:00 | |
| | Swim | | | | | 00:30 | E(Speed) | | |
| | Bike | | | | | 00:45 | E2 | | |
| | Run | | | | | | | | |
| 11 | Strength | 01:00 | PE | | | | | | |
| | Sport | | | 01:00 | | | | 01:00 | |
| | Swim | | | | | 00:30 | E(Form) | | |
| | Bike | | | | | 01:00 | E2 | | |
| | Run | | | | | | | | |
| 12 | Strength | 01:00 | PE | | | Day off | | | |
| | Sport | | | 01:00 | | | | 01:00 | |
| | Swim | | | | | | | | |
| | Bike | | | | | | | | |
| | Run | | | | | | | | |
| 13 | Strength | 01:00 | SM | | | | | | |
| | Sport | | | 01:00 | | | | 01:00 | |
| | Swim | | | | | 00:30 | E(Form) | | |
| | Bike | | | | | 01:00 | S5 | | |
| | Run | | | | | | | | |
| 14 | Strength | 01:00 | SM | | | | | | |
| | Sport | | | 01:00 | | | | 01:00 | |
| | Swim | | | | | 00:30 | E(Form) | | |
| | Bike | | | | | 01:00 | S4 | | |
| | Run | | | | | | | | |
| 15 | Strength | 01:00 | SM | | | | | | |
| | Sport | | | 01:00 | | | | 01:00 | |
| | Swim | | | | | 00:30 | E(Form) | | |
| | Bike | | | | | 01:00 | S5 | | |
| | Run | | | | | | | | |
| 16 | Strength | | | | | | | | |
| | Sport | | | | | | | | |
| | Swim | | | VACATION | | | VACATION | | |
| | Bike | | | | | | | | |
| | Run | | | | | | | | |
| 17 | Strength | 01:00 | SM | | | | | | |
| | Sport | | | 01:00 | | | | 01:00 | |
| | Swim | | | | | 00:30 | E(Form) | | |
| | Bike | | | | | 01:00 | S4 | | |
| | Run | | | | | | | | |
| 18 | Strength | 01:00 | SM | | | | | | |
| | Sport | | | 01:00 | | | | 01:00 | |
| | Swim | | | | | 00:30 | E(Form) | | |
| | Bike | | | | | 01:00 | S5 | | |
| | Run | | | | | | | | |

| Fri Time | Fri Code | Sat Time | Sat Code | Sun Time | Sun Code | Weekly Training Hours | Weekly Training Hours By Sport | |
|---|---|---|---|---|---|---|---|---|
| | | | | | | | Strength | 01:00 |
| | | | | | | | Sport | 02:00 |
| | | 00:30 | M | | | | Swim | 01:00 |
| | | 01:30 | E3 | | | | Bike | 02:15 |
| | | 00:55 | E2 | | | 07:10 | Run | 00:55 |
| | | | | | | | Strength | 01:00 |
| | | | | | | | Sport | 02:00 |
| 00:30 | E2 | | | | | | Swim | 01:00 |
| | | 01:30 | E2 | | | | Bike | 02:30 |
| | | 01:00 | E3 | | | 07:30 | Run | 01:00 |
| Day off | | | | | | | Strength | 01:00 |
| | | | | | | | Sport | 02:00 |
| | | 00:30 | M | | | | Swim | 00:30 |
| | | 01:00 | S3 | | | | Bike | 01:00 |
| | | 00:30 | E2 | | | 05:00 | Run | 00:30 |
| | | | | | | | Strength | 01:00 |
| | | | | | | | Sport | 02:00 |
| 00:30 | E1 | | | | | | Swim | 01:00 |
| | | 01:30 | E1 | | | | Bike | 02:30 |
| | | 01:00 | A1c | | | 07:30 | Run | 01:00 |
| | | Brick | | | | | Strength | 01:00 |
| | | | | | | | Sport | 02:00 |
| 00:30 | E2 | | | | | | Swim | 01:00 |
| | | 01:00 | E2 | 01:00 | E1 | | Bike | 03:00 |
| | | 00:30 | text | | | 07:30 | Run | 00:30 |
| | | | | | | | Strength | 01:00 |
| | | | | | | | Sport | 02:00 |
| 00:30 | E2 | | | | | | Swim | 01:00 |
| | | 01:30 | E4 | | | | Bike | 02:30 |
| | | 01:00 | E2 | | | 07:30 | Run | 01:00 |
| | | | | | | | Strength | 00:00 |
| | | | | | | | Sport | 00:00 |
| | VACATION | | | | VACATION | | Swim | 00:00 |
| | | | | | | | Bike | 00:00 |
| | | | | | | 00:00 | Run | 00:00 |
| | | | | | | | Strength | 01:00 |
| | | | | | | | Sport | 02:00 |
| 00:30 | T1a | | | | | | Swim | 01:00 |
| | | 01:30 | E2 | | | | Bike | 02:30 |
| | | 01:00 | M5(20) | | | 07:30 | Run | 01:00 |
| | | | | | | | Strength | 01:00 |
| | | | | | | | Sport | 02:00 |
| 00:30 | E2 | | | | | | Swim | 01:00 |
| | | 02:00 | E4 | | | | Bike | 03:00 |
| | | 01:00 | E2 | | | 08:00 | Run | 01:00 |

TABLE 16.2. MULTISPORT PERFORMANCE PLAN (CONTINUED)

| Week | Sport | Mon Time | Mon Code | Tues Time | Tues Code | Wed Time | Wed Code | Thurs Time | Thurs Code |
|---|---|---|---|---|---|---|---|---|---|
| 19 | Strength | 01:00 | SM | | | | | | |
| | Sport | | | 01:00 | | | | 01:00 | |
| | Swim | | | | | 00:30 | E(Form) | | |
| | Bike | | | | | 01:00 | S4 | | |
| | Run | | | | | | | | |
| 20 | Strength | | | | | Day off | | | |
| | Sport | | | 01:00 | | | | 01:00 | |
| | Swim | | | | | | | | |
| | Bike | | | | | | | | |
| | Run | | | | | | | | |
| 21 | Strength | 01:00 | SM | | | | | | |
| | Sport | | | 01:00 | | | | 01:00 | |
| | Swim | | | | | 00:30 | E(Form) | | |
| | Bike | | | | | 01:00 | S5 | | |
| | Run | | | | | | | | |
| 22 | Strength | 01:00 | SM | | | | | | |
| | Sport | | | 01:00 | | | | 01:00 | |
| | Swim | | | | | 00:30 | E(Form) | | |
| | Bike | | | | | 01:00 | S4 | | |
| | Run | | | | | | | | |
| 23 | Strength | 01:00 | SM | | | | | | |
| | Sport | | | 01:00 | | | | 01:00 | |
| | Swim | | | | | 00:30 | E(Form) | | |
| | Bike | | | | | 01:00 | S5 | | |
| | Run | | | | | | | | |
| 24 | Strength | 01:00 | SM | | | Day off | | | |
| | Sport | | | 01:00 | | | | 01:00 | |
| | Swim | | | | | | | | |
| | Bike | | | | | | | | |
| | Run | | | | | | | | |

your sport days happen to be Wednesday and Friday, move the workouts around so strength training days are separated by 48 hours. You may also want to move days so run workouts are separated by 48 hours as well.

As an example, an athlete using this plan might play basketball, racquetball, handball or squash on Tuesdays and Thursdays. One assumption the plan makes is that you are running around, using your legs on the sport days. Be sure to

| Fri Time | Fri Code | Sat Time | Sat Code | Sun Time | Sun Code | Weekly Training Hours | Weekly Training Hours By Sport | |
|---|---|---|---|---|---|---|---|---|
| | | Day off | | Brick or Race | | | Strength | 01:00 |
| | | | | | | | Sport | 02:00 |
| 00:30 | E1 | | | | | | Swim | 01:00 |
| | | | | 01:00 | text | | Bike | 02:00 |
| | | | | 01:00 | text | 07:00 | Run | 01:00 |
| | | | | | | | Strength | 00:00 |
| | | | | | | | Sport | 02:00 |
| 00:30 | E2 | | | | | | Swim | 00:30 |
| | | | | 01:30 | E1 | | Bike | 01:30 |
| | | 00:45 | A1c | | | 04:45 | Run | 00:45 |
| | | | | | | | Strength | 01:00 |
| | | | | | | | Sport | 02:00 |
| 00:30 | A | | | | | | Swim | 01:00 |
| | | | | 01:30 | E2 | | Bike | 02:30 |
| | | 01:00 | M5(25) | | | 07:30 | Run | 01:00 |
| | | | | | | | Strength | 01:00 |
| | | | | | | | Sport | 02:00 |
| 00:30 | E2 | | | | | | Swim | 01:00 |
| | | | | 01:30 | T2(5-8) | | Bike | 02:30 |
| | | 01:00 | E2 | | | 07:30 | Run | 01:00 |
| | | | | | | | Strength | 01:00 |
| | | | | | | | Sport | 02:00 |
| 00:30 | S3 | | | | | | Swim | 01:00 |
| | | | | 01:30 | E2 | | Bike | 02:30 |
| | | 01:00 | M2(4-5a) | | | 07:30 | Run | 01:00 |
| | | Day off | | Race or Brick | | | Strength | 01:00 |
| | | | | | | | Sport | 02:00 |
| | | | | | | | Swim | 00:00 |
| | | | | | text | | Bike | 00:00 |
| | | | | | | 03:00 | Run | 00:00 |

warm up with 10 to 20 minutes of jogging in Zones 1 and 2 before starting the game. A few short accelerations may also help sport readiness. Sport days are some mix of aerobic and anaerobic activity.

Strength training during this training block can be either the anatomical adaptation (AA) phase listed in Chapter 21 or your own program. Another option is to strength train AA on Monday and participate in a body pump or circuit training class on Wednesday. In any case, planned strength training will enhance overall sport performance.

Another feature of the overall plan is a rest week scheduled every four weeks. This allows the body a chance to recover and grow stronger. Rest is essential to improved performance in all sports.

Notice the swimming time trial in the first week. This time trial is a good measure of fitness progress. The average time for 100 yards should improve in subsequent time trials.

## Base 2

In Base 2, the strength training routine changes to maximum strength (MS). In this block of training, consider one of the MS days a BT workout. The second MS day can be a bit lighter or you can participate in body pump or circuit training. Select one sport day to be a BT day; the second one should be easy or form work. The third BT day is the Sunday bike ride. Not only is there a bit more intensity allowed in the Sunday ride, but also the ride grows in length as the weeks progress.

The Saturday run is also increasing in length, but the increments are very small, only five minutes. The rest week of this block includes a run with a short tempo segment, which should be fun.

## Base 3

Strength training in Base 3 moves to one day per week of power endurance or PE. Make the moves moderate in PE, because explosive work is already included within your sport workouts. A short bike and a short swim—or a day of golf—replaces the second strength training day. No, a swim and bike workout does not equal a golf day, but depending on your personal goals, a day of golf might be more appropriate than swimming or cycling. One swim day per week is enough to get you through the triathlon later in the summer. One bike day, Sunday, builds overall endurance and will also get you through a race. Those who decide to swim and bike instead of golf on Wednesday will likely be stronger on race day than the golfers. It is, however, possible to be an active participant in each sport.

Again, select one of the sport days to be a BT. By this time, the sport day may have changed to something like soccer, softball or inline hockey. The other BT workouts each week are both a swim and a run, or a swim and a bike ride. In week 11, the two sport days can be BTs or you can chose to make the Sunday bike ride an E3; this is left to the individual athlete.

### Build 1

In weeks 13 to 16, strength training moves to a maintenance mode, the SM phase, and remains in this mode through the end of the plan. Wednesday remains a swimming and cycling day throughout the rest of the schedule—or, as mentioned in the Base 3 description, this could be a golf day.

On Saturday of week 13, there is an optional 10km race or a fast group run. The race would be most comfortably run in Zones 1 to 3. However, a breakthrough strategy would be to begin the first quarter of the event in Zones 1 to 2, the middle half of the event in Zones 2 to 3 and the last quarter of the race in Zones 3 to 5a. A 5km could be done as well; simply add more warm-up and cool-down time to the event.

Week 14 has a brick scheduled: a bike immediately followed by a run. The bike is mostly Zone 1 to 2 effort, while the run is Zone 1 to 2 for the first 15 minutes and Zones 3 to 4 for the last 15 minutes. Be sure to walk afterwards and stretch.

The final week of this block is family vacation. Structured workouts are an option. A suggestion would be three days of running at 20 to 30 minutes per session. Workout specifics are up to you. If vacation is an active holiday with swimming, hiking, walking and other physical activities, no structured, planned workouts are necessary. If you come back totally exhausted from vacation, it would be best to insert a rest week similar to week 12 in place of week 17.

## Build 2

Special workouts of note during this block include a two-hour bike ride at the end of week 18, which could easily be one of the many fundraising activities held all summer long— a ride for a cause. The second item of note is the brick at the end of week 19. It includes an hour bike and an hour run. The first half of each sport is at Zone 1 to 2 effort and the last half is Zone 3 to 4. This brick could easily be replaced by a sprint triathlon.

The last item of note in this block is the fast run or race

on Saturday of week 20. A 5km event would be the recommended distance. Be sure to warm up before and cool down after the race.

### Build 3

The last block of this plan includes a 25-minute tempo run on Saturday of week 21 and a bicycle time trial on Sunday of week 22. The bike time trial distance can be anywhere between 5 and 8 miles. This time trial is a fun way to see how fast you can go. It can also be used to chart future training progress.

Week 23 has some running intervals on Saturday: 4 to 6 x 3 to 4 minutes, increasing heart rate into Zones 4 to 5a. Take 1 minute of easy jogging between run intervals.

The final week of this block includes a sprint triathlon. If a competition is not in your area, create your own event. Make your car the transition area. Complete a swim between 450 and 500 yards, ride 13 to 15 miles on the bike and run around 3 miles. Plan to finish your personal event with a smile on your face and perhaps a small victory dance at the car—hey, you only live once.

## QUESTIONS AND ANSWERS

**Q.** My race days do not line up with the ones on the plan; what do I do?

**A.** You can move entire weeks around or use the "three BT rule" to change the workout intensity of one or more sessions during your race week.

**Q.** My vacation is not in week 16, now what?

**A.** It would be a miracle if anyone's schedule perfectly matched the one on Table 16.2. You may need to eliminate or move some of the weeks. Be careful not to eliminate a rest week, creating a plan that spans eight or 12 weeks with no rest.

**Q.** In a rest week, it works better for me to take Thursday off and miss a sport day. What should I do on Wednesday?

**A.** Depending on the block, either strength train or swim and bike on that day, as you have done in the previous four weeks.

**Q.** A 10km is not in my dreams—perhaps only a 5km. Do I need to run an hour for my longest run?

**A.** If a 5km is your goal event, a 45-minute run will do the trick. The minimum I would suggest is 30 minutes.

# PART IV

There is only one training plan in Part IV. The original book plan had six year-long plans, one each for Olympic distance racing, duathlon, half-Ironman, Ironman, stage racing in multisport and a multisport general fitness plan. Frankly, the book would have been too large if all these plans were included. I would have had to add an extra section to the strength training chapter: "Lift the book 12 times and rest." For that reason, we decided to begin with one year-long plan, the Olympic distance one, and make the decision about writing a second book, with more year-long plans, based on the feedback and needs of the athletes.

Although it is highly unlikely you can use the plan exactly as it is, you can use the format and general design to make the plan fit your personal needs. You may need to reduce the hours of one or more of the workouts. It may be necessary to reduce the intensity of one workout per week. You may need to put hill repeats in cycling instead of running due to your personal race goals and performance limiters. Do not be afraid to make those design modifications, because the optimal design is the one that meets your personal needs.

# CHAPTER SEVENTEEN

# Olympic Distance, *One Year Plan*

*"Racing hurts. Prior to a race I usually dread the pain that I will have to push through. But once the gun goes off, my fears vanish. It is that transformation in my mind from fear and doubt into determination and desire which makes racing so attractive for me.*
*—Doug Friman,*
*Tucson, Arizona, age 25*

I t is difficult to assemble a plan for an entire year that fits most athletes—in fact, it is impossible. So why include a year-long plan? The goal for this chapter is to show how an annual plan might be designed and to give athletes a framework they can modify to meet their personal needs. Let us look at the big picture—the overview, shown in Table 17.1.

A brief description of each training period follows this paragraph. Each period will be explained in more detail within the chapter. The plan spans 52 weeks and begins with a Transition phase. The Transition period shown is four weeks long; it could easily be slightly longer or shorter. Tran-

| Week # | Month | Period | Weekly Planned Hours | Activities | Race Priority |
|---|---|---|---|---|---|
| 1 | September/October | Transition | 3:00–6:00 | | |
| 2 | October | Transition | 3:00–6:00 | | |
| 3 | October | Transition | 3:00–6:00 | | |
| 4 | October | Transition | 3:00–6:00 | | |
| 5 | October | Preparation | 08:30 | | |
| 6 | October/November | Preparation | 08:30 | | |
| 7 | November | Preparation | 08:30 | | |
| 8 | November | Preparation | 07:00 | | |
| 9 | November | Base 1 | 10:00 | | |
| 10 | November/December | Base 1 | 11:30 | | |
| 11 | December | Base 1 | 07:00 | | |
| 12 | December | Base 1 | 12:00 | | |
| 13 | December | Base 1 | 13:30 | | |
| 14 | December/January | Base 1 | 07:00 | Holiday | |
| 15 | January | Base 2 | 10:30 | | |
| 16 | January | Base 2 | 12:30 | | |
| 17 | January | Base 2 | 13:45 | | |
| 18 | January | Base 2 | 07:00 | Business trip | 5–10K, C |
| 19 | January/February | Base 3 | 11:00 | | |
| 20 | February | Base 3 | 13:30 | | |
| 21 | February | Base 3 | 15:00 | | |
| 22 | February | Base 3 | 07:00 | 1/2 Marathon | C |
| 23 | February/March | Build 1 | 12:30 | | |
| 24 | March | Build 1 | 12:30 | | |
| 25 | March | Build 1 | 07:30 | Triathlon | B |
| 26 | March | Build 2 | 12:00 | | |
| 27 | March/April | Build 2 | 12:00 | | |
| 28 | April | Build 2 | 07:00 | Triathlon | B |
| 29 | April | Peak | 10:30 | | |
| 30 | April | Peak | 08:30 | | |
| 31 | April | Race | 07:00 | Triathlon | A |
| 32 | April/May | Recover | | | |
| 33 | May | Base 3 | 11:00 | | |
| 34 | May | Base 3 | 13:30 | | |
| 35 | May | Base 3 | 15:00 | | |
| 36 | May/June | Base 3 | 07:00 | | |
| 37 | June | Build 1 | 12:30 | | |
| 38 | June | Build 1 | 12:30 | | |
| 39 | June | Build 1 | 07:00 | Vacation | C-10K |
| 40 | June/July | Build 2 | 12:00 | | |
| 41 | July | Build 2 | 12:00 | | |
| 42 | July | Build 2 | 12:00 | | |
| 43 | July | Build 2 | 07:00 | Triathlon | B |
| 44 | July | Build 3 | 12:00 | | |
| 45 | July/August | Build 3 | 12:00 | | |
| 46 | August | Build 3 | 07:00 | Triathlon | B |
| 47 | August | Peak | 10:30 | 5K | C |
| 48 | August | Peak | 08:30 | | |
| 49 | August/September | Race | 07:00 | Triathlon | A |
| 50 | September | Race | 7:00+ | | |
| 51 | September | Race | 7:00+ | | |
| 52 | September | Race | 7:00+ | | |

TABLE 17.1. PLAN OVERVIEW

sition is a time to recover from a long season of racing. It is very unstructured in nature, with the goal being rejuvenation of the body and mind.

Transition is followed by a Preparation period. Preparation is more structured than Transition and begins building the foundation for higher levels of training. It is also four weeks long, but could be a few weeks more or less. The training periods shown in this particular plan follow a pattern of two or three weeks of increasing volume or intensity followed by a rest week. The rest week allows the athlete to get stronger—to rebuild from the tearing-down process of training.

The Preparation period is followed by Base 1. The Base 1 period is six weeks long; however, it follows the pattern of two weeks of increasing volume and one week of rest. The biggest reason for Base 1 to follow this pattern, for this plan, is to enforce rest during the holiday season. As a rule of thumb, I plan an athletic rest week during times of high personal stress or other life commitments. The plan shown in this chapter plans a rest week during the Christmas holiday. Some athletes need two weeks of reduced volume during that time of the year. If that sounds like you, the plan should be modified accordingly.

After the beginning of the year, Base 2 and Base 3 follow in sequence. They are each four weeks in length. Following the Base periods, and prior to the first Peak in April, Build 1 and Build 2 are each three weeks long. Notice the second Build phase, weeks 37 to 46, has three Build periods and they vary in length from three to four weeks. This format illustrates there is more than one way to assemble a Build period. In my experience, lengthening the periods to five or more weeks results in greater risk of illness or injury.

Those are some of the major items to notice on the overview of the plan. Now let us get into more detail about the type of athlete this plan was designed for and the specifics of the training plan.

## PROFILE

This plan is designed for an experienced triathlete looking for off-season and in-season conditioning. They train about 500 hours per year and have the ability to train between seven and 15 hours per week.

## GOALS

The goals include peaking for two major Olympic distance races this season: consider these "A-priority" races. For these important events, you taper volume and rest so the races produce personal-best fitness levels and fast times. A "B-priority" race is important and will be scheduled at the end of a rest week. A "C-priority" race is for fun and may be skipped if it interferes with proper rest.

## PLAN DESCRIPTION

Table 17.1 on page 202 lists training instructions for 52 weeks. Instructions for weeks 1 to 4 are on a single line, as are those for weeks 50 to 52. Although this table details the overall plan shown on Table 17.2, some of the workouts in each period require special instructions. Those details follow.

**Transition (Weeks 1 to 4)**

As previously mentioned, Transition is a time for rejuvenation. Only work out when you feel like it, but do try to stay active. Sports other than swimming, cycling and running are acceptable and encouraged. I recommend people try to run a couple of times per week during this time to make the transition back to run training easier.

**Preparation (Weeks 5 to 8)**

This is the beginning of structured training. Sport-specific training during this phase is mostly aerobic and includes a good deal of form work. Form work is important for the development of economy and will remain in the plan all season. There is also an emphasis on strength training in the weight room, which prepares the body for more difficult training to come. During each rest week, when aerobic training decreases, also decrease the number of sets or repetitions, or both, in the weight room.

If a lactate threshold test has not been completed yet, week 8 would be a good time to test, instead of one of the time trials.

On days where running and strength training is shown, if you decide to do both activities within a single workout, run first.

**Base 1 (Weeks 9 to 14)**

In this period, strength training changes to the maximum strength (MS) phase. Most triathletes find MS difficult, as it seems to remove that light, fast feeling from the legs. To help

## TABLE 17.2. OLYMPIC DISTANCE ONE YEAR PLAN

| Week | Sport | Mon Time | Mon Code | Tues Time | Tues Code | Wed Time | Wed Code | Thurs Time | Thurs Code |
|---|---|---|---|---|---|---|---|---|---|
| 1-4 | Strength | Weeks' goals: | | | | | | | |
| | Swim | 1) Fun activities yielding 3-6 hours of physical activity per week. | | | | | | | |
| | Bike | 2) Usually run two times per week, 30-45 min ea. | | | | | | | |
| | Run | | | | | | | | |
| 5 | Strength | 01:15 | AA | | | 01:00 | AA | | |
| | Swim | | | 01:00 | E(Form) | | | 01:00 | E2 |
| | Bike | | | | | | | 00:30 | S5 |
| | Run | | | | | 00:30 | S2 | | |
| 6 | Strength | 01:15 | AA | | | 01:00 | AA | | |
| | Swim | | | 01:00 | E(Form) | | | 01:00 | E2 |
| | Bike | | | | | | | 00:30 | S5 |
| | Run | | | | | 00:30 | S2 | | |
| 7 | Strength | 01:15 | AA | | | 01:00 | AA | | |
| | Swim | | | 01:00 | E(Form) | | | 01:00 | E2 |
| | Bike | | | | | | | 00:30 | S5 |
| | Run | | | | | 00:30 | S2 | | |
| 8 | Strength | 01:00 | AA | | | 01:00 | AA | | |
| | Swim | | | 00:45 | T1b | | | 00:45 | E(Form) |
| | Bike | | | | | | | | |
| | Run | | | | | | | 00:30 | E2 |
| 9 | Strength | 01:30 | MS | | | 01:30 | MS | | |
| | Swim | | | 01:00 | E(Form) | | | 01:00 | E(Speed) |
| | Bike | | | | | | | | |
| | Run | | | 00:45 | TM#1 | | | | |
| 10 | Strength | 01:30 | MS | | | 01:30 | MS | | |
| | Swim | | | 01:00 | E(Form) | | | 01:00 | E(Speed) |
| | Bike | | | | | | | | |
| | Run | | | 00:45 | TM#2 | | | 00:30 | E1 |
| 11 | Strength | 01:00 | MS | | | 01:00 | MS | | |
| | Swim | | | 00:45 | E(Form) | | | 00:45 | E(Speed) |
| | Bike | | | | | | | | |
| | Run | | | | | | | 00:30 | E2 |
| 12 | Strength | 01:30 | MS | | | 01:30 | MS | | |
| | Swim | | | 01:00 | E(Form) | | | 01:00 | E(Speed) |
| | Bike | | | | | | | | |
| | Run | | | 01:00 | TM#3 | | | 00:30 | E2 |
| 13 | Strength | 01:30 | MS | | | 01:30 | MS | | |
| | Swim | | | 01:15 | E(Form) | | | 01:15 | E(Speed) |
| | Bike | | | | | | | | |
| | Run | | | 01:00 | TM#4 | | | 00:30 | E2 |
| 14 | Strength | 01:00 | MS | | | 01:00 | MS | | |
| | Swim | | | 00:45 | T1b | | | 00:45 | E(Form) |
| | Bike | | | | | | | | |
| | Run | | | | | | | 00:30 | E2 |

| Fri Time | Fri Code | Sat Time | Sat Code | Sun Time | Sun Code | Weekly Training Hours | Weekly Training Hours By Sport | |
|---|---|---|---|---|---|---|---|---|
| | 3) Bike or hike about an hour per week. | | | | | | Strength | tbd |
| | | | | | | | Swim | tbd |
| | 4) Swim, row or rock climb for upper body. | | | | | | Bike | tbd |
| | | | | | | 3:00–6:00 | Run | tbd |
| 01:00 | AA | | | | | | Strength | 03:15 |
| | | | | | | | Swim | 02:00 |
| | | | | 01:15 | E2 | | Bike | 01:45 |
| | | 01:00 | E2 | | | 08:30 | Run | 01:30 |
| 01:00 | AA | | | | | | Strength | 03:15 |
| | | | | | | | Swim | 02:00 |
| | | | | 01:15 | E2 | | Bike | 01:45 |
| | | 01:00 | E2 | | | 08:30 | Run | 01:30 |
| 00:45 | AA | | | | | | Strength | 03:00 |
| | | | | | | | Swim | 02:00 |
| | | | | 01:30 | E2 | | Bike | 02:00 |
| | | 01:00 | E2 | | | 08:30 | Run | 01:30 |
| | | | | | | | Strength | 02:00 |
| | | | | | | | Swim | 01:30 |
| 01:00 | S5 | | | 01:00 | T1(5 mi) | | Bike | 02:00 |
| | | 01:00 | T1(3 mi) | | | 07:00 | Run | 01:30 |
| | | | | | | | Strength | 03:00 |
| | | 01:00 | M | | | | Swim | 03:00 |
| 01:00 | S1 | | | 01:30 | E3 | | Bike | 02:30 |
| | | 00:45 | E2 | | | 10:00 | Run | 01:30 |
| | | | | | | | Strength | 03:00 |
| | | 01:15 | M | | | | Swim | 03:15 |
| 01:00 | S2 | | | 02:00 | E3 | | Bike | 03:00 |
| | | 01:00 | E2 | | | 11:30 | Run | 02:15 |
| | | | | | | | Strength | 02:00 |
| | | | | | | | Swim | 01:30 |
| 01:00 | S1 | | | 01:00 | M1(20–30) | | Bike | 02:00 |
| | | 01:00 | S2 | | | 07:00 | Run | 01:30 |
| | | | | | | | Strength | 03:00 |
| | | 01:15 | M | | | | Swim | 03:15 |
| 01:00 | S2 | | | 02:00 | E2 | | Bike | 03:00 |
| | | 01:15 | E3 | | | 12:00 | Run | 02:45 |
| | | | | | | | Strength | 03:00 |
| | | 01:15 | M | | | | Swim | 03:45 |
| 01:15 | S5 | | | 02:30 | E2 | | Bike | 03:45 |
| | | 01:30 | E3 | | | 13:30 | Run | 03:00 |
| | | | | | | | Strength | 02:00 |
| | | | | | | | Swim | 01:30 |
| 01:00 | S5 | | | 01:00 | T1(5 mi) | | Bike | 02:00 |
| | | 01:00 | T1(3 mi) | | | 07:00 | Run | 01:30 |

TABLE 17.2. OLYMPIC DISTANCE ONE YEAR PLAN (CONTINUED)

| Week | Sport | Mon Time | Mon Code | Tues Time | Tues Code | Wed Time | Wed Code | Thurs Time | Thurs Code |
|---|---|---|---|---|---|---|---|---|---|
| 15 | Strength | 01:15 | PE | | | 01:30 | PE + Plyo #1 | | |
| | Swim | | | 01:00 | E(Form) | | | 01:00 | Force |
| | Bike | | | | | | | | |
| | Run | | | 00:45 | M2(4–5a) | | | 00:30 | E1 |
| 16 | Strength | 01:15 | PE | | | 01:30 | PE + Plyo #2 | | |
| | Swim | | | 01:15 | E(Speed) | | | 01:15 | Force |
| | Bike | | | | | | | | |
| | Run | | | 01:00 | M2(4–5a) | | | 00:30 | E1 |
| 17 | Strength | 01:15 | PE | | | 01:30 | PE + Plyo #3 | | |
| | Swim | | | 01:15 | E(Form) | | | 01:15 | Force |
| | Bike | | | | | | | | |
| | Run | | | 01:00 | M2(4–5a) | | | 00:45 | E1 |
| 18 | Strength | Day off | | | | 01:30 | PE + Plyo #4 | | |
| | Swim | | | 01:00 | E(Speed) | | | 01:00 | M(Form) |
| | Bike | | | | | | | | |
| | Run | | | | | | | 00:30 | E1 |
| 19 | Strength | 01:15 | SM | | | | | | |
| | Swim | | | 00:45 | E(Form) | | | 01:00 | A |
| | Bike | | | | | 01:00 | M2(4-5a) | | |
| | Run | | | 00:45 | S1(4–6 x 20) | | | 00:30 | E1 |
| 20 | Strength | 01:15 | SM | | | | | | |
| | Swim | | | 01:15 | E(Speed) | | | 01:15 | A |
| | Bike | | | | | 01:00 | M2(4-5a) | | |
| | Run | | | 01:00 | S1(6–8 x 20) | | | 00:30 | E1 |
| 21 | Strength | 01:15 | SM | | | | | | |
| | Swim | | | 01:15 | E(Form) | | | 01:15 | A |
| | Bike | | | | | 01:30 | E2 | | |
| | Run | | | 01:00 | S1(6–8 x 20) | | | 01:00 | M1(20-25) |
| 22 | Strength | 01:00 | SM | | | | | | |
| | Swim | | | 00:45 | E(Speed) | | | 00:45 | A |
| | Bike | | | | | | | | |
| | Run | | | | | 00:30 | S2 | | |
| 23 | Strength | 01:15 | SM | | | | | | |
| | Swim | | | 01:00 | E1 | | | 01:15 | E2 |
| | Bike | | | | | 01:00 | E2 | | |
| | Run | | | 00:45 | E1 | | | 01:00 | S2 |
| 24 | Strength | 01:15 | SM | | | | | | |
| | Swim | | | 01:00 | E(Form) | | | 01:15 | E2 |
| | Bike | | | | | 01:00 | E2 | | |
| | Run | | | 01:00 | TM(Track#1) | | | 00:45 | S2 |
| 25 | Strength | 01:00 | SM | | | | | | |
| | Swim | | | 01:00 | E(Speed) | | | 00:45 | T1b |
| | Bike | | | | | | | | |
| | Run | | | | | 00:45 | S2 | | |

| Fri Time | Fri Code | Sat Time | Sat Code | Sun Time | Sun Code | Weekly Training Hours | Weekly Training Hours By Sport | |
|---|---|---|---|---|---|---|---|---|
| | | 01:00 | E2 | | | | Strength | 2:45 |
| 00:45 | E2 | | | 01:30 | E4 | | Swim | 3:00 |
| | | 01:15 | E2 | | | | Bike | 2:15 |
| | | | | | | 10:30 | Run | 2:30 |
| | | 01:15 | E2 | | | | Strength | 2:45 |
| 01:00 | E2 | | | 02:00 | E4 | | Swim | 3:45 |
| | | 01:30 | E2 | | | | Bike | 3:00 |
| | | | | | | 12:30 | Run | 3:00 |
| | | 01:15 | E2 | | | | Strength | 2:45 |
| 01:15 | E2 | | | 02:30 | E4 | | Swim | 3:45 |
| | | 01:45 | E2 | | | | Bike | 3:45 |
| | | | | | | 13:45 | Run | 3:30 |
| | | | | | | | Strength | 1:30 |
| | | | | | | | Swim | 2:00 |
| 01:00 | S5 | | | 01:00 | E2 | | Bike | 2:00 |
| | | 01:00 | A1b | | | 07:00 | Run | 1:30 |
| | | 01:00 | E2 | | | | Strength | 1:15 |
| 00:30 | E1 | | | 02:30 | E2 | | Swim | 2:45 |
| | | 01:45 | E4 | | | | Bike | 4:00 |
| | | | | | | 11:00 | Run | 3:00 |
| | | 01:15 | E2 | | | | Strength | 1:15 |
| 01:00 | S5 | | | 03:00 | E4 | | Swim | 3:45 |
| | | 02:00 | E2 | | | | Bike | 5:00 |
| | | | | | | 13:30 | Run | 3:30 |
| | | 01:15 | E2 | | | | Strength | 1:15 |
| 01:30 | E2 | | | 03:30 | E4 | | Swim | 3:45 |
| 00:30 | E1 | 01:00 | E2 | | | | Bike | 6:30 |
| | | | | | | 15:00 | Run | 3:30 |
| | | | | | | | Strength | 1:00 |
| | | | | | | | Swim | 1:30 |
| 01:00 | E1 | | | 01:00 | E1 | | Bike | 6:30 |
| | | 02:00 | Race | | | 07:00 | Run | 3:30 |
| | | 01:00 | M(OW) | | | | Strength | 1:15 |
| 01:00 | S1 | | | 03:00 | M3(4Z) | | Swim | 3:15 |
| | | 01:15 | E2 | | | | Bike | 5:00 |
| | | | | | | 12:30 | Run | 3:00 |
| | | 01:00 | M(OW) | | | | Strength | 1:15 |
| 01:00 | S1 | | | 03:00 | M4(20-30) | | Swim | 3:15 |
| | | 01:15 | E2 | | | | Bike | 5:00 |
| | | | | | | 12:30 | Run | 3:00 |
| | | | | Brick or Race | | | Strength | 1:00 |
| | | | | | | | Swim | 1:45 |
| | | 01:00 | S5 | 01:45 | text | | Bike | 2:45 |
| 00:30 | E1 | | | 00:45 | text | 07:30 | Run | 2:00 |

TABLE 17.2. OLYMPIC DISTANCE ONE YEAR PLAN (CONTINUED)

| Week | Sport | Mon Time | Mon Code | Tues Time | Tues Code | Wed Time | Wed Code | Thurs Time | Thurs Code |
|------|-------|----------|----------|-----------|-----------|----------|----------|------------|------------|
| 26 | Strength | 01:00 | SM | | | | | | |
| | Swim | | | 01:00 | E(Form) | | | 01:00 | E2 |
| | Bike | | | | | 01:00 | E1 | | |
| | Run | | | 01:00 | TM(Track#2) | | | 00:45 | S2 |
| 27 | Strength | 01:00 | SM | | | | | | |
| | Swim | | | 01:00 | E(Speed) | | | 01:00 | E2 |
| | Bike | | | | | 01:00 | E1 | | |
| | Run | | | 01:00 | TM(Track#3) | | | 00:45 | S2 |
| 28 | Strength | 01:00 | SM | | | | | | |
| | Swim | | | 01:00 | E(Speed) | | | 00:45 | T1b |
| | Bike | | | | | | | | |
| | Run | | | | | 00:45 | E2 | | |
| 29 | Strength | 01:00 | SM | | | | | | |
| | Swim | | | 01:00 | E(Form) | | | 00:45 | E2 |
| | Bike | | | | | 01:00 | E1 | | |
| | Run | | | 01:00 | TM(Track#4) | | | 00:30 | E1 |
| 30 | Strength | 00:45 | SM | | | | | | |
| | Swim | | | 00:45 | E(Speed) | | | 00:45 | E2 |
| | Bike | | | | | 00:45 | E1 | | |
| | Run | | | 00:45 | S2 | | | 00:30 | E1 |
| 31 | Strength | | | | | | | | |
| | Swim | | | 01:00 | E(Speed) | | | 00:45 | E(Speed) |
| | Bike | 01:00 | S4 | | | | | | |
| | Run | | | | | 00:45 | S2 | | |
| 32 | Strength | | | Week's goals: | | | | | |
| | Swim | | | 1) All workouts are two hours or less. | | | | | |
| | Bike | | | 2) Spend minimal time in Zone 3 and above. | | | | | |
| | Run | | | 3) Take a minimum of two days off. | | | | | |
| 33 | Strength | 01:15 | SM | | | | | | |
| | Swim | | | 00:45 | E(Form) | | | 01:00 | E2 |
| | Bike | | | | | 01:00 | E2 | | |
| | Run | | | 00:45 | S2 | | | 00:30 | E1 |
| 34 | Strength | 01:15 | SM | | | | | | |
| | Swim | | | 01:00 | E(Form) | | | 01:15 | E2 |
| | Bike | | | | | 01:15 | E2 | | |
| | Run | | | 01:00 | S2 | | | 00:45 | E2 |
| 35 | Strength | 01:15 | SM | | | | | | |
| | Swim | | | 01:15 | E(Form) | | | 01:15 | E2 |
| | Bike | | | | | 01:30 | E2 | | |
| | Run | | | 01:00 | S2 | | | 01:00 | E2 |

210

| Fri Time | Fri Code | Sat Time | Sat Code | Sun Time | Sun Code | Weekly Training Hours | Weekly Training Hours By Sport |
|---|---|---|---|---|---|---|---|
|  |  |  |  |  |  |  | Strength 1:00 |
|  |  | 01:15 | M(OW) |  |  |  | Swim 3:15 |
| 01:00 | S1 |  |  | 03:00 | A1c |  | Bike 5:00 |
|  |  | 01:00 | E2 |  |  | 12:00 | Run 2:45 |
|  |  |  |  |  |  |  | Strength 1:00 |
|  |  | 01:15 | M(OW) |  |  |  | Swim 3:15 |
| 01:00 | S2 |  |  | 03:00 | A1c |  | Bike 5:00 |
|  |  | 01:00 | E2 |  |  | 12:00 | Run 2:45 |
|  |  | Brick or Race |  |  |  |  | Strength 1:00 |
|  |  |  |  |  |  |  | Swim 1:45 |
|  |  | 01:00 | S5 | 01:30 | S4 |  | Bike 2:30 |
| 00:45 | E1 |  |  | 00:30 | S2 | 07:15 | Run 2:00 |
|  |  |  |  |  |  |  | Strength 1:00 |
|  |  | 01:00 | M(Speed) |  |  |  | Swim 2:45 |
| 00:45 | S1 |  |  | 02:30 | text |  | Bike 4:15 |
|  |  | 01:00 | E2 |  |  | 10:30 | Run 2:30 |
|  |  | Brick |  |  |  |  | Strength 0:45 |
|  |  | 01:00 | A(Form) |  |  |  | Swim 2:30 |
| 01:00 | S2 |  |  | 01:00 | text |  | Bike 2:45 |
|  |  | 00:45 | E2 | 00:30 | text | 08:30 | Run 2:30 |
| Day off |  | Brick |  | Race day! |  |  | Strength 0:00 |
|  |  |  |  |  |  |  | Swim 1:45 |
|  |  | 00:30 | S4 |  |  |  | Bike 1:30 |
|  |  | 00:10 | S2 |  |  | 04:10 | Run 0:55 |
|  |  |  |  |  |  |  | Strength tbd |
| 4) Work out only if you feel like it. |  |  |  |  |  |  | Swim tbd |
| 5) Relax, have fun. |  |  |  |  |  |  | Bike tbd |
| 6) At the end of the week, feel eager and ready to |  |  |  |  |  | 3:00- |  |
| resume structured training. |  |  |  |  |  | 7:00 | Run tbd |
|  |  |  |  |  |  |  | Strength 1:15 |
|  |  | 01:00 | M |  |  |  | Swim 2:45 |
| 01:00 | S5 |  |  | 02:30 | E4 or A1b |  | Bike 4:30 |
|  |  | 01:15 | E2 |  |  | 11:00 | Run 2:30 |
|  |  |  |  |  |  |  | Strength 1:15 |
|  |  | 01:15 | M |  |  |  | Swim 3:30 |
| 01:15 | S3(6-8) |  |  | 03:00 | E4 or A1c |  | Bike 5:30 |
|  |  | 01:30 | E4 |  |  | 13:30 | Run 3:15 |
|  |  |  |  |  |  |  | Strength 1:15 |
|  |  | 01:15 | M |  |  |  | Swim 3:45 |
| 01:30 | S5 |  |  | 03:30 | E4 or A1b |  | Bike 6:30 |
|  |  | 01:30 | E4 |  |  | 15:00 | Run 3:30 |

TABLE 17.2. OLYMPIC DISTANCE ONE YEAR PLAN (CONTINUED)

| Week | Sport | Mon Time | Mon Code | Tues Time | Tues Code | Wed Time | Wed Code | Thurs Time | Thurs Code |
|---|---|---|---|---|---|---|---|---|---|
| 36 | Strength | 01:00 | SM | | | | | | |
| | Swim | | | 01:00 | E(Speed) | | | 01:00 | T1b |
| | Bike | | | | | | | | |
| | Run | | | | | 00:45 | E1 | | |
| 37 | Strength | 01:15 | SM | | | | | | |
| | Swim | | | 01:00 | Force | | | 01:00 | E(Speed) |
| | Bike | | | | | 01:00 | M3(4–5a) | | |
| | Run | | | 01:00 | E2 | | | 00:45 | S2 |
| 38 | Strength | 01:15 | SM | | | | | | |
| | Swim | | | 01:00 | Force | | | 01:00 | E(Speed) |
| | Bike | | | | | 01:00 | M3(4–5a) | | |
| | Run | | | 01:00 | E2 | | | 00:45 | S2 |
| 39 | Strength | 01:00 | SM | | | Brick | | | |
| | Swim | | | 00:45 | E(Speed) | | | 00:45 | E(Form) |
| | Bike | | | | | 01:00 | S5 | | |
| | Run | | | | | 00:30 | S2 | | |
| 40 | Strength | 01:15 | SM | | | | | | |
| | Swim | | | 01:00 | A | | | 01:00 | E2 |
| | Bike | | | | | 01:00 | M4(20) | | |
| | Run | | | 01:00 | S1 | | | 00:45 | E3 |
| 41 | Strength | 01:15 | SM | | | | | | |
| | Swim | | | 01:00 | A | | | 01:00 | E2 |
| | Bike | | | | | 01:00 | M5(20–25) | | |
| | Run | | | 01:00 | S1 | | | 00:45 | E3 |
| 42 | Strength | 01:15 | SM | | | | | | |
| | Swim | | | 01:00 | A | | | 01:00 | E2 |
| | Bike | | | | | 01:00 | M5(20–30) | | |
| | Run | | | 01:00 | S1 | | | 00:45 | E3 |
| 43 | Strength | 01:00 | SM | | | Brick | | | |
| | Swim | | | 00:45 | M | | | 00:30 | E(Speed) |
| | Bike | | | | | 00:45 | A7 | | |
| | Run | | | | | 00:30 | S2 | | |
| 44 | Strength | 01:15 | SM | | | | | | |
| | Swim | | | 01:00 | E(Form) | | | 01:00 | E2 |
| | Bike | | | | | 01:00 | E2 | | |
| | Run | | | 00:45 | E2 | | | 01:00 | S2 |
| 45 | Strength | 01:15 | SM | | | | | | |
| | Swim | | | 01:00 | E(Form) | | | 01:00 | E2 |
| | Bike | | | | | 01:00 | E2 | | |
| | Run | | | 00:45 | E2 | | | 01:00 | S2 |

| Fri Time | Fri Code | Sat Time | Sat Code | Sun Time | Sun Code | Weekly Training Hours | Weekly Training Hours By Sport |
|---|---|---|---|---|---|---|---|
| | | | | | | | Strength 1:00 |
| | | | | | | | Swim 2:00 |
| 01:15 | E1 | | | 01:00 | T1(5 mi) | | Bike 2:15 |
| | | 01:00 | T1(3 mi) | | | 07:00 | Run 1:45 |
| | | | | | | | Strength 1:15 |
| | | 01:15 | E2 | | | | Swim 3:15 |
| 01:00 | S5 | | | 03:00 | E2 | | Bike 5:00 |
| | | 01:15 | M2(4-5a) | | | 12:30 | Run 3:00 |
| | | | | | | | Strength 1:15 |
| | | 01:15 | E2 | | | | Swim 3:15 |
| 01:00 | S5 | | | 03:00 | E2 | | Bike 5:00 |
| | | 01:15 | M2(4-5a) | | | 12:30 | Run 3:00 |
| Day off | | | | | | | Strength 1:00 |
| | | | | | | | Swim 1:30 |
| | | | | 02:00 | E2 | | Bike 3:00 |
| | | 01:00 | A1c | | | 07:00 | Run 1:30 |
| | | | | | | | Strength 1:15 |
| | | 01:00 | E(Speed) | | | | Swim 3:00 |
| 01:00 | E1 | | | 03:00 | E2 | | Bike 5:00 |
| | | 01:00 | A2(5b) | | | 12:00 | Run 2:45 |
| | | | | | | | Strength 1:15 |
| | | 01:00 | E(Speed) | | | | Swim 3:00 |
| 01:00 | E1 | | | 03:00 | E2 | | Bike 5:00 |
| | | 01:00 | A2(5b) | | | 12:00 | Run 2:45 |
| | | | | | | | Strength 1:15 |
| | | 01:00 | E(Speed) | | | | Swim 3:00 |
| 01:00 | E1 | | | 03:00 | E2 | | Bike 5:00 |
| | | 01:00 | A2(5b) | | | 12:00 | Run 2:45 |
| Day off | | | | Race day! | | | Strength 1:00 |
| | | | | | | | Swim 1:15 |
| | | 0:30 | Text | | | | Bike 0:45 |
| | | | | | | 03:30 | Run 0:30 |
| | | | | | | | Strength 1:15 |
| | | 01:00 | A | | | | Swim 3:00 |
| 01:00 | S2 | | | 03:00 | A1c | | Bike 5:00 |
| | | 01:00 | M5(15-20) | | | 12:00 | Run 2:45 |
| | | | | | | | Strength 1:15 |
| | | 01:00 | A | | | | Swim 3:00 |
| 01:00 | S1 | | | 03:00 | A1c | | Bike 5:00 |
| | | 01:00 | A2(5b) | | | 12:00 | Run 2:45 |

TABLE 17.2. OLYMPIC DISTANCE ONE YEAR PLAN (CONTINUED)

| Week | Sport | Mon Time | Mon Code | Tues Time | Tues Code | Wed Time | Wed Code | Thurs Time | Thurs Code |
|------|-------|----------|----------|-----------|-----------|----------|----------|------------|------------|
| 46 | Strength | 01:00 | SM | | | Brick | | | |
| | Swim | | | 00:45 | text | | | 00:30 | E(Speed) |
| | Bike | | | | | 00:45 | text | | |
| | Run | | | | | 00:30 | text | | |
| 47 | Strength | 01:00 | SM | | | | | | |
| | Swim | | | 01:00 | E2 | | | 00:45 | E(Speed) |
| | Bike | | | | | 01:00 | E2 | | |
| | Run | | | 01:00 | E2 | | | 00:30 | S2 |
| 48 | Strength | 00:45 | SM | | | | | | |
| | Swim | | | 00:45 | E(Speed) | | | 00:45 | E2 |
| | Bike | | | | | 01:00 | E2 | | |
| | Run | | | 00:45 | E2 | | | 00:30 | E1 |
| 49 | Strength | | | | | | | | |
| | Swim | | | 01:00 | E(Speed) | | | 00:45 | E(Speed) |
| | Bike | 01:00 | A7 | | | | | | |
| | Run | | | | | 00:30 | A7(3x90) | 00:15 | E2 |
| 50–52 | Strength | Weeks' goals: | | | | | | | |
| | Swim | 1) Do what you want, when you feel like it. Be sure to rest. | | | | | | | |
| | Bike | Fitness is quite high now, so enjoy. | | | | | | | |
| | Run | | | | | | | | |

minimize this effect, use the treadmill workouts found in Appendix H. Those with only 20-second run times help keep running form in tune. These workouts are particularly useful for people who may normally slog along in the dark or on slick streets in the evening after work. If you would rather do fast drills on land, use the S2 drills found in Chapter 20. Drills are also used on the bike and are designed to improve form.

In the first segment of Base 1, weeks 9 through 11, the breakthrough workouts (BTs) are the two strength training days and one muscular endurance day in the pool. The treadmill workouts, although challenging, should not be extremely difficult.

In the second segment of Base 1, weeks 12 through 14,

| Fri Time | Fri Code | Sat Time | Sat Code | Sun Time | Sun Code | Weekly Training Hours | Weekly Training Hours By Sport | |
|---|---|---|---|---|---|---|---|---|
| Day off | | | | Race day! | | | Strength | 1:00 |
| | | | | | | | Swim | 1:15 |
| | | 00:30 | S4 | | | | Bike | 1:15 |
| | | | | | | 04:00 | Run | 0:30 |
| | | 01:00 | M(OW) | | | | Strength | 1:00 |
| | | | | | | | Swim | 2:45 |
| 00:45 | S5 | | | 02:30 | A1d | | Bike | 4:15 |
| | | 01:00 | A1c | | | 10:30 | Run | 2:30 |
| | | | | Brick | | | Strength | 0:45 |
| | | 01:00 | M(Speed) | | | | Swim | 2:30 |
| 00:45 | S5 | | | 01:00 | text | | Bike | 2:45 |
| | | 00:45 | S2 | 00:30 | text | 08:30 | Run | 2:30 |
| Day off | | | | Race day! | | | Strength | 0:00 |
| | | | | | | | Swim | 1:45 |
| | | 00:30 | S4 | | | | Bike | 1:30 |
| | | | | | | 04:00 | Run | 0:45 |
| | | | | | | | Strength | tbd |
| 2)Race shape can be maintained for a few weeks with low | | | | | | | Swim | tbd |
| volume weekday recovery and weekend racing. | | | | | | | Bike | tbd |
| 3) Consider doing fun events. | | | | | | 07:00+ | Run | tbd |

some Zone 3 work is allowable on the long run. If this shows to be too much for you, reduce the intensity of the long run to Zones 1 and 2. If you do not want to build running volume toward a half-marathon, keep all Saturday runs in the 1:30 range, while the plan shows time building. Keep the intensity as shown on the plan.

Week 14, for this plan, happens to be Christmas week. All intensity may have to be removed from the week, as personal commitments become the priority. Not to worry, you will be fine. Reduce intensity and perhaps volume so you can enjoy family and friends. If you do not celebrate Christmas, but rather another holiday, the same comments apply for that time of the year.

### Base 2 (Weeks 15 to 18)

Strength training moves from maximum strength to power endurance (PE). An option for this period is to use the plyometric drills found in Appendix G. If you decide not to do plyometrics, simply follow the instructions for PE strength training found in Chapter 21.

Some of the run workouts need more detail. In week 15's Tuesday run, include 4 to 6 x 3' (1' RI). On Tuesday of week 16, do 4 to 5 x 4' (1' RI). On Tuesday of week 17, do 4 to 5 x 5' (1'30" RI). All of these intervals should take you into Zones 4 to 5a.

In week 18, on the Saturday run, run with a fast group or do a race of distance 10K or 5K. Always warm-up before racing, with more warm-up for shorter races.

Week 18 on the overview shows a "business trip." Any of the workouts shown on the plan can be done while traveling, if you can find access to a gym. Swimming with a new masters group can be fun as well. For running, some athletes like to jump into a weekend race in a new city. Bike rides may be done on a spin bike or exercise cycle found at most gyms. If you have to miss workouts during this week, do not fret: it is a rest week anyway.

### Base 3 (Weeks 19 to 22)

In Base 3, strength training moves to the strength maintenance (SM) phase. As implied, this workout is intended to maintain strength. Do not make the strength training so difficult that it causes lingering soreness.

Several run workouts need more detail. On the Saturday runs in weeks 19 and 20, continuous motion is not necessary during the long runs; walking breaks are fine. On Saturday in week 22, do a half-marathon race for fun or do a fast group run.

Bike workouts needing more explanation are: in week 19, on Wednesday, do 3 to 4 x 6' (2" RI); and in week 20, on Wednesday, do 3 to 4 x 6'-8' (2" RI). Heart rate should increase to Zones 4 to 5a during these intervals. In week 20, on Sunday, limit the amount of work in Zone 4 and above.

### Build 1 (Weeks 23 to 25)

Intensity is removed from the beginning of week 23 to allow for recovery from the half-marathon. The fast swim and fast bike that week should be done only if you are recovered from the race.

In this period, you will begin to work on speed or anaerobic endurance. My personal favorite way to improve speed is by using a treadmill. It is very difficult, if not impossible, for athletes to have enough self-control to run a track workout at the same intensities as the treadmill workouts provided in Appendix I. If the thought of running on a treadmill is appalling, try to do the same workouts—using the time and pace designated in the appendix—on the track. If you do chose to do the workouts on the treadmill, you may find an entirely new level of speed and mental toughness.

If you have a safe way to execute an open water swim for the M(OW) workouts during this block, swim the first half of

217

the time at Zones 1 to 2 and the second half of the time fartlek. Make the fartlek portions at race pace. If you do not have access to open water, do a similar effort in the pool. If you decide to race this week, make the week 25 Thursday swim an Endurance (Speed) workout.

On the Sunday bike in week 23, do 4 to 6 x (4'). The rest interval is equivalent to an easy spin downhill. On Sunday in week 25, you can schedule the first race of the season, or do a brick. If a brick is chosen, ride 1:45 and run 45 minutes. The ride should begin in Zones 1 and 2, finishing with a 30-minute time trial at race pace. The run should be split in half, with the first half in Zones 1 to 2 and the second half at race pace.

### Build 2 (Weeks 26 to 28)

Minimal special instructions for workouts are necessary for this training block. You have the option to race at the end of week 28 or complete the brick as shown on the plan. If you decide to race, make the Thursday swim workout of that week an Endurance (Speed) session.

### Peak and Race (Weeks 29 to 31)

As volume tapers during this time, extreme self-control will be necessary. Refrain from sneaking in extra workouts and increasing workout time. You need to rest so your body is fastest on race day, not in a training session with your buddies.

The only workout needing special instructions is the brick on Sunday of week 30. Bike for one hour and run for 30 minutes. Both are negative-split workouts, going out at Zones 1 and 2, coming back in Zones 4 to 5a or race pace.

Enjoy the race: go fast.

### Recover (Week 32)

I like to schedule a recovery week midseason for all athletes I work with. Relax, enjoy and take a break from structured training. Follow the general guidelines shown on Table 17.2.

### Base 3 (Weeks 33 to 36)

After the first Peak and Race period, a return to Base 3 training is scheduled. In this Base 3 period, fast workouts are grouped entirely on the weekend. This is done to show there are different methods to organizing fast workouts within a training block. Also, I have found that variety keeps training fun. Variety is why the S2 workouts are scheduled for Tuesday runs. You can, however, repeat the form treadmill workouts in Appendix H. Simply do them in sequence beginning with TM#1 in week 33. Athletes often find their E2 speed has increased since the first time they did these workouts back in Base 1.

### Build 1 (Weeks 37 to 39)

This particular Build period contains workouts that I would normally classify as Base 3–type work. This block is designed to illustrate there are no clear-cut rules around the periodization of workouts. The lesson is one of planned change, subjecting the athlete to increasing volume or intensity followed by rest. Each period builds on the previous one.

Bike workouts needing special instructions are these. In week 37, on Wednesday, do 3 to 4 x 4 to 6 minutes uphill, with rest interval equivalent to an easy spin downhill. In week 38, on Wednesday, do 3 to 4 x 6 to 8 minutes uphill, with rest interval equivalent to an easy spin downhill. These intervals should increase heart rate to Zones 4 to 5a.

Run workouts needing special instructions are these. In week 37, on Saturday, do 3 to 5 x 6' (2' RI). Inexperienced athletes should select the lower number of repetitions. In week 38, on Saturday, do 3 to 5 x 6' (2' RI). Try to do one more repetition than last week. These intervals should increase heart rate to Zones 4 to 5a.

Week 39 has "Vacation" listed on the plan overview. The comments relating to a vacation week are the same as those for a holiday week, such as week 14 in Base 1.

### Build 2 (Weeks 40 to 43)

The workouts needing additional details for this block include the Saturday run sessions. In week 40, do 4 to 5 x 3' (3' RI); in week 41, do 5 to 6 x 3' (3' RI); and in week 42, do 6 to 7 x 3' (3' RI). All these intervals should take you into Zone 5b.

The swim session on Tuesday of week 43 should include one segment of half the race distance at race pace. It can be broken into intervals or done as a straight swim. On Saturday of week 43, make the ride mostly easy, but run through all your gears to be sure the bike is in proper working order.

Sunday is race day, so have fun. If there is no race available, create your own brick or race simulation workout.

### Build 3 (Weeks 44 to 46)

One of the run sessions in this block builds on the previous block: on Saturday of week 45, do 6 to 7 x 3' (3' RI) into Zone 5b.

The swim on Tuesday of week 46 can be mostly easy, but include 5 x 100 yards at race pace, with 20 second rest intervals, as the main set. The brick that week is a 45-minute bike, mostly in Zones 1 to 2, with the last 15 minutes at race pace. The run is 30 minutes, mostly in Zones 1 to 2, with the last 10 minutes at race pace. This is enough intensity to keep you feeling fresh for the race this weekend. Race day comments are the same as those in Build 2.

### Peak and Race (Weeks 47 to 49)

This is the second Peak period of the season. Three workouts need extra comment. The week 47 run on Saturday can be a fast group run or a 5k race. For the week 48 brick on Sunday, bike 1:00 and run 30 minutes, both negative-split workouts—out at Zones 1 to 2 and back at race pace. On the Monday bike in week 49, do 4 x 90" with 3-minute recovery.

The final race of the season is likely on Sunday of week 49. Best wishes for fast racing, enjoy!

### Weeks 50 to 52

Many athletes find their fitness is at an excitingly high level after the last race of the season and a bit of rest. Some are able to maintain this high level of fitness for anywhere between two and six weeks. Depending on your desire to race, you may want to have a racing block at the end of the season and race every weekend. Others cannot stand the thought of packing all that gear and traveling to another event. Those who no longer want to race can still have fun by allowing some training sessions to become races—savor that hard-earned fitness.

As soon as you become stale, which will be a within a few weeks, it is time to begin the cycle all over again with a Transition period.

# PART V

This section of the book is devoted to explaining the workout codes used in each training plan. Chapter 18 is for swimming. Although "yards" are used in the text, yards and meters are interchangeable. Chapter 19 is for cycling, Chapter 20 for running and Chapter 21 for strength training. A few athletes prefer their own strength training program to the one in this book. If that is the case, be certain the program suits your goals. There are athletes who select a body building program that does develop a chiseled physique but is not optimal for multisport training. At the same time, if physique development is a higher-priority goal than endurance performance, by all means use the program that helps you reach your goal. All workouts should start out with a rating of perceived exertion of 1 and end with a perceived exertion of 1. That means do not bolt of out the starting gate and start swimming, cycling, or running as fast as you can. Allow your body a chance to warm up. Yes, that warm up and cool down time is included in the total workout time. I recommend athletes stretch after their cool down period at the end of every workout.

A second example of plan layout is Table 9.1 on page 104-105. The left column again has the week number, however each day of the week has two columns. One column lists the time of the workout in a specific sport and the second column has the workout code. Each sport or activity is listed in a separate row and repeats for each week. For example, Wednesday of week 3 will be a form workout on the bike lasting an hour and a half.

Tips for hydration and refueling are covered in Chapter 3 and apply to all the plans.

# Swim Workouts

*I have never seen a poor taper. It is simply poor training.*
*—Nick Hansen, world-caliber swim coach and*
*endurance athlete, Loveland, Colorado, age 35*

S wimming is different than cycling or running. The swim course is usually the same: 25 yards of clear water with a black line on the bottom of the pool. A variety of courses can be used to eliminate boredom in an aerobic workout in cycling or running. In the pool, a variety of workouts keeps swimming interesting.

Too often, athletes mix and match workouts or workout segments with no particular workout goal in mind. They simply swim. This habit leads to mediocre swimming. The plans within this book will use specific workout codes designed to help you change gears. Some days are for recovery, or taking it easy in the pool; other days go fast with no holding back.

## SPECIFIC WORKOUTS

The workouts are based on a combination of rating of perceived exertion (RPE) and the associated training zones on Table 1.1, page 7, as well as the results from an individual time trial (T1) detailed in this chapter. If you are just beginning to get into shape, use RPE until enough fitness has been built to do the time trial. If you have special health conditions, consult a physician about any restrictions he or she may place on exercise intensities.

## WORKOUT CODES

Sample workouts for each code are included in Appendix F. More workouts can be found in *Workouts in a Binder*™: *Swim Workouts for Triathletes*, waterproof workout cards available from VeloPress. The swimming cards are coded and can be used in conjunction with this book, *The Triathlete's Training Bible* or as stand-alone swimming workouts.

Generally, all swimming workouts will have a warm-up set, a main set and cool-down set. Workouts are categorized by a main emphasis, often designed to enhance a particular energy system; however, some workouts will have multiple goals.

### Testing

Testing will typically be done every three to four weeks, during a rest week. Some athletes prefer to test every other rest week, or each six to eight weeks. Improving T1 pace over several weeks and months of training is a marker of improved fitness and certainly a goal to shoot for.

*T1.* After a warm-up of 10 to 20 minutes, do the following:

- *T1a. If training for a sprint-distance triathlon, swim 3 x 100 with 20 seconds rest between each one. The goal of the set is to swim at the highest possible sustained speed in order to achieve the lowest average time. In other words, do not swim a fast first 100 and have the third 100 be 15 seconds slower. Watch the clock and get your time on each 100. Average the time for all three 100s to establish a T1-pace. For example, a reasonable swim might look like 1:25, 1:21 and 1:24; the T1-pace would be 1:23. One would not want to swim 1:20, 1:25 and 1:35 for a 15-second difference between the first and third 100s. It is best if all three 100s are within 5 seconds of one another.*

- *T1b. If training for an Olympic- or Ironman-distance triathlon, swim 3 x 300 with 30 seconds rest between each one. As with the 100s in the previous paragraph, the goal of the set is to swim at the highest average speed possible. An accurate test is when all three 300s are within 15 seconds of each other. In other words, do not swim a fast first 300 and have the third 300 be 20 or more seconds slower. Watch the clock and get your time on each 300. Average the time for all three 300s and divide the average by three to establish a T1-pace for a 100 yard distance. For example, if you swam 3:30, 3:25 and 3:22, the average time for the 300s is 3:27. Divide that result by three to obtain a T1-pace of 1:09. A handy reference chart for average 300 pace and T1-pace is in Table 18.1 on page 228.*

| TABLE 18.1: 300 SWIM, T-1 PACE CHART | | | |
| --- | --- | --- | --- |
| THIS CHART SHOWS 300 TIMES AND THE ASSOCIATED T1-PACE PER 100 SWIM. | | | |
| 300 Average Time | T-pace per 100 | 300 Average Time | T-pace per 100 |
| 02:42:00 | 00:54:00 | 04:21:00 | 01:27:00 |
| 02:45:00 | 00:55:00 | 04:24:00 | 01:28:00 |
| 02:48:00 | 00:56:00 | 04:27:00 | 01:29:00 |
| 02:51:00 | 00:57:00 | 04:30:00 | 01:30:00 |
| 02:54:00 | 00:58:00 | 04:33:00 | 01:31:00 |
| 02:57:00 | 00:59:00 | 04:36:00 | 01:32:00 |
| 02:57:00 | 00:59:00 | 04:39:00 | 01:33:00 |
| 03:00:00 | 01:00:00 | 04:42:00 | 01:34:00 |
| 03:03:00 | 01:01:00 | 04:45:00 | 01:35:00 |
| 03:06:00 | 01:02:00 | 04:48:00 | 01:36:00 |
| 03:09:00 | 01:03:00 | 04:51:00 | 01:37:00 |
| 03:12:00 | 01:04:00 | 04:54:00 | 01:38:00 |
| 03:15:00 | 01:05:00 | 04:57:00 | 01:39:00 |
| 03:18:00 | 01:06:00 | 05:00:00 | 01:40:00 |
| 03:21:00 | 01:07:00 | 05:03:00 | 01:41:00 |
| 03:24:00 | 01:08:00 | 05:06:00 | 01:42:00 |
| 03:27:00 | 01:09:00 | 05:09:00 | 01:43:00 |
| 03:30:00 | 01:10:00 | 05:12:00 | 01:44:00 |
| 03:33:00 | 01:11:00 | 05:15:00 | 01:45:00 |
| 03:36:00 | 01:12:00 | 05:18:00 | 01:46:00 |
| 03:39:00 | 01:13:00 | 05:21:00 | 01:47:00 |
| 03:42:00 | 01:14:00 | 05:24:00 | 01:48:00 |
| 03:45:00 | 01:15:00 | 05:27:00 | 01:49:00 |
| 03:48:00 | 01:16:00 | 05:30:00 | 01:50:00 |
| 03:51:00 | 01:17:00 | 05:33:00 | 01:51:00 |
| 03:54:00 | 01:18:00 | 05:36:00 | 01:52:00 |
| 03:57:00 | 01:19:00 | 05:39:00 | 01:53:00 |
| 04:00:00 | 01:20:00 | 05:42:00 | 01:54:00 |
| 04:03:00 | 01:21:00 | 05:45:00 | 01:55:00 |
| 04:06:00 | 01:22:00 | 05:48:00 | 01:56:00 |
| 04:09:00 | 01:23:00 | 05:51:00 | 01:57:00 |
| 04:12:00 | 01:24:00 | 05:54:00 | 01:58:00 |
| 04:15:00 | 01:25:00 | 05:57:00 | 01:59:00 |
| 04:18:00 | 01:26:00 | 06:00:00 | 02:00:00 |

## Endurance Workouts

The main emphasis of an endurance workout (E) is aerobic work. The main set of the workout is typically 20 to 40 minutes long, containing broken sets with rest intervals of 15 seconds or less. One of the main goals of this type of workout is to keep swimming. Swim at a pace that allows you to complete the entire set without taking extra rest. This speed is typically five to eight seconds per 100 slower than T1-pace.

*E1. Control the intensity of any (E) workout so RPE is in Zone 1.*

*E2. Control the intensity of any (E) workout so RPE is in Zones 1 to 2.*

*E3. Control the intensity of any (E) workout so RPE is in Zones 2 to 3.*

*E(Speed).* The main set will be mostly aerobic work; however, the end of the workout will include some very fast 25s or 50s, with an emphasis on high-speed arm turnover. Generally, there is ample rest between swim segments to allow full recovery. Neuromuscular training is more important than sustained high heart rates during the speed segment.

*E(Form).* The main set will be mostly aerobic work; however a good deal of form work will be included at the beginning or the end of the workout. Most often, speed is less important than good form. Some coaches refer to this as drill work. Again, neuromuscular training is important during the drill segment.

*E(OW).* Swim for the designated time in open water. Emphasize sighting objects (like buoys or markers on shore)

to aid in swimming a straight line. The plan may say E(OW)
(30), which means to swim for 30 minutes in open water in
training Zones 1 to 3. Of course, swimming in a safe situation
is essential, with lifeguards or other rescue persons present.

### Force Workouts

*Force.* These workouts use paddles; however a good deal
of form work will be included at the beginning or the end of
the workout.

*Force(Speed).* The main set includes paddles; however,
the end of the workout includes very fast 25s or 50s, with an
emphasis on high-speed arm turnover. Generally, there is
ample rest between swim segments to allow full recovery.
Neuromuscular training is more important than sustained
high heart rates during the speed segment.

*Force(Form).* The main set will include paddles; however,
the end of the workout will include very fast 25s or 50s, with
an emphasis on high-speed arm turnover. Generally, there is
ample rest between swim segments to allow full recovery.
Neuromuscular training is more important than sustained
high heart rates during the drill segment.

### Muscular Endurance Workouts

These workouts are often referred to as lactate threshold
or anaerobic threshold workouts. It is important to be well-
rested heading into a muscular endurance session.

*M.* This workout utilizes your T1-pace for the main set.
The main set is some combination of distances lasting 20 to

40 minutes, with a good portion of the set at T1-pace or slightly (two to five seconds) faster. Swim segments might be 50 to 200 yards or meters long, and depending on the length of each swim, rest intervals are five to 20 seconds long. The goal is to sustain T1-pace, or slightly faster.

*M(Speed).* The main set includes swims at T1-pace; however, the end of the workout includes very fast 25s or 50s, with an emphasis on high-speed arm turnover. Generally, there is ample rest between swim segments to allow full recovery. Neuromuscular training is more important than sustained high heart rates during the speed segment.

*M(Form).* The main set is at T1-pace; however, a good deal of form work will be included at the beginning or the end of the workout. Generally, there is ample rest between swim segments to allow full recovery. Neuromuscular training is more important than sustained high heart rates during the drill segment.

*M(OW).* Swim for the designated time in open water, at race pace. Emphasize sighting objects (like buoys or markers on shore) to aid in swimming a straight line. The plan may say 00:45, E(OW) (15), which means to swim for 45 minutes in open water, 15 minutes of which is at T1-pace or slightly faster. Of course, swimming in a safe situation is essential, with lifeguards or other rescue persons present.

### Anaerobic Endurance

These sessions achieve the best results if you are well-rested. The intention is to swim fast—very fast; faster than you thought possible. The main set may be quite short in yardage, but still take 20 to 40 minutes to complete.

*A—Anaerobic Endurance.* The main set includes swims typically in the 50- to 100-yard range, with rest intervals 30 to 60 seconds or longer. The main goal is to swim fast—no conserving, just go for it. In this type of work, you may find that speed decreases as the set goes on. That is okay. The fastest speed possible for that given swim is the goal. If you are unable to swim faster than T1-pace, stop the set, swim easy and try it again another day.

*A(Form).* The main set will include swims faster than T1-pace; however, a good deal of form work will be included at the beginning or the end of the workout. Generally, there is ample rest between swim segments to allow full recovery. Neuromuscular training is more important than sustained high heart rates during the drill segment.

## SAMPLE ATHLETE

To illustrate how to use the workouts to your advantage, we will follow a sample athlete, Michele. Michele swam her 3 x 300 time trial and achieved an average pace of 4:15. Her T1-pace (from the sidebar on page 233) is 1:25 per 100. In order for Michele to progress and swim faster speeds, it is important that she swim at certain goal paces for certain workouts while not compromising rest. That pace changes, depending on the goal of the workout. The pace will also change as she swims faster time trials, decreasing her T1-pace.

The chart shown below gives examples of the pace Michele should swim each workout code at her current T1-pace of 1:25. As previously mentioned, these goal times will decrease as she gains more fitness and speed.

| TABLE 18.2. MICHELE'S SWIMS | | | |
|---|---|---|---|
| THIS CHART SHOWS 300 TIMES AND THE ASSOCIATED T1-PACE PER 100 SWIM. | | | |
| Workout Code | Description | Example of Main Set | Example Speeds |
| T1-pace | Time trial | 3 x 300 (30-second rest interval) Result: 4:17, 4:15, 4:13 Average 300 time of 4:15 | Resulting T1-pace of 1:25 per 100 |
| The example speeds below are based on the results of the time trial above. When the time trial speed decreases, the goal speeds below will decrease as well. | | | |
| E1 | Endurance | 8 x 200 | Goal: Ignore the clock, make RPE Zone 1 |
| E2 | Endurance | 8 x 200 on a 3:20 swim interval | Goal: Hold 1:30–1:35 pace per 100 |
| E3 | Endurance | 8 x 200 on a 3:15 swim interval | Goal: Hold 1:25–1:30 pace per 100 or 2:50–3:00 per 200 |
| Force | Force | 5 x 200 with paddles on a 3:15 swim interval | Goal: Hold 1:20–1:25 pace per 100 or 2:40–2:50 per 200 |
| M | Muscular Endurance | 5–6 x 200 on a 3:05 swim interval | Goal: Hold 1:20–1:25 pace per 100 or 2:40–2:50 pace per 200 |
| A | Anaerobic Endurance | 8 x 50 on a 2:30 swim interval | Goal: Hold under 0:35 pace per 50 |

# Bike Workouts

*The counterintuitive thing that I learned with a structured training plan is that you have to go easy to see how hard you can really go. Before working off a structured plan, I went too hard on my easy days and thus too easy on my hard days. As a result I was never really reaching peak performance. I needed a structured plan from an objective, knowledgeable trainer. Using this approach, I was able to meet my 5-year-long goal to place in my age group at a World Championship Duathlon.*
*—Robin Steele, Fort Collins, Colorado*

All of the workouts are based on the training zones determined by doing one of the tests in Chapter 1. If you have zero fitness, do not do the lactate threshold test, and consult a physician before beginning any exercise program. If you have any special health conditions, it would be wise to consult a physician about restrictions they may place on your exercise intensities.

## WARM-UP AND COOL-DOWN

The workout time listed in any plan includes warm-up and cool-down. A warm-up is typically between 10 and 30 minutes, depending on the particular workout and how much time is assigned. If the ride is mostly Zone 1 to Zone 2, begin and end the ride in Zone 1. Before beginning intervals, tempo rides or races, be certain to include a good warm-up. If the workout is a high intensity session, begin the ride in Zone 1 and slowly increase speed, so that heart rate is close to the zone in which you will be doing the work intervals. If you are unable to get your heart rate into the specified zone by the third interval, quit trying, spin easy and head home; it was not your day.

After all workouts and races, take an easy spin to cool down. By the end of the cool-down, heart rate should be Zone 1 or less. Stretch muscles shortly after cool-down.

## WORKOUT CODES

### Endurance Workouts

*E1.* Ride in the small chain ring on a flat course, keeping heart rate in Zone 1.

*E2.* This level is used for aerobic maintenance and endurance training. Heart rate should stay primarily in Zones 1 to 2. How much time is spent in each zone depends on how you feel that day. The goal of an E2 ride is not to see how much time you can spend in Zone 2. Ride on a rolling course if possible, with grades up to 4 percent. For reference, most highway off-ramps are 4-percent grade. Riding in a slightly larger gear can simulate a gentle hill, if there are no hills where you live. Remain in the saddle on the hills. If you ride with a group, inner discipline is necessary to let the group go if they want to hammer.

*E3.* This workout is used for endurance training and the beginning of lactate threshold training. Ride a rolling course in Zones 1 to 3. Stay seated on the hills to build/maintain hip power. Ride a course and use gearing that allows work intensity into Zone 3, but not so hard you dip into Zones 4 and 5.

*E4.* This is a multifaceted workout for building endurance, speed and strength. The first time you do an E4 workout, keep heart rate in Zones 1 to 4. As training progress continues, and depending on the specifics of the plan, you can spend some time in Zone 5. As fitness increases, it is possible to spend progressively larger amounts of time in Zones 4 and 5. This progression is not detailed in the plans and is left to the individual athlete—begin conservatively.

### Form or Speed Workouts

*S1—Spin Step-ups.* This workout is intended to work on pedaling form and neuromuscular coordination. On an indoor trainer: Warm up with low resistance and a pedaling cadence of 90 rpm. After 15 to 20 minutes of warm-up, increase cadence to 100 rpm for 3 minutes, 110 rpm for 2 minutes and 120+ rpm for 1 minute. If time allows, spin easy for 5 minutes to recover and repeat. If just beginning to increase pedaling speed, it may be best to cut all of the times in half in order to maintain the recommended speeds. It is important that resistance is low, to allow a focus on the speed of the feet and not force on the pedals. This workout can be done on the road if the road is flat or slightly downhill.

*S2—Isolated Leg.* This workout helps work the dead spot out of a pedal stroke. After a warm-up on an indoor trainer with light resistance, do 100 percent of the work with one leg while the other leg is resting on a stool. The bottom of the stroke is similar to the motion of scraping mud off the bottom of your shoe. The top of the stroke can be improved by driving toes forward. In all positions, keep the toes relaxed. Do not allow them to curl-up and clench the bottom of your shoe.

This can be done outdoors by relaxing one leg while the other leg does 90 percent of the work. Change legs when fatigue sets in, or set a specific time interval to prevent excess fatigue. Work your way up to a work interval of 30 to 60 seconds per leg. After doing a work segment with each leg, spin easy with both legs for a minute and then go back to single legwork.

Stop pedaling with one leg when form becomes sloppy. Do not worry about achieving any particular heart rate; smooth pedaling form is most important. Begin with a cumulative time of 3 to 5 minutes on each leg and build time as you become stronger.

*S3—Accelerations.* This workout is intended to work on leg speed and neuromuscular pathways. Warm up well, then complete the specified number of 30-second accelerations, spinning an easy 2 minutes and 30 seconds (2' 30") between each acceleration. The end of the 30 seconds should be faster than the beginning. On the plans, the code looks something like S3(4–6), which means do 4 to 6 times 30-second accelerations, with 2-minute-and-30-second rest intervals between each one. If only S3 appears on the plan, the total number of repeats is left to your discretion.

*S4—Fartlek.* Ride mostly in Zones 1 to 2 with a few short (10- to 20-second) accelerations placed throughout the workout, your choice. This workout can be used as a prerace bike check. If using it as a prerace bike check, run through all the gears at some point during the ride to ensure smooth shifting.

*S5—Cadence.* With heart rate in Zones 1 to 2, the entire ride is at 90 rpm or greater. If cadence is not at least 90, coast until legs are recovered. This is best done on a flat course.

### Muscular Endurance Workouts

*M1—Tempo.* This workout is the beginning of lactate threshold speed work and is used for a good portion of training for events lasting more than three hours. After a warm-up, on a mostly flat course, ride in Zone 3 for the time indicated on the plan. For example M1(15) means ride 15 minutes, steady, in Zone 3.

*M2(3Z)—Cruise Intervals.* These intervals will also begin work on lactate threshold speed. On a mostly flat course or indoor trainer, complete the number of intervals given on the plan, allowing heart rate to rise into Zone 3 over the course of the interval. For example, 4–5 x 4' (1' RI) means after the warm-up, ride 4 or 5 times 4 minutes, allowing pulse to rise into Zone 3 and no higher. After heart rate is in Zone 3, try to hold it there until the end of the interval. Begin timing the interval as soon as you begin an increased effort—do not wait to begin the clock until your heart rate reaches Zone 3. All work intervals begin when effort is increased and end when effort is decreased. Spin easy and recover for 1 minute between efforts.

*M2(4–5a)—Cruise Intervals.* These intervals work on lactate threshold speed, as the season and your fitness progress. On a mostly flat course or indoor trainer, complete the number of intervals shown on the plan (or detailed within each plan's chapter), allowing heart rate to rise into Zones 4 to 5a over the course of the interval. For example, 4–5 x 4' (1' RI) means after warm-up, ride 4 or 5 times 4 minutes, allowing pulse to rise into Zones 4 to 5a and no higher. After heart rate is in Zones 4 to 5a, try to hold it there until the end of the interval. Take 1 minute of easy spinning between work intervals to recover.

*M3(3Z)—Hill Cruise Intervals.* Same as M2(3Z) except on a long hill with a 2- to 4-percent grade.

*M3(4Z)—Hill Cruise Intervals.* Same as M2(4–5a) except on a long hill with a 2- to 4-percent grade.

*M4—Criss-cross Threshold.* On a mostly flat or rolling course, begin with a warm-up and slowly increase heart rate to Zone 4. Once Zone 4 is attained, begin timing. Gradually build speed until the top of Zone 5a is achieved. Then, gradually reduce speed until the bottom of Zone 4 is achieved. The build and reduction time segments should take about two minutes. Continue to criss-cross from low Zone 4 to high Zone 5a for the time specified on the plan. For example, the plan may say M4(20), which means criss-cross the indicated zones for 20 minutes.

***M5—Tempo.*** This workout improves lactate threshold speed. After a warm-up on a mostly flat course, ride in Zones 4 to 5a for the time indicated on the plan. For example, M5(15) means ride 15 minutes, steady, in Zones 4 to 5a.

### Speed Endurance (Anaerobic) and Taper Workouts

Some of the workouts specify a rolling course or a hilly course. "Hilly" is relative to where you live. In general, a rolling course has grades up to about 4 percent and a hilly course has steeper grades. If you live in Flat City, simulate pedaling up hills by shifting up a gear or two.

***A1a—Easy Group Ride.*** This particular workout is not anaerobic, but is part of a series of group rides. Ride with a group and stay mostly in Zones 1 to 3.

***A1b—Faster-paced Group Ride.*** Ride with a group and stay mostly in Zones 1 to 4. Some time can be spent in Zone 5, but keep it minimal.

***A1c—Fast, Aggressive Group Ride.*** Ride with a group, and ride in all zones. Be aggressive and power up the hills, chase riders who might have been faster than you in the past, and have fun.

***A1d—Ride As You Feel.*** If you are feeling great, ride aggressively with some time in all zones; if tired, take it easy.

***A2(5bZ)—Speed Endurance Intervals.*** After a good warm-up on a mostly flat course, do the specified number of intervals, allowing heart rate to climb into Zone 5b. The intervals may be done on a flat course or slight uphill. For example, 4–5 x 3' (3' RI) means do 4 or 5 times 3 minutes, getting heart rate into Zone 5b and keeping it there until the end of the interval. Timing begins when effort is increased and ends when effort ends. Take 3 minutes between intervals.

*A6(5b–cZ) —Hill Reps.* After a good warm-up, ride a 6- to 8-percent grade hill and complete the specified number of hill repetitions. Stay seated for the first 60 seconds as you build to Zone 5b, then shift to a higher gear, stand, and drive the bike to the top, allowing heart rate to climb into Zone 5c. Recover completely for 3 to 4 minutes between repetitions.

*A7—Taper Intervals.* After a good warm-up, complete the specified number of 90-second accelerations, getting heart rate into Zones 4 to 5a. Take three full minutes to recover and get heart rate back to Zone 1 before going to the next interval. On the plans, the intervals may look like 4–5 x 90" (3' RI). If the number is not specified on the plan, do three to five repeats. Remember that more is not necessarily better. These intervals help keep legs feeling fresh and speedy while volume is tapering prior to a race or important ride.

## Test Workouts

*T1(5), T1(8), T1(10)—Aerobic Time Trial (ATT).* This is best done on a CompuTrainer or a trainer with a rear-wheel computer pick-up. It can also be done on a flat section of road, but weather conditions will affect the results. After a warm-up, ride 5, 8, or 10 miles with your heart rate 9 to 11 beats below lactate threshold heart rate. Distance of the time trial may be designated or left to your own descretion, by simply T1, on the plan. Use a single gear and do not shift during the test. Record the gear used, time and how you felt in your training journal. Each time you repeat the test, try to make testing conditions the same. As aerobic fitness improves, the time should decrease.

*T2—As-fast-as-you-can-go Time Trial (TT).* After a 15- to 30-minute warm-up, complete a 5- to 8-mile time trial, as fast as you can possibly ride. If you are a novice, use 5 miles. You may need to use a distance somewhere between 5 and 8 miles, because the available course dictates the exact length. Your course needs to be free of stop signs and heavy traffic. You can use a course with a turn-around point. Use any gear you wish and shift any time. Each time you repeat the test, try to make testing conditions as similar as possible (this includes wind, temperature, subjective feelings and outside stressors).

### Cross-training

*XT.* Some of the plans show an option of cross-training, such as aerobics, cross-country skiing and rollerblading, to name a few. Keep in mind your cross-training sport heart rates will not match cycling heart rate. Use rating of perceived exertion (RPE) to estimate correct training zones. These workouts should be mostly easy.

## REFERENCES

Bernhardt, G. *The Female Cyclist: Gearing up a Level.* Boulder, CO: VeloPress, 1999.

Friel, J. *The Triathlete's Training Bible.* Boulder, CO: VeloPress, 1998.

# CHAPTER TWENTY

# Run
# Workouts

*If you keep running fun, you will remain a kid forever—*
*at least on the inside.*

—Ðon Ļorenzen (a.k.a. Goatman),
Ļoveland, Colorado, age 50

A ll of the workouts are based on the training zones determined by doing one of the tests in Chapter 1. If you have zero fitness, do not do the lactate threshold test, and consult a physician before beginning any exercise program. If you have any special health conditions, it would be wise to consult a physician about restrictions they may place on your exercise intensities.

## WARM-UP AND COOL-DOWN

The workout time in any plan includes warm-up and cool-down. A warm-up is typically between 10 and 30 minutes, depending on the particular workout and how much time is assigned. If the run is mostly Zone 1 to Zone 2, begin and end the run in Zone 1. Before beginning intervals, tempo runs or races, be certain to get a good warm-up. If the workout is a high intensity session, begin the run in Zone 1 and slowly increase speed so that heart rate is close to the zone in which you will be doing the work intervals. If you are unable to get your heart rate into the specified zone by the third interval, quit trying, jog easy and head home; it was not your day.

After all workouts and races, take an easy jog or walk to cool down. By the end of the cool-down, heart rate should be Zone 1 or less. Stretch muscles shortly after cool-down.

## WORKOUT CODES

### Endurance Workouts

*E1.* Run on a flat course—a soft surface would be best (grass, dirt or a treadmill)—keeping heart rate in Zone 1.

*E2.* This level is used for aerobic maintenance and endurance training. Heart rate should stay primarily in Zones 1 to 2. How much time is spent in each zone depends on how you feel that day. The goal of an E2 run is not to see how much time you can spend in Zone 2. Run a rolling course if possible, with grades up to 4 percent. For reference, most highway off-ramps are 4-percent grades. For those living in vertically deficient cities, changing the grade on a treadmill can simulate hills. If you run with a group, inner discipline is necessary to let the group go if they turn a training run into a race.

*E3.* This workout is used for endurance training and the beginning of lactate threshold training. It is also used for a good portion of half- and full-marathon training. Run a rolling or hilly course in Zones 1 to 3. Allow heart rate to rise into Zone 3, but do not force it there. If running a mountainous course, walk the steep hills, if necessary, to keep heart rate out of the Zones 4 and up.

*E4.* This is a multifaceted workout that is for building endurance, speed and strength. Run a hilly course allowing heart rate to rise into all zones. The first time an E4 workout is done, keep heart rate in Zones 1 to 4, and limit total Zone 4 time to 15 to 20 minutes. Be cautious on the downhill sections, keeping speed under control to minimize pounding on your knees. As fitness increases, it is possible to spend progressively larger amounts of time in Zones 4 and 5. This progression is not detailed in the plans and is left to the individual athlete—begin conservatively.

### Form or Speed Workouts

*S1—Strides.* This workout is intended to work on running form and neuromuscular coordination. After 15 to 20 minutes of warm-up, do the fast run segments on a soft, flat surface, such as a grassy park or football field. Run 20 to 30 seconds four to eight times as indicated on the plan. For example, the plan may say something like 4–6 x 20", which means do somewhere between four and six 20-second runs. Walk or slowly jog back to the start position, taking a minute-and-a-half to two minutes to do so. As you gain experience, an option is to run on a gentle downhill at a park or golf course. The emphasis is on quick cadence and proud posture. This workout is for form, so trying to spend every moment above Zone 1 is not important. If heart rate drops below Zone 1 during recovery, it is okay. Cool down with 5 to 10 minutes of easy jogging.

*S2—Pick-ups.* Within a run that is mostly Zones 1 to 2 intensity, insert several 20- to 30-second accelerations. Finish the acceleration faster than you began. Quick cadence and proud posture are important. Jog easy for two or more minutes between accelerations.

### Muscular Endurance Workouts

*M1—Tempo.* This workout is the beginning of lactate threshold speed work. On a mostly flat course, after a warm-up, run in Zone 3 for the time indicated on the plan. For example, M1(15) means run 15 minutes, steady, in Zone 3.

*M2(3Z)—Cruise Intervals.* These intervals will also begin work on lactate threshold speed. On a mostly flat course or treadmill, complete the number of intervals given on the plan, allowing heart rate to rise into Zone 3 over the course of the interval. For example, 4–5 x 4' (1' RI) means after warm-up, run 4 or 5 times 4 minutes, allowing pulse to rise into Zone 3 and no higher. After heart rate is in Zone 3, hold it there until the end of the interval. Begin timing the interval as soon as effort is increased—do not wait to begin the clock when heart rate reaches Zone 3. All work intervals begin when effort is increased and end when effort is decreased. Jog easy and recover for 1 minute between efforts.

*M2(4–5a)—Cruise Intervals.* These intervals improve lactate threshold speed as the season and your fitness progress. On a mostly flat course or treadmill, complete the number of intervals given on the plan, allowing heart rate to rise into Zones 4 to 5a over the course of the interval. For example, 4–5 x 4' (1' RI) means after warm-up, run 4 or 5 times 4 minutes, allowing pulse to rise into Zones 4 to 5a and no higher. After heart rate is in Zones 4 to 5a, try to hold it there until the end of the interval. Take 1 minute of easy jogging to recover between work intervals.

Advanced athletes can use pace instead of heart rate to guide the intervals. Run the intervals at an open 10K pace, which is roughly 20 seconds faster per mile than 10K pace completed at the end of a triathlon.

*M3(3Z)—Hill Cruise Intervals.* Same as M2(3Z), except on a long hill with a 2- to 4-percent grade.

*M3(4Z)—Hill Cruise Intervals.* Same as M2(4–5a), except on a long hill with a 2- to 4-percent grade. Using 10K speed does not work well here.

*M5—Tempo.* This workout is for lactate threshold speed. After warm-up on a mostly flat course, run in Zones 4 to 5a for the time indicated on the plan. For example, M5(15) means run 15 minutes, steady, in Zone 4 to 5a.

### Speed Endurance (Anaerobic) and Taper Workouts

Some of the workouts specify a rolling course or a hilly course, which is relative to where you live. In general, a rolling course has grades up to about 4 percent and a hilly course has steeper grades. If you live in Flat City, simulate hills by changing the incline on a treadmill.

*A1a—Easy Group Run.* This particular workout is not anaerobic, but is part of a series of group runs. Run with a group and stay mostly in Zones 1 to 3.

*A1b—Faster-paced Group Run.* Run with a group and stay mostly in Zones 1 to 4. Time can be spent in Zone 5, but keep it minimal.

*A1c—Fast, Aggressive Group Run or Race.* Run with a group in all zones. Be aggressive and power up the hills, chase runners who might have been faster than you in the past and have fun. Or, run a race of a distance around 50 to 75 percent of the total time indicated on the plan.

*A1d—Run As You Feel.* If you are feeling great, run aggressively with some time in all zones; if tired, take it easy.

*A2(5bZ)—Speed Endurance Intervals.* After a good warm-up on a mostly flat course (a track or treadmill works well), do the specified number of intervals, allowing heart rate to climb into Zone 5b. The intervals may be done on a flat course or slightly uphill. For example, 4 to 5 x 3' (3' RI) means do 4 or 5 times 3 minutes, getting heart rate into Zone 5b and keeping it there until the end of the interval. Take 3 minutes recovery between intervals.

*A6(5b–cZ)—Hill Reps.* After a good warm-up, run up a hill with a 6- to 8-percent grade and complete the specified number of hill repetitions. Recover completely for 3 to 4 minutes between repetitions.

*A7—Taper Intervals.* After a good warm-up, do the specified number of 90-second accelerations, getting heart rate into Zones 4 to 5a. Take 3 full minutes to recover and get heart rate back to Zone 1 before going to the next interval. On the plans, the intervals will look like 4–5 x 90" (3' RI). If the number is not specified on the plan, do three to five repeats. Remember that more is not necessarily better. These intervals help keep your legs feeling fresh and speedy while volume is tapering prior to a race.

### Test Workouts

*T1—Aerobic Time Trial (ATT).* This is best done on a track or very flat section of road. After a warm-up, run one to three miles with heart rate 9 to 11 beats below your lactate threshold heart rate. The distance is typically specified on the schedule, such as T1(3) for a 3-mile time trial. Record time and the conditions. Each time you repeat the test, try to make test conditions the same, including the amount of time since the last BT workout. As aerobic fitness improves, the time should decrease.

*T2—As-fast-as-you-can-go Time Trial (TT).* After a 15- to 30-minute warm-up, complete a 1.5-mile time trial as fast as you can possibly run. As with the aerobic time trial, record time and the conditions. Each time you repeat the test, try to make testing conditions the same, including the amount of time since the last BT workout. As race fitness improves, the time should decrease.

*TT.* Time trial of length designated within the text of each plan.

### Cross-training

*XT.* Some of the plans show an option of cross-training, such as aerobics, cross-country skiing and in-line skating, to name a few. Keep in mind your cross-training sport heart rates will not match your running heart rate. Use rating of perceived exertion to estimate correct training zones. These workouts should be mostly easy.

## REFERENCES

Bernhardt, G. *The Female Cyclist: Gearing up a Level.* Boulder, CO: VeloPress, 1999.

Friel, J. *The Triathlete's Training Bible.* Boulder, CO: Velo-Press, 1998.

# CHAPTER TWENTY-ONE

# Strength Training and Stretching

*Ve vaunt to pomp you awp!*
*–Hans and Franz,*
*personal trainers from* Saturday Night Live

More athletes are turning to strength training to enhance their performance in endurance events. Others are still holdouts, fearing the gym may turn them into hulking-human specimens, capable of power-lifting small cars. Not to worry; multisport athletes should not weight train like power lifters or body builders because their fitness goals are different.

Consider that our natural maximal muscular strength is achieved somewhere in our 20s or early 30s. For this reason, I suggest anyone over 30 years old invest some time in a strength training program. The older you are, the more you need the gym.

Women tend to be approximately 50 percent weaker in the upper body and 30 percent weaker in the lower body than men. This measure is for average males and average females and is in terms of absolute strength. Athletic women are generally stronger than nonathletic women are; however, they are generally not as strong as athletic males in the same sport. Much of this strength difference is due to hormonal factors, which give males greater muscle mass. Although women may not have goals to be as strong as men within their sport, they can, however, use a weight training program to increase their strength per pound of body mass and their lean muscle mass.

Some of the adaptations that occur when we strength train include increased muscle fiber size, increased muscle contractile strength and increased tendon, bone and ligament tensile strength. These changes are thought to improve physical capacity, economy and metabolic function, decrease injury risk and help you look darn good.

"I might look good, but will I be faster?" There have been studies on trained and untrained (sedentary) cyclists, with both groups experiencing positive results. In one study, untrained cyclists who strength trained for 12 weeks improved their cycling endurance by 33 percent and lactate thresholds by an average of 12 percent, while their control group, who did no training, made no gains.

In a separate study on trained cyclists, the addition of a strength training program increased their cycling endurance by 20 percent, allowing them to pedal 14 minutes longer before fatigue set in. They also increased short-term, high-intensity endurance (performance in the 4- to 8-minute range) by 11 percent.

In addition to performance increases, a weight training program can prevent bone loss and even increase bone mass, which is critical to the prevention of osteoporosis in both men and women. How important a weight training program might be to multisport athletes is not quantitatively known at this time.

## STARTING A STRENGTH TRAINING PROGRAM

No one was born with the knowledge to use all the pieces of equipment in the gym, nor were they born with perfect weight-lifting form. When just beginning a weight-training program, ask for help. Good form is critical. This book provides guidelines on which exercises to use. To find illustrations and specific instructions on how to do each exercise, consult a qualified trainer at the gym or the illustrations and instructions in my book *The Female Cyclist* or Joe Friel's *The Triathlete's Training Bible.* When seeking help at the gym, ask someone you trust to recommend a trainer and ask the trainer for his or her credentials.

The strength training exercises in this book are intended to augment your multisport program, specifically triathlon or duathlon. Because multisport athletes are trying to juggle fitness, family and job responsibilities, this particular strength training program minimizes weight room time while maximizing the benefits to a multisport program. Some plans include provisions for other sports such as soccer, softball, racquetball and others. This particular plan may not be optimal for those sports.

Some guidelines for this program:

- *Focus on the muscle groups that do the majority of work in swimming, cycling and running.*
- *When appropriate, mimic the positions and movements of swimming, cycling or running as closely as possible.*
- *Make multijoint exercises the priority and do single-joint exercises as time allows. For example, squats use three joints—the hip, knee and ankle. Knee extensions use only the knee joint.*
- *Always include abdominal exercises to strengthen your torso.*
- *Include exercises to strengthen the lower back. Seated rowing does work the lower back; however, some athletes find including back extensions as well minimizes back fatigue—particularly for cycling in the hills.*
- *Separate strength training sessions by at least 48 hours.*
- *Maintain good postural alignment whenever possible. This means when standing in a normal, relaxed position, the head is supported by the neck, which has a normal curvature. The neck, which is part of the spine, also has a curvature that is normal for you. For example, when doing squats, the head and neck should be in a position that allows the curvature of your neck to be in a normal position. The head is not craned towards the ceiling, nor is the chin pointed at the chest.*

• *Always, always, always maintain control of the weight on the concentric and the eccentric actions. This means using muscles, not momentum, to lift the weight. It means lowering the weight using muscles to control the speed, not allowing gravity to do most of the work and only using muscles to stop the weight at the end of the motion.*

## THE PROGRAM IN DETAIL

Table 21.1 shows an overview of the strength training program. This table can be copied and taken to the gym for reference. It can be stored in the journal you use to track strength training progress.

### Strength Training Phases

Only three exercises—a hip extension exercise, seated row and standing bent-arm lat pull-down—change phases. The rest of the exercises remain at the same number of sets and loads as recommended in the AA phase. The only change to these exercises is decreasing the number of repetitions to between 15 and 20, which may require a slight increase in weight.

*AA—Anatomical Adaptation.* This is the initial phase of strength training, which is included at the beginning of a racing season or when someone is just beginning a strength training program. It is typically used in Base or preseason training. Its purpose is to prepare tendons and muscles for greater loads in the next strength training phases.

*MS—Maximum Strength.* This phase is used to teach the

## TABLE 21.1. STRENGTH TRAINING

| Phase | AA | MS1 | PE1 | ME1 | SM1 |
|---|---|---|---|---|---|
| **Total sessions** per phase | 8–12 | 8–12 | 6–8 | 4–8 | 4+ |
| **Days per week** | 2–3 | 2 | 1–2 | 1–2 | 1–2 |
| **Exercises** (in order of completion) | 1 2 3 4 5 6 7 8 Circuit | **[1 2][7 6][5 8]** | **[1 2][7 6][5 8]** | **[1 2][7 6][5 8]** | **[1 2][7 6][5 8]** |
| **Load** (percent of 1 Rep Max) | 40–60 | **80–95** | **65–85** | **30–50** | **Sets 1–2 at 60 Set 3 at 80** |
| **Sets per session** | 3–5 | **3–6** | **3–5** | **2–4** | **2–3** |
| **Reps per set** | 20–30 | **3–6** | **8–15** | **40–60** | **Sets 1–2 at 12 Set 3 at 6–8** |
| **Speed of movement** | Slow | **Slow-Moderate** | **Moderately fast or Explosive²** | **Moderate** | **Slow-Moderate** |
| **Minutes of recovery** (between sets) | 1–1.5 | **2–4** | **3–5** | **1–2** | **1–2** |

**Triathlon Exercises:**
(In order of completion)
**1. Hip extension (squat, leg press or step-up)**
**2. Standing bent-arm lat pull-down**
3. Hip extension (different from #1)
4. Chest press or push-ups
**5. Seated row**
6. Personal weakness
   (hamstring curl, knee extension
   or heel raise)
7. Abdominal exercise
8. Optional—back extension

**Duathlon Exercises:**
(In order of completion)
**1. Hip extension (squat, leg press or step-up)**
**2. Upper body choice—lat pull-down or
   standing row**
3. Hip extension (different from #1)
4. Chest press or push-ups
**5. Seated row**
6. Personal weakness
   (hamstring curl, knee extension
   or heel raise)
7. Abdominal exercise
8. Optional—back extension

**Notes:**
1. Bold-faced exercises follow the guidelines for each particular phase. All other exercises remain at AA sets and loads. Repetitions for all other exercises move to 15 to 20.
2. Explosive movements are only done if equipment described in the chapter is available, otherwise movements are moderately fast speeds.
3. Do not continue any exercise that causes pain. This includes joints that "pop" or "crack" and any exercise that causes sharp pain during the exercise or lasting for days after the strength training session.
4. Before each strength training session, warm up with 10 to 20 minutes of aerobic activity. Cool down with 10 to 20 minutes of easy spinning on the bike. Do not use running to cool down.
5. Exercises in brackets [ ] can be done in a superset manner, alternating between the two exercises.

central nervous system to recruit high numbers of muscle fibers. For exercises designated MS, do one warm-up set with a light weight—something it is possible to lift around 15 or 20 times. As you add more weight, begin the first set conservatively. Use a weight you are certain you can lift six to eight times.

After a rest and stretching, add five to 10 pounds and lift again. Continue these sequences until six sets are complete. At some point, it may be impossible to add more weight and you top out, having to lift the final two or three sets at the same weight. That is fine. If you find the last set was easy, begin the entire sequence five to 10 pounds heavier at the next strength training session.

As for form on the MS phase, slowly exert force on the weight to move it. Do not use an explosive force to move the weight, like a rocket booster on the leg press machine. Using explosive force to get a heavy weight up will more than likely lead to knee or back problems. Going slower may lead to a bit of a struggle to get the weight up the first time; that is okay.

Many athletes find this phase fun because strength gains come quickly as loads increase. Be cautious not to extend this phase beyond the recommended number of sessions. Continuation of this phase for too long may result in muscle imbalances, particularly in the upper leg, which could lead to hip or knee injuries.

*PE—Power Endurance.* The PE strength-training phase is intended to combine strength with velocity. Making fast movements with weights, however, is controversial. At least one study has shown that when lifters were asked to move a weight as quickly as possible while maintaining contact with the weight-bar, power actually decreased. On a separate occasion, the same group was asked to move the weight as quickly as possible, but to release the weight. Their power and speed of movement increased in the second scenario.

In theory, the body was trying to protect itself in the first scenario, attempting to keep joints from being injured. It appears that the body was using opposing muscles to slow the weight down, actually decreasing power. So, when you begin to do the PE phase, you must ask yourself if the particular piece of equipment or exercise you are using will increase or decrease your power.

One of the best options for a hip extension exercise with fast movements is a leg press machine that allows you to explosively jump off of the platform with a load, and return to the start position at a moderate speed. In other words, it does not allow the entire load to come slamming down on your shoulders. The type of equipment I am most familiar with has the athlete on an incline bench, with the travel of the platform parallel to the ground. If your gym does not have such a leg press machine, it is best to moderate your speed to reduce the risk of injury and to be certain you are not losing power.

The jumping exercise explained in the last paragraph is a form of plyometrics. Plyometrics are exercises or drills aimed at linking strength with speed of movement to produce power. It used to be thought that plyometrics was only for sprinters and football players, but a recent study showed that

5km running performance was improved in well-trained endurance athletes using plyometrics.

An example of a plyometric exercise for the upper body is using a medicine ball in place of lat pull-downs. While standing, hold the medicine ball above your head and, as fast and forcefully as possible, slam the ball into the ground. A plyometric exercise to mimic rowing is difficult to duplicate. One option is to lie face-down on a bench, hanging one side of the body off the bench. Quickly lift a medicine ball off the ground and release it at maximum height. Another upper body option includes quickly tossing a medicine ball between two people, keeping the elbows high, similar to a chest press position.

There simply was not enough room in this book to go into multiple, detailed plyometric programs. One option for plyometrics (for advanced athletes) is included in Appendix G. Plyometrics are recommended only on particular plans. If the plan you are using does not call for plyometrics, simply do PE strength training exercises at a moderate speed. For more information on plyometrics, consult Donald A. Chu's *Jumping into Plyometrics,* published by Leisure Press.

***ME—Muscular Endurance.*** The ME phase follows PE and trains the body to manage fatigue at moderately high load levels by increasing capillary density and the number and size of mitochondria (energy production sites within the muscle cells). While this phase is beneficial to those who lack race endurance, some athletes find muscular endurance is better developed actually doing each particular sport. Others prefer one day of PE and one day of ME for a four-week period. Each plan will make recommendations on what format to use.

*SM—Strength Maintenance.* As the name implies, this phase is intended to maintain strength. A day of SM training should not be exhausting. Save your energy for sport-specific exercises.

### Exercises

The recommended exercises are listed on Table 21.1. Some exercises have more than one option shown. While it is not possible to show all available options for each exercise, it is advantageous for athletes to have more than one choice for each exercise, particularly for the times when the gym gets busy. Additionally, exercises that are slightly different, like the squat and leg press, stimulate muscles in different manners. The end result is a greater number of muscle fibers stimulated by slightly varying the routine either within a week or from week to week. For example, if you lift on Tuesday and Thursday, during the PE phase, use squats on Tuesday and leg press on Thursday.

In the AA phase, lifting can be completed in a "circuit," which means completing the first set of all the exercises before completing the second set. Sometimes this is a problem in a busy weight room, particularly for hip-extension exercises. For example, if people circle the squat machine like buzzards while you are trying to complete the program, go ahead and complete all of the sets of hip extension before moving to the next exercise.

The order of completion of exercises in the other phases is such that all sets and repetitions of each exercise are completed before moving on to the next exercise. The exceptions are the exercises in [brackets] that can be completed in "superset" format. Supersetting means alternating between the exercises within the brackets before moving on to the next group of exercises.

## Load

The load estimates are given in terms of 1 Rep Max, or the maximum weight you could lift only once. It is not recommended to attempt to find 1 Rep Max; rather, estimate it by finding the amount of weight you can lift 10 times, then divide that number by 0.75. For example, if you can leg press 150 pounds 10 times, maybe 11, but no more, divide 150 by 0.75 to estimate 1 Rep Max as 200 pounds.

Another way to estimate load is to begin with a weight that is embarrassingly easy. Slowly keep increasing the weight until you can only lift the number of repetitions listed for any particular phase.

## Sets

This means the number of repeated lifting bouts done on any particular exercise.

## Repetitions per Set

This is the number of repetitions done within each set at any particular exercise. For example, during the PE phase, complete a hip extension exercise set three to five times, and lift the weight eight to 15 times each time the exercise is done.

## Speed of Movement

The recommended speed is subjective; however, the weight must be controlled in both directions of movement. The phase requiring the most concern is the PE phase; please refer to the PE details for more information. Novice athletes (those in their first two years of strength training) should not try for highly explosive moves.

## Minutes of Recovery

Each phase has recommended recovery times between sets. These times are important for each phase. For example, the MS phase is compromised if the athlete shortens the 2- to 4-minute recovery times. A shortened recovery time means the athlete would have to reduce the weight, not making full use of the MS phase.

During the recovery time, stretch. Stretching exercises are outlined later in the chapter.

## Recovery Weeks

As part of your periodization plan, some weeks will reduce the volume of training to rest and recover. This can be applied to strength training by reducing the number of strength training days that week, reducing the time spent in each strength session by reducing the number of sets within a workout, slightly reducing the weight lifted on each exercise, or a combination of any of these three methods.

## STRETCHING

Those who stretch are religious about their routine. Those who do not stretch do not see any benefit to doing so, nor do they associate any negative consequences with not stretching. Flexibility has been shown to improve neuromuscular coordination and physical efficiency, increase the supply of blood and nutrients to joint structure, improve balance and muscular awareness, and improve performance and strength. Improve strength?

A study of swimmers, football players and runners had them do contract-relax flexibility training for the knee extensors and flexors. Contract-relax flexibility training involves a passive stretch of a muscle after an isometric contraction. The athletes did flexibility training for 8 weeks, 3 days per week. The researchers found flexibility training to increase the range of motion of the knee joint by about 6 percent. The scientists also found the stretching to improve knee joint torque. Eccentric knee extension torque increased between 19 and 25 percent, depending on the particular velocity of the measurement. Eccentric knee flexion torque increased by between 16 and 18 percent, again depending on the velocity of the measurement. Concentric knee flexion torque increased by between 8 and 10 percent, while knee flexion isometric torque increased by 11 percent.

In summary, the contract-relax flexibility training increased the strength of the knee flexors and extensors (hamstrings and quadriceps, respectively, to name some of the major muscles involved) during eccentric actions. The training also increased the strength of the knee flexors during concentric actions.

There are two basic types of flexibility: static flexibility and dynamic flexibility. Static flexibility is the range of motion relative to a joint, with little emphasis on speed of movement. An example is the combination of hamstring, back and upper back flexibility needed by people riding in a time-trial position or enduring a long ride. Dynamic flexibility is resistance to motion at the joint and involves speed during physical performance. An example of the use of dynamic flexibility is a cyclist's jumping out of the saddle to aggressively climb a hill or sprint to catch an opponent. A good endurance athlete must have both types of flexibility.

### How to Stretch

There are many methods to stretch. The one recommended in this book is called "proprioceptive neuromuscular facilitation" (PNF). There are also many variations on this technique. One easy-to-follow version is this:

1. *Static-stretch (stretch and hold) the muscle for about 8 seconds. Remember to breathe.*
2. *Contract the same muscle for about 8 seconds. (Leave out the contraction step when stretching during the rest interval of strength training and just hold static stretches for about 15 seconds.)*
3. *Stretch and hold the stretch again for about 8 seconds. Breathe.*
4. *Continue alternating muscle contractions and stretches*

## TABLE 21.2. STRETCHING GUIDE

| When to Stretch | Muscles to Stretch |
|---|---|
| **During weight training rest intervals** | |
| 1. Hip extension (squat, leg press or step-up) | Quadriceps, hamstrings, gluteus |
| 2. Standing bent-arm lat pull-down | Latissimus dorsi, biceps |
| 3. Hip extension (different from #1) | Quadriceps, hamstrings, gluteus |
| 4. Chest press or push-ups | Biceps, triceps, pectoralis |
| 5. Seated row | Upper and lower back, latissimus dorsi, biceps |
| 6. Personal weakness | |
|    hamstring curl | Hamstrings |
|    knee extension | Quadriceps |
|    calf raise | Calves |
| 7. Abdominal exercise | Abdominals |
| 8. Optional—back extension | Back, particularly the lower back |
| | |
| **After swimming** | Select exercises that stretch arms and the entire shoulder area including, but not limited to: triceps, latissimus dorsi, biceps, trapezius and deltoids |
| **After cycling** | Quadriceps, hamstrings, gluteus, calves, the lower back and the muscles listed for swimming |
| **After running** | Quadriceps, hamstrings, gluteus, calves, the lower back and optional stretches including those listed for swimming |

*until you have completed between four and eight static stretches. End with a stretch and not a contraction.*

You should find you are able to stretch farther, or increase your range of motion, each time you repeat the stretch.

### Stretches for Cycling and Weight Room

Table 21.2 provides suggestions for muscle groups to stretch, including when to stretch them. To find illustrations and specific instructions on how to stretch particular muscles and groups of muscles, consult a qualified trainer at the gym or the illustrations and instructions in my book *The Female Cyclist* or Joe Friel's *The Triathlete's Training Bible.* A couple of good resources for more ideas for stretching exercises are *Sport Stretch* by Michael J. Alter and *Stretching* by Bob Anderson.

## REFERENCES

Anderson, B. *Stretching.* Bolinas, California: Shelter Publications, 1980.

Alter, M. J. *Sport Stretch.* Champaign, IL: Human Kinetics, 1998.

American Council on Exercise. *Personal Trainer Manual.* San Diego, CA: The American Council on Exercise, 1992.

Bell, F. Program Director of Colorado Acceleration Program, McKee Medical Center Sports Medicine, Loveland, CO. Interviews by Gale Bernhardt, July 1998.

Bernhardt, G. *The Female Cyclist: Gearing Up a Level.* Boulder, CO: VeloPress, 1999.

Friedlander, A. L., et al. "A Two-Year Program of Aerobics and Weight Training Enhances Bone Mineral Density of Young Women." *Journal of Bone and Mineral Research 10,* no. 4 (April 1995): 574–585.

Friel, J. *The Triathlete's Training Bible.* Boulder, CO: VeloPress, 1999.

Handel, M., et al. "Effects of Contract-Relax Stretching Training on Muscle Performance in Athletes." *European Journal of Applied Physiology 76,* no. 5 (1997): 400–408.

Hickson, R. C. "Potential for Strength and Endurance

Training to Amplify Endurance Performance." *Journal of Applied Physiology 65*, no. 5 (November 1988): 2285–2290.

Kerr, D., et al. "Exercise Effects on Bone Mass in Postmenopausal Women Are Site-Specific and Load-Dependent." *Journal of Bone and Mineral Research 11*, no. 2 (February 1996): 218–225.

Kraemer, W. J. and S. J. Fleck. "Exercise Technique: Seated Cable Row." *Strength and Health Report 1*, no. 3 (June 1997).

Kraemer, W. J. and S. J. Fleck. "Exercise Technique: Classic Lat Pull-Down." *Strength and Health Report 1*, no. 6 (June 1997).

Kraemer, W. J. and S. J. Fleck. "Exercise Technique: Machine Standing Calf Raise." *Strength and Health Report 2*, no. 1 (March 1998).

Marcinik, E. J., et al. "Effects of Strength Training on Lactate Threshold and Endurance Performance." *Medicine and Science in Sports and Exercise 23*, no. 6 (June 1991): 739–743.

McArdle, William D., et al. *Exercise Physiology, Energy, Nutrition, and Human Performance.* 3rd ed. Malvern, PA: Lea & Febiger, 1991.

Puhl, J., et al. *Sport Science Perspectives for Women.* Human Kinetics, 1988.

McCarthy, J. P., et al. "Compatibility of Adaptive Responses with Combining Strength and Endurance Training." *Medicine and Science in Sports and Exercise 27*, no. 3 (March 1995): 429–436.

Newton, et al, "Kinematics, Kinetics, and Muscle Activation During Explosive Upper Body Movements: Implications for Power Development." *Journal of Applied Biomechanics 12*, no. 1 (1996): 31–43.

Paavolainen L., et al. "Explosive-Strength Training Improves 5-Km Running Time by Improving Running Economy and Muscle Power." *Journal of Applied Physiology 5*, no. 86 (May 1999): 1527–33.

Pearl, B. and G. T. Morgan. *Getting Stronger.* Shelter Publications, 1986.

Tanaka, H. and T. Swensen. "Impact of Resistance Training on Endurance Performance. A New Form of Crosstraining?" *Sports Medicine 25*, no. 3 (March 1998): 191–200.

Wallin D., et al. "Improvement of Muscle Flexibility. A Comparison Between Two Techniques." *American Journal of Sports Medicine 13*, no. 4 (July-August 1985): 263–268.

# APPENDIX A
## TESTS FOR ESTIMATING LACTATE THRESHOLD HEART RATE ON THE BIKE

## INDOOR TEST FOR ESTIMATING CYCLING LACTATE THRESHOLD HEART RATE

One way to estimate lactate threshold (LT) heart rate involves a CompuTrainer. The newer models of CompuTrainers have a calibration feature, so the instrument can be calibrated for each test and accurate retesting can be done at a later date. The use of the CompuTrainer method makes it easy for a coach or assistant to note athletes' ventilatory threshold (VT) and perceived exertion by standing next to them. Exertion and noticeable change in ventilation are best recorded while the test is in progress, instead of trying to recall the information later.

For those of you who already have a CompuTrainer, note that this test is different than the one in the instruction manual using Ergometer/Calibration Software. I use this test because the athlete controls the power output, instead of the assistant.

### EQUIPMENT, SET-UP AND ASSISTANCE

*1. Recruit an assistant with clipboard, paper, pencil, a heart rate monitor and a CompuTrainer. It is best to position the heart rate monitor read out where both the athlete and the assistant can see it. You can create your own data sheet using the piece of paper, or make a copy of the Lactate Threshold Test Data Sheet on page 279 in this appendix.*

2. *Warm up on the CompuTrainer for around 10 minutes and calibrate according to the instructions in the manual. Reinsert the Nintendo stereo jack into the handlebar control unit.*

3. *Set "Program" to "Road Races/Courses," program 70.*

4. *Program the course to 10 miles, although you will not use the entire distance.*

5. *Input your body weight plus the bike weight and record this data on the log sheet for later reference.*

6. *Turn "Drafting" off.*

### PROCEDURE

7. *During the test, hold a predetermined power level (plus or minus 5 watts) as displayed on the TV screen. Begin the test at 50 watts and increase by 20 watts every minute, until you can no longer continue—meaning you cannot sustain the power plus or minus 5 watts or the rating of perceived exertion is too high. Stay seated throughout the test. You can change gears any time. Highly fit or professional athletes may need to begin the test at more than 50 watts; perhaps 110 watts would be more appropriate.*

8. *At the end of each minute, tell the assistant how great your rating of perceived exertion is for the particular wattage just completed. Use the Borg scale in Table A.1. In other words, on a scale of 6 to 20, 6 being very easy and 20 being very, very hard, how hard does holding a particular wattage feel to you? Keep the scale easily visible, so you can grade your exertion.*

| TABLE A.1. The Borg Rating of Perceived Exertion (RPE) Scale and training zones. | | | |
|---|---|---|---|
| | Zone | RPE | Description |
| 1 | Recovery | 6 | |
| 1 | Recovery | 7 | Very, very light |
| 1 | Recovery | 8 | |
| 2 | Extensive endurance | 9 | Very light |
| 2 | Extensive endurance | 10 | |
| 2 | Extensive endurance | 11 | Fairly light |
| 3 | Intensive endurance | 12 | |
| 3 | Intensive endurance | 13 | Somewhat hard |
| 3 | Intensive endurance | 14 | |
| 4 | Threshold | 15 | Hard |
| 5a | Threshold | 16 | |
| 5b | Anaerobic endurance | 17 | Very hard |
| 5b | Anaerobic endurance | 18 | |
| 5c | Power | 19 | Very, very hard |
| 5c | Power | 20 | |

9. *The assistant will record your exertion rating and your heart rate at the end of the minute and instruct you to increase power to the next level. She or he can also encourage you to keep your power at the designated intensity. If you have no assistant, but do have a heart rate monitor such as the Polar Accurex XTrainer Plus, keep your own heart rate stored at each "lap" minute. Mentally note perceived exertion or, better, try to jot it down on a copy of the data sheet on page 279 (Figure A.3).*

10. *The assistant will listen closely to your breathing to detect when it becomes labored and deep. She or he will note the associated heart rate with the beginning of labored breathing and note "VT."*

11. *Continue until you can no longer hold the power level for at least 15 seconds or feel you do not want to go on.*

## FIGURE A.1 LACTATE THRESHOLD TEST DATA SHEET

NAME _BG_

DATE _9/6/00_

BIKE AND RIDER WEIGHT _128 + 23 = 151_

| WATTS | HEARTRATE | RATING OF PERCEIVED EXERTION |
|-------|-----------|------------------------------|
| 50 | 106 | 6 |
| 70 | 109 | 7 |
| 90 | 118 | 7 |
| 110 | 125 | 9 |
| 130 | 130 | 10 |
| 150 | 134 | 10 |
| 170 | 142 | 12 |
| 190 | 147 | 12 |
| 210 | 154 | 13 |
| 230 | 157 | 14 |
| 250 | 159 | 15 |
| 270 | 164 | 16 |
| 290 | 165 | 16  *Noted VT |
| 310 | 166 | 17 |
| 330 | 169 | 19 |
| 350 | 170 | 19 |
| 370 | | |
| 390 | | |
| 410 | | |
| 430 | | |
| 450 | | |
| 470 | | |
| 490 | | |
| 510 | | |
| 530 | | |
| 550 | | |
| 570 | | |

| ZONE | RPE | BREATHING |
|------|-----|-----------|
| 1 | 6-9 | Hardly noticeable |
| 2 | 10-12 | Slight |
| 3 | 13-14 | Aware of breathing a little harder |
| 4 | 15-16 | Starting to breathe hard |
| 5a | 17 | Breathing hard |
| 5b | 18-19 | Heavy, labored breathing |
| 5c | 20 | Maximal exertion noted in breathing |

Notes about bike set-up, current training status, how you feel:

1) BG felt good and well-rested

2) VT seemed to occur at 290 watts

Use this chart, the power you achieved at lactate threshold and current body weight for benchmarks of improvement.

12. *The data should look similar that shown in Figure A.1. VT heart rate and power is usually comparable to a rating of perceived exertion in the range of 15 to 17, and is a close estimate of LT. One indication of this is that ath-*

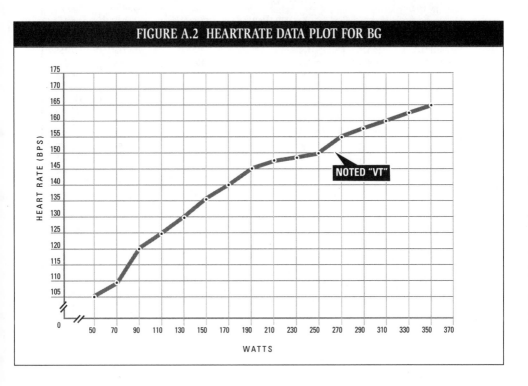

FIGURE A.2  HEARTRATE DATA PLOT FOR BG

letes are seldom able to go more than three to five minutes beyond their lactate threshold on this test.

13.Create an "XY" graph with the vertical coordinate representing heart rate and the horizontal coordinate representing wattage. Plot the data points from the test onto
a chart and connect them, as shown in the chart shown
on Figure A.2. Lactate threshold can be estimated by
using three references:

a. Note the heart rate at which breathing becomes
labored (ventilatory threshold), which is quite subjective.

b. Lactate threshold is usually between 15 and 17 on the
rating of perceived exertion scale.

c. Lactate threshold is usually no more than three to five
data points from the end of the test—that is, when the

# TABLE A.2  CYCLING HEART RATE ZONES

| 1 ZONE | 2 ZONE | 3 ZONE | 4 ZONE | 5a ZONE | 5b ZONE | 5c ZONE |
|--------|--------|--------|--------|---------|---------|---------|
| Recovery | Aerobic | Tempo | Sub-Threshold | Super-Threshold | Aerobic Capacity | Anaerobic Capacity |
| 90-108 | 109-122 | 123-128 | 129-136 | **137-140** | 141-145 | 146-150 |
| 91-109 | 110-123 | 124-129 | 130-137 | **138-141** | 142-146 | 147-151 |
| 91-109 | 110-124 | 125-130 | 131-138 | **139-142** | 143-147 | 148-152 |
| 92-110 | 111-125 | 126-130 | 131-139 | **140-143** | 144-147 | 148-153 |
| 92-111 | 112-125 | 126-131 | 132-140 | **141-144** | 145-148 | 149-154 |
| 93-112 | 113-126 | 127-132 | 133-141 | **142-145** | 146-149 | 150-155 |
| 93-112 | 113-127 | 128-133 | 134-142 | **143-145** | 146-150 | 151-156 |
| 94-113 | 114-128 | 129-134 | 135-143 | **144-147** | 148-151 | 152-157 |
| 95-114 | 115-129 | 130-135 | 136-144 | **145-148** | 149-152 | 153-158 |
| 95-115 | 116-130 | 131-136 | 137-145 | **146-149** | 150-154 | 155-159 |
| 97-116 | 117-131 | 132-137 | 138-146 | **147-150** | 151-155 | 156-161 |
| 97-117 | 118-132 | 133-138 | 139-147 | **148-151** | 152-156 | 157-162 |
| 98-118 | 119-133 | 134-139 | 140-148 | **149-152** | 153-157 | 158-163 |
| 98-119 | 120-134 | 135-140 | 141-149 | **150-153** | 154-158 | 159-164 |
| 99-120 | 121-134 | 135-141 | 142-150 | **151-154** | 155-159 | 160-165 |
| 100-121 | 122-135 | 136-142 | 143-151 | **152-155** | 156-160 | 161-166 |
| 100-122 | 132-136 | 137-142 | 143-152 | **153-156** | 157-161 | 162-167 |
| 101-123 | 124-137 | 138-143 | 144-153 | **154-157** | 158-162 | 163-168 |
| 101-124 | 125-138 | 139-144 | 145-154 | **155-158** | 159-163 | 164-169 |
| 102-125 | 126-138 | 139-145 | 146-155 | **156-159** | 160-164 | 165-170 |
| 103-126 | 1267-140 | 141-146 | 147-156 | **157-160** | 161-165 | 166-171 |
| 104-127 | 128-144 | 142-147 | 148-157 | **158-161** | 162-167 | 168-173 |
| 104-128 | 128-142 | 143-148 | 148-158 | **159-162** | 163-168 | 169-174 |
| 105-129 | 130-143 | 144-148 | 149-159 | **160-163** | 164-169 | 170-175 |
| 106-129 | 130-143 | 144-150 | 151-160 | **161-164** | 165-170 | 171-176 |
| 106-130 | 131-144 | 145-151 | 152-161 | **162-165** | 166-171 | 172-177 |
| 107-131 | 132-145 | 146-152 | 153-162 | **163-166** | 167-172 | 173-178 |
| 107-132 | 133-146 | 147-153 | 154-163 | **164-167** | 168-173 | 174-179 |
| 108-133 | 134-147 | 148-154 | 155-164 | **165-168** | 169-174 | 175-180 |
| 109-134 | 135-148 | 149-154 | 155-165 | **166-169** | 170-175 | 176-181 |
| 109-134 | 135-148 | 149-154 | 155-165 | **166-169** | 170-175 | 176-181 |
| 109-135 | 136-149 | 150-155 | 156-166 | **167-170** | 171-176 | 177-182 |
| 110-136 | 137-150 | 151-156 | 157-167 | **168-171** | 172-177 | 178-183 |
| 111-137 | 138-151 | 152-157 | 158-168 | **169-172** | 173-178 | 179-185 |
| 112-138 | 139-151 | 152-158 | 159-169 | **170-173** | 174-179 | 180-186 |
| 112-139 | 140-152 | 153-160 | 161-170 | **171-174** | 175-180 | 181-187 |
| 113-140 | 141-153 | 154-160 | 161-171 | **172-175** | 176-181 | 182-188 |
| 113-141 | 142-154 | 155-161 | 162-172 | **173-176** | 177-182 | 183-189 |
| 114-142 | 143-155 | 156-162 | 163-173 | **174-177** | 178-183 | 184-190 |
| 115-143 | 144-156 | 157-163 | 164-174 | **175-178** | 179-184 | 185-191 |
| 115-144 | 145-157 | 158-164 | 165-175 | **176-179** | 180-185 | 186-192 |
| 116-145 | 146-158 | 159-165 | 166-176 | **177-180** | 181-186 | 187-193 |
| 116-146 | 147-159 | 160-166 | 167-177 | **178-181** | 182-187 | 188-194 |
| 117-147 | 148-160 | 161-166 | 167-178 | **179-182** | 183-188 | 189-195 |
| 118-148 | 149-160 | 161-167 | 168-179 | **180-183** | 184-190 | 191-197 |
| 119-149 | 150-161 | 162-168 | 169-180 | **181-184** | 185-191 | 192198 |
| 119-150 | 151-162 | 163-170 | 171-181 | **182-185** | 186-192 | 193-199 |
| 120-151 | 152-163 | 164-171 | 172-182 | **183-186** | 187-193 | 194-200 |
| 121-152 | 153-164 | 165-172 | 173-183 | **184-187** | 188-194 | 195-201 |
| 121-153 | 154-165 | 166-172 | 173-184 | **185-188** | 191-195 | 196-202 |
| 122-154 | 155-166 | 167-173 | 174-185 | **186-189** | 190-196 | 197-203 |
| 122-155 | 156-167 | 168-174 | 175-186 | **187-190** | 191-197 | 198-204 |
| 123-156 | 157-168 | 169-175 | 176-187 | **188-191** | 192-198 | 199-205 |
| 124-157 | 158-169 | 170-176 | 177-188 | **189-192** | 193-199 | 200-206 |
| 124-158 | 159-170 | 171-177 | 178-189 | **190-193** | 194-200 | 201-207 |
| 125-159 | 160-170 | 171-178 | 179-190 | **191-194** | 195-201 | 202-208 |
| 125-160 | 161-171 | 172-178 | 179-191 | **192-195** | 196-202 | 203-209 |
| 126-161 | 162-172 | 173-179 | 180-192 | **193-196** | 197-203 | 204-210 |
| 127-162 | 163-173 | 174-180 | 181-193 | **194-197** | 198-204 | 205-211 |
| 127-163 | 164-174 | 175-181 | 182-194 | **195-198** | 199-205 | 206-212 |

*test subject wishes to stop. If ventilatory threshold, found in (a), does not agree with (b) and (c), disregard it.*

14. *Now that you have an estimate for your LT heart rate, use Table A.2 to calculate training zones. Find your lactate threshold heart rate (bold) in the "5a Zone" column. Read across, left and right, for training zones. The training zones will need to be confirmed: compare the heart rates and perceived exertion you achieved during the test with exertion levels and heart rates during workouts and races. Based on training and racing information, the zones may need slight modification. Be aware that LT can change with improved fitness, particularly for beginners.*

## OUTDOOR TEST FOR ESTIMATING CYCLING LACTATE THRESHOLD HEART RATE

Find an 8-mile course you can ride where there are no stop signs and limited traffic. After a good warm-up, do a time trial on the course. This means "all out," as fast as you can go for eight miles. You will need to either mentally notice the average heart rate during the time trial or use a heart rate monitor with an average function. It is best to have the averaging function. Do not use the maximum heart rate you saw during the test as the average. After the test, recall your average heart rate for the eight miles. This average heart rate is approximately 101 percent of LT. For example, if your average heart rate for the test was 165, 165 divided by 1.01 = 163 for LT heart rate.

If you happen to do an eight-mile time trial in some sort of a race, use 105 percent as your multiplier. In the example

| TABLE A.3. PREDICTING LACTATE-THRESHOLD PULSE RATE FROM AN INDIVIDUAL TIME TRIAL AVERAGE HEART RATE | | |
| --- | --- | --- |
| **DISTANCE OF ITT** | **AS RACE** | **AS WORKOUT** |
| 5k | 110% of LT | 104% of LT |
| 10k | 107% of LT | 102% of LT |
| 8-10 miles | 105% of LT | 101% of LT |
| 40k | 100% of LT | 97% of LT |

mentioned in the last paragraph, you would use 165 divided by 1.05 = 157. Why use a different multiplier if the time trial was an actual race compared to a workout? It is because we are typically able to push ourselves much harder in a race than in a workout.

What if your optimal course is shorter than eight miles; can that be used? Yes: a list of time trial distances and their various multipliers are listed in Table A.3. If you are in the beginning stages of improving your cycling, you might be better off to use one of the shorter time trial distances, such as 5km (3.1 miles). As you improve season after season, increase the time trial distance or continue to use a distance in the 3.1- to 4-mile range.

## FIGURE A.3. LACTATE THRESHOLD TEST DATA SHEET

NAME _____

DATE _____

BIKE AND RIDER WEIGHT _____

| WATTS | HEARTRATE | RATING OF PERCEIVED EXERTION |
|-------|-----------|------------------------------|
| 50 | | |
| 70 | | |
| 90 | | |
| 110 | | |
| 130 | | |
| 150 | | |
| 170 | | |
| 190 | | |
| 210 | | |
| 230 | | |
| 250 | | |
| 270 | | |
| 290 | | |
| 310 | | |
| 330 | | |
| 350 | | |
| 370 | | |
| 390 | | |
| 410 | | |
| 430 | | |
| 450 | | |
| 470 | | |
| 490 | | |
| 510 | | |
| 530 | | |
| 550 | | |
| 570 | | |

| ZONE | RPE | BREATHING |
|------|-----|-----------|
| 1 | 6-9 | Hardly noticeable |
| 2 | 10-12 | Slight |
| 3 | 13-14 | Aware of breathing a little harder |
| 4 | 15-16 | Starting to breathe hard |
| 5a | 17 | Breathing hard |
| 5b | 18-19 | Heavy, labored breathing |
| 5c | 20 | Maximal exertion noted in breathing |

Notes about bike set-up, current training status, how you feel:

_____

_____

_____

_____

_____

_____

_____

# APPENDIX B
## FIELD TESTS FOR ESTIMATING LACTATE THRESHOLD ON THE RUN

### INDOOR TEST FOR ESTIMATING RUNNING LACTATE THRESHOLD

This test involves running on a treadmill. You and your assistant should be familiar with the operation of the treadmill you will use and you must have experience running on a treadmill. This test has some risks associated with it; be responsible for your own safety. If you begin to feel dizzy or light-headed during the test, stop the test before the treadmill shoots you off the back.

#### EQUIPMENT, SET-UP AND ASSISTANCE

1. *A treadmill with a top speed of at least 10 mph is necessary. If your treadmill has a slower max speed, it should have a variable grade mode.*

2. *Also needed is an assistant, a heart rate monitor, a clipboard, paper and a pencil. The assistant holds the heart rate monitor wrist receiver during the test.*

#### PROCEDURE

3. *With the assistant, read all of the instructions before starting.*

4. *Warm up for 10 to 15 minutes, gradually elevating heart rate to a comfortable and easy effort.*

5. *Once the test begins, the assistant will operate the treadmill. He or she should stand so he or she can easily reach the stop control button.*

6. *Begin the test at 6 mph on a level treadmill (if it has 10 mph as the max speed) or at 6 mph on a 2-percent grade (if the treadmill has less than 10 mph max speed).*

7. *Every minute, your assistant increases the speed by 0.2 mph.*

8. *Just before each of these speed increases, the assistant records your heart rate, rating of perceived exertion (Borg Scale) and the current speed in mph. The data will look something like this:*

| Speed | Heart Rate | Rating of Perceived Exertion |
|-------|------------|------------------------------|
| 6.0   | 130        | 8                            |
| 6.2   | 133        | 9                            |
| 6.4   | 134        | 11                           |
| 6.6   | 137        | 13                           |

9. *Both you and the assistant should pay close attention to your breathing. When it becomes labored for the first time (when there's a lot of air being moved), the assistant should note the heart rate at that point on the data sheet. This data point is your "VT" or ventilatory threshold heart rate.*

10. *The test stops when you decide you have gone far enough. Tell the assistant to stop the treadmill or stop it yourself. Decide ahead of time how this will be done.*

11. *Create an "XY" graph with the vertical coordinate representing heart rate and the horizontal coordinate representing speed cubed.*

12. *Plot the data points from the test onto this chart and connect them. As with the cycling test, if there is a point at which the line deflects or bends sharply, the heart rate associated with this deflection is assumed to be LT pulse.*

## TABLE B.1. RUNNING HEART RATE ZONES

Find your lactate threshold heart rate (bold) in the "5a Zone" column.
Read across to left and right for training zones.

| 1 Zone Recovery | 2 Zone Extensive Endurance | 3 Zone Intensive Endurance | 4 Zone Sub-Threshold | **5a Zone Super-Threshold** | 5b Zone Anaerobic Endurance | 5c Zone Power |
|---|---|---|---|---|---|---|
| 93-119 | 120-126 | 127-133 | 134-139 | **140-143** | 144-149 | 150-156 |
| 94-119 | 120-127 | 128-134 | 135-140 | **141-144** | 145-150 | 151-157 |
| 95-120 | 121-129 | 130-135 | 136-141 | **142-145** | 146-151 | 152-158 |
| 95-121 | 122-130 | 131-136 | 137-142 | **143-146** | 147-152 | 153-159 |
| 96-122 | 123-131 | 132-137 | 138-143 | **144-147** | 148-153 | 154-160 |
| 96-123 | 124-132 | 133-138 | 139-144 | **145-148** | 149-154 | 155-161 |
| 97-124 | 125-133 | 134-139 | 140-145 | **146-149** | 150-155 | 156-162 |
| 97-124 | 125-134 | 135-140 | 141-146 | **147-150** | 151-156 | 157-163 |
| 98-125 | 126-135 | 136-141 | 142-147 | **148-151** | 152-157 | 158-164 |
| 99-126 | 127-135 | 136-142 | 143-148 | **149-152** | 153-158 | 159-165 |
| 99-127 | 128-136 | 137-143 | 144-149 | **150-153** | 154-158 | 159-166 |
| 100-128 | 129-137 | 138-144 | 145-150 | **151-154** | 155-159 | 160-167 |
| 100-129 | 130-138 | 139-145 | 146-151 | **152-155** | 156-160 | 161-168 |
| 101-130 | 131-139 | 140-146 | 147-152 | **153-156** | 157-161 | 162-169 |
| 102-131 | 132-140 | 141-147 | 148-153 | **154-157** | 158-162 | 163-170 |
| 103-131 | 132-141 | 142-148 | 149-154 | **155-158** | 159-164 | 165-172 |
| 103-132 | 133-142 | 143-149 | 150-155 | **156-159** | 160-165 | 166-173 |
| 104-133 | 134-143 | 144-150 | 151-156 | **157-160** | 161-166 | 167-174 |
| 105-134 | 135-143 | 144-151 | 152-157 | **158-161** | 162-167 | 168-175 |
| 105-135 | 136-144 | 145-152 | 153-158 | **159-162** | 163-168 | 169-176 |
| 106-136 | 137-145 | 146-153 | 154-159 | **160-163** | 164-169 | 170-177 |
| 106-136 | 137-146 | 147-154 | 155-160 | **161-164** | 165-170 | 171-178 |
| 107-137 | 138-147 | 148-155 | 156-161 | **162-165** | 166-171 | 172-179 |
| 108-138 | 139-148 | 149-155 | 156-162 | **163-166** | 167-172 | 173-180 |
| 109-139 | 140-149 | 150-156 | 157-163 | **164-167** | 168-174 | 175-182 |
| 109-140 | 141-150 | 151-157 | 158-164 | **165-168** | 169-175 | 176-183 |
| 110-141 | 142-151 | 152-158 | 159-165 | **166-169** | 170-176 | 177-184 |
| 111-141 | 142-152 | 153-159 | 160-166 | **167-170** | 171-177 | 178-185 |
| 111-142 | 143-153 | 154-160 | 161-167 | **168-171** | 172-178 | 179-186 |
| 112-143 | 144-154 | 155-161 | 162-168 | **169-172** | 173-179 | 180-187 |
| 112-144 | 145-155 | 156-162 | 163-169 | **170-173** | 174-179 | 180-188 |
| 113-145 | 146-156 | 157-163 | 164-170 | **171-174** | 175-180 | 181-189 |
| 114-145 | 146-156 | 157-164 | 165-171 | **172-175** | 176-182 | 183-191 |
| 115-146 | 147-157 | 158-165 | 166-172 | **173-176** | 177-183 | 184-192 |
| 115-147 | 148-157 | 158-166 | 167-173 | **174-177** | 178-184 | 185-193 |
| 116-148 | 149-158 | 159-167 | 168-174 | **175-178** | 179-185 | 186-194 |
| 117-149 | 150-159 | 160-168 | 169-175 | **176-179** | 180-186 | 187-195 |
| 117-150 | 151-160 | 161-169 | 170-176 | **177-180** | 181-187 | 188-196 |
| 118-151 | 152-161 | 162-170 | 171-177 | **178-181** | 182-188 | 189-197 |
| 118-152 | 153-162 | 163-171 | 172-178 | **179-182** | 183-189 | 190-198 |
| 119-153 | 154-163 | 164-172 | 173-179 | **180-183** | 184-190 | 191-199 |
| 120-154 | 155-164 | 165-173 | 174-180 | **181-184** | 185-192 | 193-201 |
| 121-154 | 155-165 | 166-174 | 175-181 | **182-185** | 186-193 | 194-202 |
| 121-155 | 156-166 | 167-175 | 176-182 | **183-186** | 187-194 | 195-203 |
| 122-156 | 157-167 | 168-176 | 177-183 | **184-187** | 188-195 | 196-204 |
| 123-157 | 158-168 | 169-177 | 178-184 | **185-188** | 189-196 | 197-205 |
| 123-158 | 159-169 | 170-178 | 179-185 | **186-189** | 190-197 | 198-206 |
| 124-159 | 160-170 | 171-179 | 180-186 | **187-190** | 191-198 | 199-207 |
| 124-159 | 160-170 | 171-179 | 180-187 | **188-191** | 192-199 | 200-208 |
| 125-160 | 161-171 | 172-180 | 181-188 | **189-192** | 193-200 | 201-209 |
| 126-161 | 152-172 | 173-181 | 182-189 | **190-193** | 194-201 | 202-210 |
| 126-162 | 163-173 | 174-182 | 183-190 | **191-194** | 195-201 | 202-211 |
| 127-163 | 164-174 | 175-183 | 184-191 | **192-195** | 196-202 | 203-212 |
| 127-164 | 165-175 | 176-184 | 185-192 | **193-196** | 197-203 | 204-213 |
| 128-165 | 166-176 | 177-185 | 186-193 | **194-197** | 198-204 | 205-214 |
| 129-165 | 166-177 | 178-186 | 187-194 | **195-198** | 199-205 | 206-215 |
| 129-166 | 167-178 | 179-187 | 188-195 | **196-199** | 200-206 | 207-216 |
| 130-167 | 168-178 | 179-188 | 189-196 | **197-198** | 199-207 | 208-217 |
| 130-168 | 169-179 | 180-189 | 190-197 | **198-201** | 202-208 | 209-218 |
| 131-169 | 170-180 | 181-190 | 191-198 | **199-202** | 203-209 | 210-219 |
| 132-170 | 171-181 | 182-191 | 192-199 | **200-203** | 204-210 | 211-220 |

*Confirm this by comparing it with the VT heart rate and your heart rate when perceived exertion was the range of 15 to 17. (Be aware that you may not have a deflection point on the graph.)*

*13. Use your LT heart rate and Table B.1 to determine your training zones. Notice the run and bike percents are slightly different. These zones were based on the work done by Peter Janssen and his book* **Training Lactate Pulse Rate.**

## OUTDOOR TEST FOR ESTIMATING RUNNING LACTATE THRESHOLD

Find a three-mile course you can run where there are no stop signs and limited traffic. A track can be used. As with the cycling time trial, after a good warm-up, do a running time trial on the course. This means "all out," as hard as possible, as if it were a race. You will need to either mentally notice the average heart rate during the time trial (which is highly inaccurate) or use a monitor with an average function. It is best to have the averaging function. After the test, recall average heart rate for the test. That average heart rate is approximately 101 percent of LT.

For example, if average heart rate for the test was 172, 172 divided by 1.01 equals 170 for LT heart rate. If you happen to do a 5K running race, use 105 percent as your multiplier. In the example mentioned in the last paragraph, you would use 172 divided by 1.05 to equal 164 for LT heart rate. This difference is because we tend to push ourselves much harder in a race than in a workout.

# APPENDIX C
# TRAINING WITH POWER

If you own a CompuTrainer or a Power-Tap, you can use them with some of the intensive endurance and lactate threshold endurance workouts in this book. For Ironman distance racing, intensive endurance training will be used. For Olympic distance events, lactate threshold endurance or improved power output at lactate threshold heart rate is the long-term goal. To use power measurements for some of the heart rate intervals given in this book, use the guidelines that are covered in the paragraphs that follow.

## COMPUTRAINER

When you tested for lactate threshold on the Compu-Trainer, lactate threshold heart rate was achieved at a particular power output. This value is lactate threshold power (LTP). When a training plan in one of the chapters designates a particular number of intervals or minutes at Zones 4 to 5a, you can use LTP plus or minus 5 percent—instead of heart rate—as the goal. For example, if lactate threshold power is 300 watts, the interval power range is 285 to 315 watts. If the workout calls for 4 x 6 minutes in Zones 4 to 5a, instead of shooting for a heart rate, aim for 285 to 315 watts. Typically, you'll find the first interval or two seem too easy and that it takes a good deal of time for your heart rate to climb into Zone 4. By the last interval, however, heart rate is well into Zones 4 to 5a and it is a challenge to hold power constant to the end of the designated time.

It is best to start with power on the low side and increase or build to the end of the interval. If power fades at the end of a given set, or heart rate climbs over Zone 5a early in the set, the goal power level is too high and needs to be adjusted.

Some intervals may be designated in Zone 3. The best way to determine Zone 3 power is by conducting an aerobic time trial (ATT) and using the average power produced during the time trial, plus or minus 5 percent. Instructions for conducting an ATT are in Chapter 19.

## POWER-TAP

This relatively new training tool has made training with power on the bicycle, both indoors and outdoors, much more affordable. When intervals in this book are designated in Zones 4 to 5a, use the results from the critical power test for 30 minutes (CP30) from the Power-Tap training manual. Use CP30 plus or minus 5 percent. For example, if CP30 is 300 watts, the interval power range is 285 to 315 watts. If the workout calls for 4 x 6 minutes in Zones 4 to 5a, aim for 285 to 315 watts instead of shooting for a heart rate. Typically, you'll find the first interval or two seem too easy and that it takes a good deal of time for heart rate to climb into Zone 4. By the last interval, however, heart rate is well into Zones 4 to 5a, and it is a challenge to hold power constant to the end of the designated time.

For athletes who have both systems, it is important to note that power output on CompuTrainer is relative to CompuTrainer and power output on Power-Tap is relative to

Power-Tap. This means that power output from the two systems may not match.

As for Zone 3 intervals utilizing Power-Tap, again, an aerobic time trial is the best way to determine the power range to shoot for. The aerobic time trial is described in Chapter 19.

## WHY USE POWER AND NOT HEART RATE?

I have found that using heart rate as a tachometer for high-end speed training (Zones 4 to 5) can be inaccurate and difficult to monitor. In fact, for short sprints, a heart rate monitor is useless. For longer intervals, many athletes ride the first couple of intervals too fast and end up with fading speed at the end of the set. A power meter allows the athlete to be more consistent with energy and speed, aiming for a strong finish.

# APPENDIX D
# GENERAL QUESTIONS
# AND ANSWERS

*"Most of the time our bodies are so willing to do what we want them to do, with little or no complaining. When our bodies ask for rest, I think we should listen."*
*Tara Walhart, Middletown, New Jersey*

*Q1. Should I always shoot for the highest number when a range is given?*
A1. No. A range is given on some workouts to allow you to customize the workout for how you feel. Also, if you are in a time crunch and have to cut the workout short, go for fewer repetitions.

*Q2. If a workout prescribes two hours and I am feeling great, can I just go ahead and do three hours?*
A2. Generally speaking, on two-hour rides, try not to go over or under more than about 15 minutes. On three-hour and longer rides, shoot for plus or minus 20 to 30 minutes. On shorter weekday rides, try to stay within around 10 minutes plus or minus.

*Q3. What happens if I get in a real time crunch and can only do 30 minutes of a 60-minute workout or I have to skip it altogether?*
A3. Realistically, you will probably miss a few workouts. If you are going to skip a workout, try to make it E1 that is an hour or less. The priority workouts are usually the long week-

end workouts that are continuously building volume, week-day intervals and strength sessions.

*Q4. Can I rearrange the workouts within the week? I work weekends.*

A4. Rearranging the workouts is fine, with a few guidelines:

• Keep at least 48 hours between strength training sessions.

• Try to keep BT workout sessions separated by 48 hours unless otherwise called for in the original plan.

• Do not try to make up missed weekday workouts on the weekend. In other words, don't try ride for six hours on Saturday if you missed three one-hour workouts during the week and you have a three-hour Saturday ride scheduled.

*Q5. I can only make it to the gym once a week. Is one strength training session really worth it?*

A5. Strength can be maintained by lifting once per week.

*Q6. What if I get sick; can I still train?*

A6. If your symptoms are above the neck and minimal (runny nose, headache, scratchy throat) go ahead and work out if you feel up to it. Cut your intensity to Zones 1 and 2. Reduce the total workout time or stop altogether if you feel bad once you get the workout started.

If your symptoms are below the neck or intense (cough, chills, vomiting, achy muscles, fever, sore throat) do not even start the workout. A virus likely causes these symptoms. Ignoring the symptoms and trying to train through the illness carries the risk of a more serious illness that can have you literally sidelined for months. Missing a few days of training to get well is your best investment of time.

*Q7. What happens if I miss some training days due to illness?*
A7. If you miss 1 to 3 days, resume your training as shown on the plan, skipping the workouts you missed. If you miss a week or more, consider pushing your goal forward. Depending on how you recover, you may want to repeat a week or two of training, to get you back on track. Whatever you do, take it easy coming back—you do not want another setback.

*Q8. If a swim then a run is shown on a particular day, do they have to be done in that order?*
A8. No. If your masters swimming group meets in the evening and you run in the morning, that is fine.

*Q9. If I miss a Thursday run or bike and Friday is shown as a day off, can I move the missed workout to Friday?*
A9. Yes, just be careful not to start "stacking" workouts on top of each other. Missing several workouts during the week cannot be made up in a couple of days on the weekend.

# APPENDIX E
## INSTRUCTIONS FOR THE
## HEALTH QUESTIONNAIRE

The health questionnaire is intended to help you record health risks related to heredity and current health condition. This information will need to be updated as more information becomes available about family members and as your personal health changes.

Sometimes athletes unwittingly put the goal to be thin ahead of the goal to be healthy. Severely restricting calories will affect current health and will certainly affect future health if wellness does not become the number one priority.

Each question was designed to prompt thoughts about personal health and genetic risks and to convey the idea that nutrition affects several areas of overall health. These areas can be used as markers to determine if a change in nutrition habits should be considered. Physical well-being, athletic performance, mental attitude and nutrition are synergistic. They each need to be optimized in order for the athlete to perform at peak capability. The questionnaire appears in condensed form later in this appendix; first, here's a bit more detail about what information each question should elicit.

1. Knowing your family health history is important when making decisions about nutrition and any type of supplementation. Record any major health problems among your grandparents, parents and siblings in this section.

2. Record the history of any health problems you have had in past years.

3. Do you currently have any health problems? Is your overall health improving or declining?

4. Describe your current diet. It is best to have a food log, giving details, but you can also describe how you eat. Do you eat highly processed foods? Do you eat out? If so, how many times each week? How many times each day do you eat? Do you eat because you are hungry, tired, stressed or nervous? Do you eat a wide variety of foods or do you tend to eat the same things each day?

5. Has your diet always been like it is now or have you made recent changes? Why did the changes happen? Have the changes improved how you feel?

6. What does your blood chemistry work say? Are there any items that are outside the recommended ranges? If so, can the answers to questions 1 through 5 yield any help to correcting the problem?

Questions 1 through 6 are intended to stimulate thoughts about overall health over a period time. The answer to any one of the questions may not yield valuable information, but the answers to all the questions together may help you and your health care providers to flesh out solutions to any problems.

Questions 7 through 14 are subtle questions. The answers may suggest something is wrong with your health. These small details, again, when examined in total, may tell a tale of good health or impending trouble. When seeking the help of a physician, take the answers from this questionnaire along, as they can give a small snapshot of your health.

# HEALTH QUESTIONNAIRE

Questions 1 through 6 give you a health snapshot, including hereditary health issues.

1. What is my family history of health disorders?

2. What is my personal health history? What problems have I had in past years?

3. What health problems do I currently have?

4. What is my diet currently like?

5. Have I made recent changes to my diet?

6. What does my most recent blood chemistry work say about my health?

If you answer "yes" to several of the following questions, your diet may not be serving your needs. Chapter 3 can help you modify your diet; alternatively, consider seeking the help of a registered dietitian specializing in sports nutrition.

7. Am I frequently awake throughout the night?

8. Does my hair grow slowly, or is it dry or brittle?

9. Do I have acne, or wounds that heal slowly?

10. Are my nails weak and brittle?

11. Am I frequently ill or injured?

12. Am I often tired or do I often have low energy?

13. Do I often have to skip training or reduce the intensity because I have no energy?

14. (Women) Are my periods irregular, often skipping months?

# APPENDIX F
# SAMPLE SWIM WORKOUTS

The workouts in this appendix are examples for some of the codes used in the plans. All workouts are freestyle and two levels are given for each workout, an "A" level and a "B" level. The A level is more advanced. Depending on your personal speed, the workouts take around 45 to 60 minutes to complete. More workouts are available from VeloPress in *Workouts in a Binder*™ (VeloPress).

The values in the "workouts" section will not specify meters or yards, as the two can be used interchangeably. For reading ease, yards are referenced in the "definitions" section.

## DEFINITIONS

*W/U.* Warm-up segment, with gradually increasing speeds throughout. All workouts in this appendix have the same warm-up for both A-level and B-level swimmers.

*C/D.* Cool-down segment; Zone 2 finishing with Zone 1 rating of perceived exertion.

*T1-pace.* The pace you held in the time trial (T1 for swimming). For example, if T1-pace was 1:20 per 100 yards, then T1-pace for 200 is 2:40 and T1-pace for 50 yards is 40 seconds.

*Rest Interval.* Some swim sets will have a designated rest interval, such as (0:25 RI), which means a 25-second rest after each swim or repetition. For example:

200 (0:20 RI)
300 (0:25 RI)
200 (0:20 RI)…

In this set, the swimmer would swim 200 yards, rest 20 seconds, swim 300 yards, rest 25 seconds, swim 200 yards, rest 20 seconds and continue with the set. Once you begin rolling on the main set of the workout, the idea is to take only the amount of rest designated on the workout.

*Swim Interval.* Some workouts will have a designated swim interval, which includes the swim time and the rest time. A swim interval may be designated by a code such as "(T1-pace + 0:25 SI)." For example, assuming a T1-pace of 1:20 again, 4 x 100 (T1-pace + 0:25 SI) means swim 4 x 100 on a 1:40 interval. If the 100 is swum at a 1:20 pace, there will be 20 seconds of rest. If the 100 is swum at a 1:18 pace, there will be 22 seconds of rest. Typically, the idea behind this type of set is to swim at T1-pace or slightly—one to three seconds—faster.

The second way a swim interval may be designated is with a code such as "(1:00 SI)," which means the swim and rest must be completed within a minute. For example, 10 x 50 (1:00 SI) means to swim 10 repeats of 50 yards, starting every 60 seconds.

*No Rest Interval Designated.* Rest as long as you please.

*Rt Arm.* This drill is freestyle with only one arm working—the right arm. With the left arm at your side (not out front), a moderate kick and normal body position and roll, the right arm performs a perfect stroke for the designated distance. That distance is typically 25 yards.

*Lt Arm.* This drill is freestyle with only one arm working—the left arm. With the right arm at your side (not out front), a moderate kick and normal position and roll, the left arm performs a perfect stroke for the designated distance. That distance is typically 25 yards.

**Pull.** The swim is done with pull buoys, and paddles are optional. Paddles are used when working on force.

**Kick.** No arms; kick only: can be done with or without a kickboard. If kicking without a kickboard, try to simulate normal swimming body position and keep arms streamlined. Arms can be streamlined along the body or in front. Either way, they should be quiet. In other words, if your arms are in front of the body, do not do a breast stroke pull, short or long, to get a breath. A slight press with locked hands and a quick breath will do. Or, keep your arms at your sides and roll the body to the side for a breath.

**DPS.** Distance per stroke: work on maximizing the distance each arm can propel the body. Count the number of strokes per 25 yards.

**Cruise.** A moderate pace; a Zone 3-type effort.

**Max Speed.** All-out fast, no holding back.

**Build.** Get faster within the designated swim. For example, "25 Build" means to get faster throughout the entire 25 yards. The last 5 yards should be the fastest swimming of that particular 25.

**Easy.** Zone 1 rating of perceived exertion.

**B-3.** Breathe every third stroke.

# WORKOUTS

### Endurance Form—E(Form)

W/U:    200 swim, 200 kick, 200 pull

6 x 75 : 25 Rt arm, 25 Lt arm, 25 DPS

| Main Set: | A | B |
|---|---|---|
| | 200 (0:15 RI) | 200 (0:20 RI) |
| | 300 (0:15 RI) | 300 (0:25 RI) |
| | 400 (0:20 RI) | 200 (0:20 RI) |
| | 400 (0:20 RI) | 300 (0:25 RI) |
| | 300 (0:15 RI) | 200 |
| | 200 | |

| C/D: | A | B |
|---|---|---|
| | 200 | 100 |

Total: 3050–2350

---

### Endurance Speed—E(Speed)

W/U:    300 swim, 200 kick, 100 pull

| Main Set: | A | B |
|---|---|---|
| | 600 (0:30 RI) | 300 (0:25 RI) |
| | 300 (0:20 RI) | 300 (0:25 RI) |
| | 300 (0:20 RI) | 200 (0:20 RI) |
| | 150 (0:15 RI) | 200 (0:20 RI) |
| | 150 150 (0:15 RI) | 150 |

Speed Set: 6 x 75: 25 cruise, 25 strong build, 25 easy (0:25 RI)

C/D:                    Your choice

Total: 2550+–2350+

## Force

W/U:     (100 swim, 100 kick, 100 pull) x 2, 300 build

| Main Set: | A | B |
|---|---|---|
| | 200 (0:20 RI) | 100 (0:20 RI) |
| | 4 x 100 (0:15 RI) | 4 x 50 (0:15 RI) |
| | 50 (0:30 RI) | 50 (0:30 RI) |

Special instructions: Increase speed each time. The fourth set should produce faster speeds than the first set. Do not take additional rest after the 50—rest only 30 seconds and roll right back into the first long swim. Paddles are optional and recommended for working on force.

C/D:              300 easy swim

Total: 2600–2300

---

## Muscular Endurance—M

W/U:     (150 swim, 75 kick, 75 build) x 2

| Main Set: | A | B |
|---|---|---|
| | 6 x 100 @ (T1-pace + 0:25) SI | 4 x 100 @ (T1-pace + 0:25) SI |
| | 100 easy | 100 easy |
| | 6 x 100 @ (T1-pace + 0:20)SI | 4 x 100 @ (T1-pace + 0:20) SI |
| | 100 easy | 100 easy |
| | 6 x 100 @ (T1-pace + 0:15) SI | 4 x 100 @ (T1-pace + 0:15) SI |

Special instructions: The swims should be at T1-pace, at least for the first set. A slight increase in speed (1 to 2 seconds per 100) can be attempted on the second and third sets, but do not increase the rest time. The 100 swims are active recovery and easy, but not enough time for coffee!

C/D:              200 easy

Total: 2600–2200

## Anaerobic Endurance—A(Form)

W/U:    200 swim, 200 kick, 200 pull, 100 swim , 100 kick, 100 pull, 50 swim, 50 kick, 50 pull

Main Set:

| | A | B |
|---|---|---|
| | 2 x 100 (1:00 RI) | 2 x 100 (1:00 RI) |
| | 2 x 75 (0:45 RI) | 2 x 75 (0:45 RI) |
| | 2 x 50 (0:30 RI) | 2 x 50 (0:30 RI) |
| | 4 x 25 (0:30 RI) | 4 x 25 (0:30 RI) |

Special instructions: Every swim listed above is all-out fast—no holding back. Both groups intentionally swim the same distances.

6 x 75: (25 kick, 50 B-3 with perfect stroke) (0:20 RI)

C/D:                     Your choice

Total: 2050+

# APPENDIX G
# GENERAL INSTRUCTIONS FOR PLYOMETRIC WORKOUTS

Plyometric workouts need to be done on a good jumping surface. Concrete or other very hard floors should be avoided. Also, a good pair of cross-training or court shoes should be used for plyometric (plyo) workouts.

Warm up 10 to 20 minutes on a bike or running before starting plyo workouts. Do plyos first, then weights (typically PE). When jumping, imagine energy is stored in your legs, like a spring. On the four-square plyos, accuracy is first, then speed. Taping two pieces of athletic tape together, sticky side to sticky side, can make a portable four-square. Or, a square can be made on the floor by simply taping the pattern on flat carpeting or a wooden floor. Also, the lines on a basketball court can be used.

For counting on the four-square, if the pattern calls for square 1 to 2, a count of "one" is when your feet return to square 1. Rest between jumps until fully recovered—about 1 to 3 minutes. When doing single leg jumps, alternate right leg, then left leg. Do not do all right leg sets before going to the left leg. Rest 2 or 3 minutes after both legs have completed one set.

Record the number of jumps completed in the given time on the line provided For example, Number 1 to 2, 20 seconds, both legs 22.

Athletes just beginning plyometrics should do the lower number of sets indicated. An additional option for beginners is to cut the time in half, jumping 10 seconds instead of 20.

Week 3 includes one set of more advanced jumping over foam blocks. Foam blocks can be obtained from an upholstery shop.

## BEGINNING PLYOMETRIC FLOORWORK
## FOUR-SQUARE PATTERN

```
  2  |  3
-----+-----
  1  |  4
```

### Week 1

#### A. BOTH LEGS

1. Number 1 to 2, 20 seconds, 2–4 sets
Record number of jumps                    _____ _____

2. Number 1 to 4, 20 seconds, 2–4 sets
Record number of jumps                    _____ _____

3. Number 1 to 2 to 3 to 4, three times
around, 2 sets
Record time                               _____ _____

4. Number 1 to 4 to 3 to 2, three times
around, 2 sets
Record time                               _____ _____

## Week 2

**A. BOTH LEGS**

1. Number 1 to 2, 20 seconds, 1–2 sets        _____ _____

2. Number 1 to 4, 20 seconds, 1–2 sets        _____ _____

3. Number 1 to 3, 20 seconds, 1–2 sets        _____ _____
(Be sure to jump diagonally, keeping hips and toes pointed
forward.)

4. Number 4 to 2, 20 seconds, 1–2 sets        _____ _____
(Be sure to jump diagonally, keeping hips and toes pointed
forward.)

**B. SINGLE LEGS**                            **RIGHT LEFT**

1. Number 1 to 2, 10 seconds, 2 sets          _____ _____
                                              _____ _____
2. Number 1 to 4, 10 seconds, 2 sets          _____ _____
                                              _____ _____

## Week 3

### A. Both legs

1. Number 1 to 2, 20 seconds, 1–2 sets  _____  _____

2. Number 1 to 4, 20 seconds, 1–2 sets  _____  _____

3. Number 1 to 2, 10 seconds, 1–2 sets  _____  _____
(Jump over a 6-inch foam block*)

4. Number 1 to 4, 10 seconds, 1–2 sets  _____  _____
(Jump over a 6-inch foam block)

### B. Single legs                          RIGHT LEFT

1. Number 1 to 2, 5 seconds, 1–2 sets  _____  _____
(Jump over a 6-inch foam block)

2. Number 1 to 4, 5 seconds, 1–2 sets  _____  _____
(Jump over a 6-inch foam block)

### C. Both legs

5. Number 1 to 2, 20 seconds, 1–2 sets  _____  _____
(No foam—go fast!)

6. Number 1 to 4, 20 seconds, 1–2 sets  _____  _____
(No foam—go fast!)

*A piece of 6-inch x 6-inch x 2-foot foam block can be obtained from an upholstery shop. Beginning plyometric athletes may want to omit the foam blocks.*

## Week 4

### A. BOTH LEGS

3. Number 1 to 2, 20 seconds, 1–2 sets     _____ _____

4. Number 1 to 4, 20 seconds, 1–2 sets     _____ _____

5. Number 1 to 2, 20 seconds, 1–2 sets     _____ _____
(Hold 5- to 10-pound weights in each hand.)

6. Number 1 to 4, 20 seconds, 1–2 sets     _____ _____
(Hold 5- to 10-pound weights in each hand.)

### B. SINGLE LEGS        RIGHT LEFT

7. Number 1 to 2, 10 seconds, 2 sets     _____ _____
(Hold 5- to 10-pound weights in each hand.)

8. Number 1 to 2, 10 seconds, 2 sets     _____ _____
(Hold 5- to 10-pound weights in each hand.)

9. Number 1 to 2, 10 seconds, 2 sets     _____ _____
(No weights—go fast!)

10. Number 1 to 2, 10 seconds, 2 sets     _____ _____
(No weights—go fast!)

### C. BOTH LEGS

11. Number 1 to 2, 20 seconds, 1 set     _____
(No weights—go fast!)

12. Number 1 to 4, 20 seconds, 1 set     _____
(No weights—go fast!)

# APPENDIX H
# INSTRUCTIONS FOR
# TREADMILL WORKOUTS

Warm up for 10 to 20 minutes before all treadmill workouts. Begin with a speed that will keep you in Zone 1 for 5 to 10 minutes. Slowly increase the speed so you are running in Zone 2 for a steady 5 to 10 minutes before the treadmill intervals. Note the treadmill speed that allows you to comfortably run in Zone 2; this is your "2-zone" speed for all the treadmill workouts. Keep this speed the same for all workouts.

For example, if your 2-zone speed is 6.5 mph, on TM#1 do three to six repeats of 6.5 mph at a 7.5-percent incline, running for 20 seconds. After each and every run, get off of the treadmill, walk around and stretch before the next interval. This should take about 1 to 2 minutes; do not worry if heart rate drops below Zone 1. These workouts are for form and neuromuscular effect. One of the biggest mistakes made is to continue running between the intervals, not allowing full recovery. I know this is not the type of running workout you are used to, but just trust me—at least for the first workout, so you can see the effects for yourself.

After doing three to six sets, increase the elevation to 10 percent and run three to six repetitions of 20 seconds at the new incline. Change the incline one more time, running only two to four repeats.

The final run is at 1.0 mph faster than your 2-zone speed.

### Treadmill Workout #1 (TM#1)

| Set | Speed | Elevation | Time | Repeats |
|---|---|---|---|---|
| 1 | 2-zone | 7.5 | 20 sec | 3–6 |
| 2 | 2-zone | 10 | 20 sec | 3–6 |
| 3 | 2-zone | 12.5 | 20 sec | 2–4 |
| 4 | 2-zone + 1.0 mph | 0 | Until heart rate exceeds Zone 3 | 1 |

### Treadmill Workout #2 (TM#2)

| Set | Speed | Elevation | Time | Repeats |
|---|---|---|---|---|
| 1 | 2-zone + 0.5 mph | 7.5 | 20 sec | 3–6 |
| 2 | 2-zone + 0.5 mph | 10 | 20 sec | 4–8 |
| 3 | 2-zone + 0.5 mph | 12.5 | 20 sec | 2–4 |
| 4 | 2-zone + 1.0 mph | 0 | Until heart rate exceeds Zone 3 | 1 |

### Treadmill Workout #3 (TM#3)

| Set | Speed | Elevation | Time | Repeats |
|---|---|---|---|---|
| 1 | 2-zone + 0.5 mph | 7 | 20 sec | 3–6 |
| 2 | 2-zone + 0.5 mph | 11 | 15 sec | 4–8 |
| 3 | 2-zone + 1.0 mph | 11 | 12-15 sec | 2–4 |
| 4 | 2-zone + 1.0 mph | 13 | 12-15 sec | 2–4 |
| 5 | 2-zone + 1.5 mph | 10 | 10 sec | 2–4 |
| 6 | 2-zone + 1.0 mph | 0 | Until heart rate exceeds Zone 3 | 1 |

### Treadmill Workout #4 (TM#4)

| Set | Speed | Elevation | Time | Repeats |
|---|---|---|---|---|
| 1 | 2-zone + 1.0 mph | 7 | 20 sec | 3–6 |
| 2 | 2-zone + 1.0 mph | 11 | 15 sec | 4–8 |
| 3 | 2-zone + 1.5 mph | 11 | 10sec/10sec/10sec* | 2–4 |
| 4 | 2-zone + 1.5 mph | 13 | 10 sec | 2–4 |
| 5 | 2-zone + 2.0 mph | 10 | 12–15 sec | 2–4 |
| 6 | 2-zone + 1.5 mph | 0 | Until heart rate exceeds Zone 3 | 2 |

*8 to 10 seconds running, 10 seconds off, 8 to 10 seconds running

Run at this speed until heart rate reaches the end of Zone 3. Running at this new speed should feel very easy, like running downhill. If it does not feel as described, you did something wrong (I suspect you ran during your rest intervals.) Record this time in a journal. Get off the treadmill, walk 5 to 10 minutes to cool down and stretch.

When you do TM#2, use the same warm-up routine and the same 2-zone speed that was used in TM#1. This time increase speeds a bit more with the elevation changes.

TM#3 builds on #2 and TM#4 builds on #3. On the third set of TM#4, run for 8 to 10 seconds, then hop off the treadmill for just 10 seconds and back on for another 8 to 10 seconds. The final run on TM#4 is the fastest yet.

Of course, be cautious mounting and dismounting the treadmill each time. There is plenty of rest time, so there is no need to hurry back onto the treadmill. Take your time and be safe. If you have problems getting on and off of a moving treadmill, perhaps it is best not do these workouts.

# APPENDIX I
## INSTRUCTIONS FOR TREADMILL TRACK WORKOUTS

When looking at the workouts in this appendix, perhaps the thought crosses your mind, "Why are the interval times so strange? Why not nice round numbers?" The workouts in this appendix were originally designed for a runner with an open 10K speed of approximately 50 minutes. The times are approximate values for the time it would take such a runner to accomplish standard track distances. That design is where the name for the workouts came from, Treadmill Track. For your own use, the values in the chart—as is—will work. If you

| TREADMILL TRACK WORKOUT #1 | | | | | | | |
|---|---|---|---|---|---|---|---|

**Name:**_____

**Date:**_____

**W/U 20-30 Min**_____

Treadmill speed is 8% faster than open 10K pace or 8% faster than lactate threshold speed. Heart rate should climb into 5b-c, PostHR. Rest interval equals the work interval. C/D 10-15 min

| Set | Speed | Elevation | Run Time | Number | PreHR | PostHR | Comments |
|---|---|---|---|---|---|---|---|
| 1 | | 0 | 03:30 | 1 | | | |
| | | 0 | 03:30 | 2 | | | |
| | | 0 | 03:30 | 3 | | | |
| 2 | | 0 | 02:35 | 1 | | | |
| | | 0 | 02:35 | 2 | | | |
| | | 0 | 02:35 | 3 | | | |
| 3 | | 0 | 01:44 | 1 | | | |
| | | 0 | 01:44 | 2 | | | |
| | | 0 | 01:44 | 3 | | | |
| 4 | | 0 | :50 | 1 | | | |
| | | 0 | :50 | 2 | | | |
| | | 0 | :50 | 3 | | | |

## TREADMILL TRACK WORKOUT #2

**Name:**_____

**Date:**_____

**W/U 20-30 Min**_____

Treadmill speed is 8% faster than open 10K pace or 8% faster than lactate threshold speed. Heart rate should climb into 5b-c, PostHR. Rest interval equals the work interval. C/D 10-15 min

| Set | Speed | Elevation | Run Time | Number | PreHR | PostHR | Comments |
|-----|-------|-----------|----------|--------|-------|--------|----------|
| 1 | | 0 | 04:18 | 1 | | | |
| | | 0 | 04:18 | 2 | | | |
| 2 | | 0 | 03:27 | 1 | | | |
| | | 0 | 03:27 | 2 | | | |
| 3 | | 0 | 02:35 | 1 | | | |
| | | 0 | 02:35 | 2 | | | |
| 4 | | 0 | 01:44 | 1 | | | |
| | | 0 | 01:44 | 2 | | | |
| optional 5 | | 0 | 00:50 | 1 | | | |
| | | 0 | 00:50 | 2 | | | |

## TREADMILL TRACK WORKOUT #3

**Name:**_____

**Date:**_____

**W/U 20-30 Min**_____

Treadmill speed is 8% faster than open 10K pace or 8% faster than lactate threshold speed. Heart rate should climb into 5b-c, PostHR. Rest interval equals the work interval. C/D 10-15 min

| Set | Speed | Elevation | Run Time | Number | PreHR | PostHR | Comments |
|-----|-------|-----------|----------|--------|-------|--------|----------|
| 1 | | 0 | 05:10 | 1 | | | |
| 2 | | 0 | 04:18 | 1 | | | |
| | | 0 | 04:18 | 2 | | | |
| 3 | | 0 | 03:27 | 1 | | | |
| | | 0 | 03:27 | 2 | | | |
| 4 | | 0 | 02:35 | 1 | | | |

**Name:**_____

**Date:**_____

**W/U 20-30 Min**_____

Treadmill speed is 8% faster than open 10K pace or 8% faster than lactate threshold speed. Heart rate should climb into 5b-c, PostHR. Rest interval equals the work interval. C/D 10-15 min

| Set | Speed | Elevation | Run Time | Number | PreHR | PostHR | Comments |
|-----|-------|-----------|----------|--------|-------|--------|----------|
| 1 |  | 0 | 05:10 | 1 |  |  |  |
|  |  | 0 | 05:10 | 2 |  |  |  |
| 2 |  | 0 | 04:18 | 1 |  |  |  |
|  |  | 0 | 04:18 | 2 |  |  |  |
| 3 |  | 0 | 03:27 | 1 |  |  |  |
| 4 |  | 0 | 02:35 | 1 |  |  |  |

need nice round numbers to be at ease, feel free to round the run time up or down one to 10 seconds. For example, in Set No. 2 of Treadmill Track No. 1, rounding 2:35 to 2:30 is fine.

Each treadmill workout can be copied and taken to the gym. It is best to record workout particulars on a copied sheet if you plan to use the appendix workouts in the future. These workouts are anaerobic endurance workouts versus the sessions designed to improve form, displayed in Appendix H.

*An explanation of each column:*

• *Set: Includes time-specified repetitions*

• *Speed: Record the speed you set the treadmill at. Start with a speed that is 8-percent faster than your open 10K time. (A 10K run without swimming and cycling first.) This speed is roughly 20 seconds per mile faster than the 10K speed at the end of an Olympic distance triathlon.*

• *Elevation: Set elevation at zero to approximate a track ele-*

*vation. Some people prefer a 1- to 2-percent grade, which will work as well.*
- *Time: The time you run on the treadmill at the designated speed.*
- *Number: The repetition number within a given set.*
- *PreHR: Heart rate prior to stepping on the treadmill for each repetition.*
- *PostHR: Heart rate immediately after stepping off the treadmill for each repetition.*
- *Comments: How did you feel?*

Warm up for 10 to 20 minutes before all treadmill workouts. If you are doing the workout correctly, heart rate should be close to Zone 5b by the end of the first repetition of the first set. If heart rate is low, say barely making Zone 4, increase the treadmill speed by 10 seconds per mile. For example if you begin at an 8-minute pace per mile and it was too slow, increase the treadmill speed to a 7:50 pace per mile. Be cautious not to increase speed too much. If unable to stay on the treadmill for the designated time (in other words, if you get spit off the back), the speed is too fast.

Record PostHR after each repetition and between repetitions; jog easy in Zone 1 for a time that is equal to the previous interval. Hence, rest interval equals work interval.

The overall goal of each workout session is to run the final repetitions, of the final set, faster than the repetitions of the first set. This is accomplished by gently increasing the speed on the second repetition of subsequent sets. An example is given on page 312.

## TREADMILL TRACK WORKOUT #4

**Name:**_____

**Date:**_____

**W/U 20–30 Min**_____

Treadmill speed is 8% faster than open 10K pace or 8% faster than lactate threshold speed. Heart rate should climb into Zones 5b–c, PostHR. Rest interval equals the work interval. C/D 10–15 min

| Set | Speed | Elevation | Run Time | Number | PreHR | PostHR | Comments |
|---|---|---|---|---|---|---|---|
| 1 | 08:00 | 0 | 03:30 | 1 | 130 | 171 | Felt hard |
|   | 08:00 | 0 | 03:30 | 2 | 120 | 172 | Felt easier |
|   | 08:00 | 0 | 03:30 | 3 | 135 | 175 | Got in a rhythm |
| 2 | 08:00 | 0 | 02:35 | 1 | 130 | 170 | Time went fast |
|   | 07:50 | 0 | 02:35 | 2 | 115 | 173 | okay |
|   | 07:50 | 0 | 02:35 | 3 | 120 | 175 | okay |
| 3 | 07:50 | 0 | 01:44 | 1 | 120 | 169 | Feeling good |
|   | 07:40 | 0 | 01:44 | 2 | 125 | 173 | okay |
|   | 07:40 | 0 | 01:44 | 3 | 130 | 173 | okay |
| 4 | 07:40 | 0 | :50 | 1 | 130 | 170 | I'm faster! |
|   | 07:30 | 0 | :50 | 2 | 135 | 175 | good |
|   | 07:30 | 0 | :50 | 3 | 130 | 175 | good |

# EPILOGUE

*Swimming will continue to be a huge challenge for me. I never find it easy, but I have gotten faster and it feels great to have overcome my fears and to have improved. I have a long way to go but am confident now that with a lot of hard work, dedication and determination I can do it!*

*So can you! As long as you have the courage, the belief in yourself and the desire to get better, you can and will improve—with lots of hard work and persistence. Never give up, never stop believing, push your limits and reach for the stars! Anything is possible!*

*—Siri Lindley, Boulder, Colorado,*
*First alternate to the 2000 triathlon Olympic team, age 30*

To end this book, I go back to the beginning of my coaching experience. I recognize the words between the covers would not have been possible without the trust of all the people who allowed me to help them along their athletic journey. I value their trust, and many of the lessons we learned are reflected in each chapter.

When Siri forwarded her words of wisdom to me, I thought it was fitting text with which to close the book. She is a top contender for the U. S. Olympic team and an athlete looking for continuous improvement. The best athletes are always looking to make themselves just a fraction better. My desire is that this book will give you training ideas and abet your journey of continuous athletic improvement.

# GLOSSARY

***Aerobic; aerobic metabolism.*** Requiring oxygen for energy transfer.

***Aerobic capacity.*** A term used in reference to $VO_2$ max. Aerobic capacity training is in the range of 90 to 100 percent of $VO_2$ max pace, or 95 to 98 percent of maximal heart rate in women (90 to 95 percent in men.)

***Anaerobic; anaerobic metabolism.*** Describes energy transfers that do not require oxygen.

***Arteries.*** Blood vessels rich in oxygen that conduct blood away from the heart to the body.

***ATP—adenosine triphosphate.*** Molecules where potential energy is stored for use at the cellular level.

***Atherosclerosis.*** The accumulation of fat inside the arteries.

***Circulatory.*** Refers to blood flow throughout the body.

***Concentric contraction.*** Process during which a muscle contracts, exerts force, shortens and overcomes a resistance. For example, concentric contraction occurs in the quadricep muscles when lifting the weight in a knee extension exercise.

***DNA—deoxyribonucleic acid.*** The molecules that determine our heredity; the units of heredity are the genes on our chromosomes. Each gene is a portion of the DNA molecule.

***Eccentric contraction.*** Process during which a muscle contracts, exerts force, lengthens and is overcome by a resistance. For example, eccentric contraction occurs in the quadricep muscles when lowering the weight in a knee extension exercise.

**Economy.** When referenced in exercise, this term usually means the highest level of exercise achievable at the lowest energy cost.

**Extension.** Movement about a joint that increases the angle between the bones on either side of the joint.

**Fartlek.** Swedish for "speed play." It is intervals at a fast pace, inserted into a workout at the athlete's will or desire. Full recovery follows each fast bout.

**Flexion.** Movement about a joint that brings the bones on either side of the joint closer together.

**HDL.** High density lipoprotein, considered the "good" cholesterol, or that which helps prevent atherosclerosis.

**Hemoglobin.** The oxygen-transporting component of red blood cells.

**Isometric contraction.** A muscular contraction where the muscle exerts force but does not change in length.

**Lactate.** A salt of lactic acid formed when lactic acid from within the cells enters the bloodstream and lactate ions separate from hydrogen ions.

**Lactate threshold.** The point during exercise where increasing intensity causes blood lactate levels to accumulate.

**Lactic acid.** An organic acid produced within the cell from anaerobic carbohydrate metabolism.

**LDL.** Low density lipoprotein, considered the "bad" cholesterol, or that which contributes to atherosclerosis.

*Measures.*

| METRIC TO STANDARD | STANDARD TO METRIC |
|---|---|
| CONVERSION FACTORS | CONVERSION FACTORS |
| 1 kilometer (km) = 0.62 mile (mi) | 1 mi = 1.61 km |
| 1 meter (m) = 1.09 yards (yd) | 1 yd = 0.914 m |
| 1 centimeter (cm) = 0.934 inches (in) | 1 in = 2.54 cm |
| 1 millimeter (mm) = 0.039 in | 1 in = 25.4 mm |
| 1 kilogram (kg) = 2.205 pounds (lb) | 1 lb = 0.4536 kg |
| 1 liter (l or L) = 0.264 gallons (gal) | 1 gal = 3.785 L |
| 1 liter = 1.057 quarts (qt) | 1 qt = 0.946 L |
| | |
| METRIC CONVERSIONS | |
| 1 cm = 0.01 m | 1 m = 100 cm |
| 1 mm = 0.001 m | 1 m = 1000 mm |
| 1 ml = 0.001 L | 1L = 1000 mL |

*Mitochondria.* Organelles within the cells responsible for ATP generation for cellular activities.

*Myoglobin.* Oxygen-binding matter in muscle.

*Negative-split.* A workout or interval that is split in half, with the second half executed faster than the first half.

*Plasma.* The nonliving fluid component of blood. Suspended within the plasma are the various solutes and formed elements.

*Torque.* A measure of a force that rotates the body upon which it acts about an axis. It is commonly expressed in pound-feet, pound-inches, kilogram-meter and other similar units of measure.

*Triglycerides.* Often called "neutral fats," these are the most plentiful fats in the body—more than 95 percent of the body fat is in the form of triglycerides. They are the body's most concentrated source of energy fuel.

*Veins.* Blood vessels returning blood from the body to the heart.

*Ventilation.* The circulation of air through—in this context—the lungs. Ventilatory threshold is the rate of exercise where the relationship between ventilation and oxygen consumption deviates from a linear function. Breathing rate at ventilatory threshold becomes noticeably labored.

*VO$_2$ max.* A quantitative measure of an individual's ability to transfer energy aerobically. The value is typically expressed in terms of (ml $\Sigma$ kg-1 $\Sigma$ min-1), or milliliters of oxygen consumed per kilogram of body weight, per minute. The maximum value can be measured in a laboratory, where resistance is incrementally increased on a bicycle ergometer and the test subject's oxygen consumption is constantly measured. As the workload increases, there is a point where the test subject's oxygen consumption no longer increases to meet the increasing demand of the workload. The maximum oxygen consumption value achieved is considered VO$_2$ max.

*Work-to-Rest Ratio.* The ratio of fast swimming, running, or cycling to easy recovey in the same sport. For example, a 4:1 work-to-rest ratio could be 4 minutes of fast running followed by 1 minute of easy jogging.

## REFERENCES

American Council on Exercise. *Personal Trainer Manual.* San Diego, CA: The American Council on Exercise, 1992.

Eastman Kodak Company. *Ergonomic Design for People at Work. Vol. 2.* Van Nostrand Reinhold Company Inc., 1986.

Ganong, W. F. *Review of Medical Physiology.* Ninth Ed. Stamford, CT: Lange Medical Publications, 1979.

Martin, David E. and Peter N. Coe. *Better Training for Distance Runners.* Second Ed. Champaign, IL: Human Kinetics, 1997.

McArdle, W. D., et al. *Exercise Physiology, Energy, Nutrition, and Human Performance.* 3d ed. Malvern, PA: Lea & Febiger, 1991.

Oberg, E., et al. *Machinery's Handbook: A Reference Book for the Mechanical Engineer, Draftsman, Toolmaker and Machinist.* New York, NY: Industrial Press Inc., 1980.

Vickery, D. M., and J. F. Fries. *Take Care of Yourself.* Reading, MA: Addison-Wesley Publishing Company, 1994.

# INDEX

# ABOUT THE AUTHOR

Gale has been instructing or coaching athletes since 1974. She has a Bachelor of Science degree in Mechanical Engineering from Colorado State University, is a personal trainer certified by the American Council on Exercise and is certified as an Elite Coach by USA Cycling and USA Triathlon. Her collegiate coursework included design of artificial kidneys and hearts; however, her passion remains with the heart and soul of athletes.

She uses her education and experience to help endurance athletes meet their race-related goals. Her athletes include professional cyclists, Olympic hopefuls, top national-level masters road racers, ultraendurance cyclists and multisport racers. Her clients have placed at National Championships in road cycling, mountain biking and triathlon. She has coached multisport athletes to podium finishes at world championship events while others have gone to the Hawaiian Ironman.

She is a regular columnist for *Triathlete* magazine and frequently contributes feature articles for several other publications. Her training plans and coaching advice in *Triathlete* magazine have earned her the title of "Everybody's Coach." She is recognized as a "world-renowned coach" by *Inside Triathlon* magazine, speaking at the "Science of Speed" seminar at the 20th Anniversary of the Hawaiian Ironman Triathlon.

Living and training in Loveland, Colorado, with her husband Delbert, she is available for personal coaching and seminars addressing athletic and business subjects. She can be reached through her Web site www.galebernhardt.com.